Roger Allen provides a comprehensive introductory survey of literary texts in Arabic, from their unknown beginnings in the fifth century AD to the present day. The volume focuses on the major genres of Arabic literature, dealing with Islam's sacred text, the Qur'ān, and a wealth of poetry, narrative prose, drama and criticism. Allen reveals the continuities that link the creative output of the present day to the illustrious literary heritage of the past and incorporates an enormously rich body of popular literature typified most famously by *The Arabian Nights*. The volume is informed by Western critical approaches, but within each chapter the emphasis is on the texts themselves, with extensive quotations in English translation. Reference features include a chronology and a guide to further reading. A revised and abridged version of Allen's acclaimed study, *The Arabic Literary Heritage*, this book provides an invaluable student introduction to a major non-Western literary tradition.

ROGER ALLEN is Professor of Arabic at the University of Pennsylvania. He is author of *The Arabic Literary Heritage* (1998), *The Arabic Novel* (1982) and *A Period of Time* (1992). He has published more than forty journal articles on Arabic literature and translated a number of modern Arabic narratives including Najib Mahfuz's *Mirrors* (1977) and *Autumn Quail* (1985).

AN INTRODUCTION TO ARABIC LITERATURE

ROGER ALLEN

CAMBRIDGE
UNIVERSITY PRESS

PUBLISHED BY THE PRESS SYNDICATE OF THE UNIVERSITY OF CAMBRIDGE
The Pitt Building, Trumpington Street, Cambridge, United Kingdom

CAMBRIDGE UNIVERSITY PRESS
The Edinburgh Building, Cambridge CB2 2RU, UK www.cup.cam.ac.uk
40 West 20th Street, New York, NY 10011-4211, USA www.cup.org
10 Stamford Road, Oakleigh, Melbourne 3166, Australia
Ruiz de Alarcón 13, 28014 Madrid, Spain

First published 2000

Printed in the United Kingdom at the University Press, Cambridge

Typeface Monotype Baskerville 11/12½ pt. *System* QuarkXPress™ [SE]

A catalogue record for this book is available from the British Library

Library of Congress cataloguing in publication data

Allen, Roger M. A.
An introduction to Arabic literature / Roger Allen.
p. cm.
Includes bibliographical references and index.
ISBN 0 521 77657 0 (pbk.) – ISBN 0 521 77230 3 (hbk.)
1. Arabic literature – History and criticism. I. Title.
PJ7510.A43 2000
892.709–dc21 99-053418

ISBN 0 521 77230 3 hardback
ISBN 0 521 77657 0 paperback

Contents

Preface

As a scholar in Arabic literature and the teacher of a university-level course on Arabic literary history, I have for some time been experimenting with different ways of presenting the subject to university students with a broad range of humanistic interests and also to a more general reading public. I have often asked my own students to comment on the merits of previous attempts at writing a history of Arabic literature and to prepare outlines for a new approach to the topic. I am therefore especially pleased to acknowledge here that many of the principles used in preparing this work are as much a reflection of classroom debates and essay responses as of profitable discussions with academic colleagues.

I have written this book without resorting to footnotes, and so I cannot acknowledge in the time-honoured fashion the debt that I owe to numerous colleagues whose critical studies of the Arabic literary tradition are reflected in the pages that follow. I can only express the hope that the guide to further reading listed at the end of the work will convey some idea of the extent to which I am grateful for their insights. I might perhaps take a leaf out of the book of the Middle East's primary jokester, Juḥā, and suggest that those who know what those sources of my inspiration are might tell those who do not.

Several of my colleagues have done me the great service of reading portions of this work in advance of its publication. I would like to take this opportunity to thank them all for their wise counsel and gentle correction, while absolving them of all responsibility for the result: Geert Jan van Gelder, Peter Heath, Salma Khadra al-Jayyusi, Hilary Kilpatrick, Everett Rowson, Yasir Saqr, Michael Sells, and William Smyth.

Note on translation, transliteration, and further reading

A few words need to be said about various aspects of the text and the conventions that it uses. Firstly, translation: except where indicated in the text itself, the translations in the book are my own.

Secondly, on transliteration: the literary works that are the focus of this volume have been composed in Arabic. Thus, in discussing them in English, a system of transliteration is needed whereby the written symbols of Arabic are represented from the repertoire of the English alphabet. Scholars working in Arabic studies have devised a number of different systems for doing this, in part reflecting the conventions of writing and pronunciation within their own language systems. In English scholarly discourse on this field, the system of transliteration that is most widespread is the one devised by the Library of Congress in the United States, also used with minor adjustments by the British Library. The basic outlines of this system are used in this book.

The Library of Congress system uses a written symbol from the English alphabet to replicate an equivalent written symbol in Arabic. It makes no attempt to reproduce exactly the way in which the Arabic words are pronounced. Thus, while the Arabic names and titles transliterated in this book will give some idea of how the written symbols will sound, the equivalence is not (and cannot be) anything approaching complete. Beyond the usual English alphabet set, two other symbols are used: the left-facing single quotation-mark (ʾ) represents the Arabic glottal stop (called *hamzah*), such as is represented by the hyphen in the word re-enter; and the superscript c (ʿ) represents a sound for which English has no equivalent, but which linguists term a pharyngeal plosive (the name of the Arabic phoneme is ʿ*ayn*). Furthermore, the Arabic language makes use of several written symbols and pronounced sounds that are not found in the English language system. To represent these sounds and symbols in transliteration, the Library of Congress system makes use of a series of supplementary markings (usually called diacritics) in order to indicate the presence of these intrinsically Semitic phenomena: dots under certain consonants to indicate that they are emphatic and elongation signs (macrons) over vowels to show that their pronunciation time is longer than that of the short vowels.

Lastly, regarding the Guide to Further Reading: bearing in mind the nature and breadth of the subject matter of this work, it is obviously impossible to provide anything approaching a complete bibliography on any topic or even sub-topic; I might note that the reasons lie not only in the bulk of what would result, but the extreme inaccessibility of some of the sources involved. The Guide to Further Reading, which is divided into sections relating to the various chapters, is thus intended to give samples of work on the particular genre and subject involved; it is my hope that readers who find their interests aroused by this book may use such studies and translations as a trigger to yet further investigations.

Chronology

Note: In the case of authors, the dates involved are the approximate year of death

Historical events/people		Literary events/people
500		al-Muhalhil
533		Imru᾽ al-Qays
c. 570	Birth of Muḥammad	al-Shanfarā (?) Ta᾽abbaṭa sharran (?) al-Muraqqish Ṭarafah
600		
		ʿAmr ibn Kulthūm al-Ḥarith ibn Ḥillizah ʿAmr ibn Qamīʾah ʿAdī ibn Zayd Zuhayr ibn Abī Sulmā ʿAntarah
622	*Hijrah* from Mecca to Medina	Durayd ibn al-Ṣimmah
632	Death of Muḥammad	Al-Aʿshā
635	Capture of Damascus by Muslims	
636	Battle of Qàdisiyyah; defeat of Sāsānī (Persian) army	al-Khansā᾽
637–44	Conquests of Syria, Iraq, Egypt	
640	Establishment of al-Kūfah and al-Baṣrah as garrison cities in Iraq	Qays ibn Mulawwaḥ (?)
650	Standardisation of Qur᾽ānic text	
656	Murder of Caliph ʿUthmān	
657	Battle of Ṣiffīn	
661	Assassination of Caliph ʿAlī; beginning of Umawī dynasty	Labīd al-Ḥutay᾽ah

	Historical events/people	Literary events/people
670	Establishment of Qayrawān in Tunisia	Ḥassān ibn Thābit
680	Battle of Karbalā'	
685–91	Dome of the Rock built in Jerusalem	
700		
		Jamīl Laylā al-Akhyaliyyah
705	Building of Great Mosque in Damascus	al-ʿAjjāj
710	Ṭāriq crosses into Spain	al-Akhṭal
705–15	Capture of Bukhārā and Samarkand	
732	Battle of Tours; Charles Martel defeats Muslims	ʿUmar ibn Abī Rabīʿah Kuthayyir Jarīr al-Farazdaq al-Ṭirimmāḥ 'Dhū al-Rummah' al-ʿArjī
747	Beginning of ʿAbbāsī revolt in Khūrāsān	al-Walīd ibn Yazīd
750	Fall of Umawī caliphate; ʿAbbāsī caliphs come to power	ʿAbd al-ḥamīd al-kātib
755–1031	Umawī dynasty in Cordoba	ibn al-Muqaffaʿ
762	Foundation of Baghdād	Abū Ḥanīfah Abū ʿAmr ibn al-ʿAlā' Ḥammād al-Rāwiyah ibn Isḥāq Bashshār ibn Burd al-Mufaḍḍal al-Ḍabbī
785	Work begins on Great Mosque in Cordoba	al-Khalīl ibn Aḥmad
786–809	Caliphate of Hārūn al-Rashīd	Malik ibn Anas Khalaf al-aḥmar Sībawayh
800		Rābiʿah al-ʿAdawiyyah
803	Fall of Barmakī family in Baghdād	Abū Nuwās ʿAbbās ibn al-Aḥnaf Ibrāhīm al-Mawṣilī

Historical events/people		Literary events/people
827	Caliph al-Maʾmūn declares Muʿtazilī doctrine to be orthdoxy; conquest of Sicily	al-Shāfiʿī Muslim ibn al-Walīd
832	Foundation of Bayt al-Ḥikmah library in Baghdād	Abū al-ʿAtāhiyah al-Aṣmaʿī ibn Hishām Ibrāhīm ibn al-Mahdī al-Kindī
836–89	Foundation of Samarrāʾ as Abbāsī capital	Aḥmad ibn Ḥanbal Abū Tammām ibn Sallām al-Jumaḥī al-Khwārizmī Isḥāq al-Mawṣilī Ziryāb Dhū al-nūn al-Miṣrī
869–83	Zanj rebellion	al-Jāḥiẓ ibn Qutaybah al-Mubarrad
871	Sack of al-Baṣrah by Zanj forces	al-Bukhārī al-Kindī al-Balādhurī ibn al-Rūmī al-Buḥturī ibn Abī al-Dunyā ibn Abī Ṭāhir Ṭayfūr
900		Thaʿlab al-Yaʿqūbī
901	Establishment of Zaydī state in Yemen	ibn al-Muʿtazz
908	Ibn al-Muʿtazz is caliph for one day	
909	Fāṭimī caliphate in Tunisia	
922	Execution of mystic, al-Ḥallāj	al-Ṭabarī Qudāmah ibn Jaʿfar ibn ʿAbd Rabbihi
945	Būyids assume control in Baghdād	al-Ashʿarī al-Mutanabbī al-Fārābī al-Masʿūdī

Historical events/people		Literary events/people
		al-Iṣṭakhrī Abū Bakr al-Ṣūlī Muḥammad al-Niffarī al-Qālī Abū Firās Abū al-faraj al-Iṣfahānī
969	Conquest of Cairo by Fāṭimī general, Jawhar	
973	Foundation of al-Azhar mosque-university in Cairo	ibn Hāniʾ al-Āmidī al-Ṣāḥib ibn ʿAbbād ibn Ḥawqal
998–1030	Maḥmūd of Ghaznah rules in Eastern Iran	
		al-Tanūkhī ibn al-Nadīm
1000		
		al-Qāḍī al-Jurjānī Abū Bakr al-Khwārizmī Abū Hilāl al-ʿAskarī Badīʿ al-zamān al-Hamadhānī al-Bāqillānī al-Sharīf al-Raḍī ibn Darrāj ibn Shuhayd Abū Ḥayyān al-Tawḥīdī
1031	Collapse of Umawī caliphate in Cordoba	Miskawayh al-Thaʿālibī ibn Khafājah ibn Sīnā
1052	Migration of Banī Hilāl across North Africa	al-Bīrūnī Abū al-ʿAlāʾ al-Maʿarrī
1055	Saljuq Turks capture Baghdād	
1071	Battle of Manzikert: Saljuqs occupy Anatolia	ibn Ḥazm ibn Rashīq al-Qushayrī ʿAbd al-qāhir al-Jurjānī Wallādah

Historical events/people		Literary events/people
1085	Christians in Spain capture Toledo	ibn Zaydūn
1091	Loss of Sicily to Normans	
1092	Niẓām al-mulk murdered by Assassins	
1095	Pope Urban calls for Crusade	
1099	Crusaders capture Jerusalem	
1100		
		al-Ghazālī
		ʿUmar al-Khayyām
		al-Aʿmā al-Tuṭīlī
		ibn Ḥamdīs
1147	Second Crusade	al-Ḥarīrī
		ʿAbd al-qādir al-Jīlānī
		al-Idrīsī
		al-Zamakhsharī
1171	End of Fāṭimī caliphate	ibn Quzmān
1174–93	Reign of Ṣalāḥ al-dīn (Saladin)	
		Aḥmad al-Rifāʿī
		ibn Ṭufayl
1187	Crusaders defeated by Ṣalāḥ al-dīn	
		ibn Rushd
		Usāmah ibn Munqidh
		Shihāb al-dīn Yaḥyā al-Suhrawardī
1200		
		ibn al-Jawzī
		al-Qāḍī al-Fāḍil
		ʿImād al-dīn al-Iṣfahānī
		Maimonides
		ibn Jubayr
		ibn Sanāʾ al-Mulk
1219	Mongols under Jingiz Khān invade Islamic lands	
		ʿAṭṭār
1229	Jerusalem handed over to Christians	Yāqūt
		Shihāb al-dīn ʿUmar al-Suhrawardī

Historical events/people		Literary events/people
1236	Christians in Spain capture Cordoba	ibn al-Fāriḍ
1248	Christians in Spain capture Seville	ibn al-ʿArabī
1250	Mamlūks come to power in Cairo	
1254	King Alfonso establishes school in Seville	al-Tīfāshī
1256–60	Hūlāgū Khān leads Mongol army to Baghdād	
1258	End of ʿAbbāsī caliphate	
1260	Battle of ʿAyn Jālūt; Mongols defeated by Mamlūks under Baybars	
1261–1520	Mamlūk dynasty rules Egypt	Jalāl al-dīn Rūmī
		al-Shustarī
		ibn Mālik
		ibn Ṣayqal al-Jazarī
		al-Shābb al-Zarīf
		al-Bayḍāwī
1291	Expulsion of Crusaders from Palestine	ibn Khallikān
		al-Būṣīrī
1300		
1303	Mongols defeated by Mamlūks in Egypt	ibn Manẓūr ibn Dāniyāl
1324	Mansā Mūsū, King of Mālī; University of Timbuktū	ibn Taymiyyah
		al-Nuwayrī
1348	Black Death reaches Egypt	Ṣafī al-dīn al-Ḥillī
1349	Muslim missionaries in Nigeria (Kano)	
		Ṣalāḥ al-dīn al-Ṣafadī
		ibn Qayyim al-Jawziyyah
1369	Tīmūr Lang occupies Khūrāsān	ibn Nubātah
1370–80	Tīmūr Lang conquers much of Central Asia	Lisān al-dīn ibn al-Khaṭīb ibn Baṭṭūṭah
1380–87	Tīmūr conquers Īrān	
		Ḥāfiẓ
1400		
		al-Fayrūzābādī

Historical events/people		Literary events/people
1400	Islām reaches Java	ibn Khaldūn
1402	Death of Tīmūr Lang	al-Maqrīzī al-Ghuzūlī al-Qalqashandī al-Ibshīhī ibn ʿArabshāh
1453	Capture of Constantinople by Ottomans	
1499	Ismāʿīl establishes Ṣafavī dynasty in Īrān	
1500		
1508	Ṣafavīs capture Baghdād	
		al-Suyūṭī ibn Mālik al-Ḥamawī
1516	Selīm the Grim captures Cairo	
1520–66	Reign of Ottoman Sultan Sulaymān the Magnificent	
1521	Ottoman capture of Belgrade	
1522	Ottoman conquest of Rhodes	ibn Iyās
1529	Ottoman siege of Vienna	
1549	Ottoman forces reach Yemen	
1550	Sinan builds Suleymaniye Mosque in Istanbul	
1556–1605	Akbar assumes power in Mughal India	al-Shaʿrānī
1600		
1622	English capture Hormuz	al-Maqqarī
1653	Tāj Mahal completed by Shāh Jihān	Shihāb al-dīn al-Khafājī
1668	Ottoman conquest of Crete	
1683	Ottomans besiege Vienna	
1699	Treaty of Karlowitz	
1700		
		ʿAbd al-ghanī al-Nābulusī Bishop Germanus Farḥāt

Historical events/people		Literary events/people
1745	Wahhābīs established at Darʿiyyah, Arabia	
1765	English East India Company takes over administration of Bengal	al-Amīr al-Ṣanʿānī
1770–89	Yūsuf Shihāb, Amīr of Lebanon	al-Idkāwī
1773	Saʿūdī dynasty in al-Riyāḍ	al-Zabīdī
1774	Treaty of Kuchuk Kaynarji between Russia and Ottomans	
1783	Russia seizes Crimea	
1789–1807	Reign of Selīm III, Ottoman Sultan	
1798	Napoleon's invasion of Egypt	
1796	Qajar dynasty in Īrān	
1800		
1803–4	Wahhābīs capture Mecca and Medina	
1805–48	Muḥammad ʿAlī viceroy of Egypt	
1806	Wahhābīs capture Mecca	
1811	Mamlūks massacred on orders of Muḥammad ʿAlī	Aḥmad al-Tījānī
1820–23	Egyptians conquer Sudan	al-Jabartī
1823	Arabic press in Cairo	
1830	French invade Algeria	
1834	Arabic press in Beirut	Shaykh Ḥasan al-ʿAṭṭār Mārūn al-Naqqāsh
1860–61	Civil War in Syria	
1866	Foundation of Syrian Protestant College in Beirut (AUB)	Nāṣīf al-Yāzijī
1869	Suez Canal opened	Rifāʿah al-Ṭahṭāwī
1877	Anglo-French control of Egyptian finances	
1881	French occupy Tunisia; ʿUrabī Revolt in Egypt	
1882	British occupy Egypt	
1885	Mahdī's revolt in Sudan; General Gordon killed in al-Kharṭūm	Aḥmad Fāris al-Shidyāq Ḥusayn al-Marṣafī

	Historical events/people	Literary events/people
1893	French arrive in Timbuktū	Muḥammad ʿUthmān Jalāl
1898	Defeat of Sudanese forces by General Kitchener	Jamāl al-dīn 'al-Afghānī'
1900		ʿAbd al-raḥmān al-Kawākibī Abū Khalīl al-Qabbānī Muḥammad ʿAbduh Maḥmūd Sāmī al-Barūdī
1908	Ottoman Sultan ʿAbd al-ḥamīd deposed by Young Turks	
1909	Anglo-Persian Oil Company founded	
1912	Franco-Spanish protectorate of Morocco	Yaʿqūb Ṣannūʿ
1915	Arab revolt against Ottoman government	
1916	Sykes–Picot Agreement regarding disposition of Middle East following First World War	
1917	Balfour Declaration	Shiblī Shumayyil Shaykh Salāmah al-Ḥijāzī Muḥammad Taymūr
1919	Popular uprising in Egypt; first proclamation of Muṣṭafā Kemāl (Ataturk) in Turkey	
1920	Turkish War of Independence; revolt in Iraq; French capture Damascus	
1921	Reza Shāh Pahlevī assumes power in Iran	
1922	Discovery of Tutankhamūn's tomb in Egypt	Faraḥ Anṭūn
1923	Declaration of Turkish Republic	
1924	Abolition of the caliphate; first Egyptian parliament	Muṣṭafā Luṭfī al-Manfalūṭī Shaykh Aḥmad Bamba
1927	Beginnings of Muslim Brethren in Egypt	Saʿd Zaghlūl
1929	Growing unrest in Palestine	Muḥammad al-Muwayliḥī

Historical events/people		Literary events/people
1932	Foundation of Arab Academy in Cairo	Khalīl Jubrān Ḥāfiẓ Ibrāhīm Aḥmad Shawqī
1933	ʿAbd al-ʿazīz becomes King of Saʿūdī Arabia	Abū al-qāsim al-Shabbī
1935	Italy invades Ethiopia	Rashīd Riḍā Jamīl Ṣidqī al-Zahāwī
1938	Death of Ataturk	Mayy Ziyādah Muḥammad Iqbāl
1945	League of Arab States created in Cairo	Maʿrūf al-Ruṣāfī
1947	Independence of India; creation of Pakistan	Salāmah Mūsā
1948	War in Palestine; State of Israel established	Anṭūn Saʿādah Ḥasan al-Bannā Khalīl Muṭrān Khalīl Baydas ʿAlī al-Duʿājī
1951	Muḥammad Mosaddeg Prime Minister of Īrān; Ḥusayn becomes King of Jordan	
1952	Revolution in Egypt	
1954	Jamāl ʿAbd al-nāṣir (Nasser) comes to power; beginning of Algerian War of Independence; Czech arms agreement with Egypt	Maḥmūd Ṭāhir Lāshīn
1955	Afro-Asian Conference in Bandung, Indonesia	
1956	Egypt nationalises Suez Canal; Tripartite (British, French, Israeli) invasion of Suez; Sudan, Tunisia, and Morocco gain independence	Muḥammad Ḥusayn Haykal Iliyyā Abū Māḍī
1958	Revolution in Iraq; United Arab Republic (Egypt & Syria) created; Lebanese political unrest	Jūrj Abyaḍ
1961	Kuwait independence; Socialist Laws in Egypt; revolution in Yemen	Bayram al-Tūnisī
1962	End of Algerian War; independence	Aḥmad Luṭfī al-Sayyid Mārūn ʿAbbūd

	Historical events/people	Literary events/people
1964	PLO established; King Saʿūd of Saʿūdī Arabia replaced by King Fayṣal	ʿAbbās Maḥmūd al-ʿAqqād Sayyid Quṭb Badr Shākir al-Sayyāb
1967	June War between Israel and Arab states	Muḥammad Mandūr Ḥusayn Muruwwah
1968	Ḥāfiẓ al-Asad becomes President of Syria; Yāsir ʿArafāt leader of PLO	Bishārah al-Khūrī
1969	General Numayrī seizes power in the Sudan; Libyan revolution led by Muʿammar al-Qadhdhāfī	
1970	Aswan High Dam completed; fighting in Jordan (Black September); death of ʿAbd al-nāṣir; Anwar al-Sādāt President of Egypt	
1971	Establishment of United Arab Emirates in Gulf	Tawfīq Ṣāyigh
1973	October crossing (Ramaḍān/Yom Kippur War)	Ṭāhā Ḥusayn Maḥmūd Taymūr
1975–88	Lebanese civil war	
1976	Fall of Tall al-Zaʿtar Palestinian refugee camp	
1977	Camp David accords between Egypt and Israel	
1979	Revolution in Īrān brings Imām Khomeinī to power	
1975–88	Lebanese civil war	
1981	Assassination of President Anwar al-Sādāt	Ṣalāḥ ʿAbd al-Ṣabūr
1982	Israel invades Lebanon; Sabra and Shatilah Camp massacres	Khalīl Ḥāwī
1987	Palestinian intifāḍah	Michel ʿAflaq Tawfīq al-Ḥakīm Yūsuf al-Khāl
1988		Nobel Award to Najīb Maḥfūẓ Mīkhā'īl Nuʿaymah Dhū al-nūn Ayyūb Tawfīq Yūsuf ʿAwwād

Historical events/people		Literary events/people
1990–91	Gulf War: Western forces attack Iraq after its occupation of Kuwait	
		Yūsuf Idrīs
		Yaḥyā Ḥaqqī
1994		Jabrā Ibrāhīm Jabrā
1996		Emil Ḥabībī

CHAPTER I

An essay on precedents and principles

In this chapter I will make use of several of the terms found in the title and subtitle as conduits for a brief discussion of the book's aims and methods.

'Arabic' announces clearly the language in which the literary materials that constitute my primary topic have been composed, but the dual significance of the Arabic equivalent of that adjective, '*ʿarabī*' – referring to both a language and its people – also introduces the notion that this work will be one of 'translation' in the most literal sense: I will be attempting to 'carry' one literary tradition 'across' cultural boundaries into the milieu of English-speaking readers at the onset of the twenty-first century and, more particularly, the comparative framework of world literature studies. For most of the period under consideration (the sixth century CE till the present), the relationship between the Arab-Islamic world and the West has been one of almost continuous confrontation, with a concomitant and anticipatable obfuscation of some unpleasant truths on both sides. The Crusades and the reconquest of Spain leading to the fall of Granada in 1492, for instance, both of them traditionally recounted as glorious episodes in the history of Western Europe, take on a quite different significance if viewed from outside such a context. With this background in mind, it is the purpose of the second chapter of this book to provide an environmental, linguistic, and historical context for a series of discussions of the literary genres in Arabic.

Dictionary definitions of 'literary' (linked to the field of 'literature') refer initially to anything that is written about a particular topic, but, alongside this broad definition a more limited one has been developed, reflected by the entry in the *Oxford English Dictionary*, 'writings whose value lies in beauty of form or emotional effect'. The aesthetic dimension of that definition links the concept closely to that of the French term, 'belles-lettres', one that is often employed in English writing on the topic of literature. While in contemporary critical writings the Arabic word for 'literature', '*adab*', is essentially coterminous with the concept of 'belles-lettres', it has arrived at that meaning via an interesting route, one that begins with something very akin to education and manners before being used to describe the varied activities of those important contributors to the cultural values of Arab society who have for many centuries been dignified by the designation *udabā'* (sing. *adīb*) – practitioners, preservers, and teachers of *adab*. The development of this concept, *adab*, is itself a primary topic of the fifth chapter.

Having linked the discussion of 'literature' and '*adab*' in this way, I might perhaps place them both into a single context by drawing attention to the way in which recent intellectual trends in Western literary theory and criticism have challenged some of the notions connected with the belletristic approach to the topic, particularly insofar as the privileged position of the literary text, the question of evaluation, and the concept of canon are concerned. In the trans-cultural context of this book on Arabic literary genres and its organising principles, there is perhaps an irony in the fact that the variety of texts and topics which today are potentially subject to critical analysis within the realm of Western literature studies is such that the resulting scenario tends to reflect, albeit by way of different criteria, the very same generic and topical breath that interested the *adīb* during the classical period of Arabic literature.

The title of this book avoids the use of the term 'history'. During the swirling debates over issues of literary theory in recent times, the notion of literary history has been both challenged and refined. Between the variety of approaches that have emerged from this process the present work seeks to strike a balance, one that will privilege the literary dimension over the historical. The chronological dimension will always be implicit. The difference that I hope to establish can be illustrated by considering the organising principles applied in many other works on this topic in Arabic and other languages, and in particular the method of periodisation that, *mutatis mutandis*, has been applied in most cases.

The first great temporal divide is one that constitutes an important aspect of Islamic history: that between the Islamic and pre-Islamic periods, the latter being also referred to as the 'period of ignorance' (Arabic, *Jāhiliyyah*). Here a period of indeterminate duration is defined by its status as antecedent. The denomination 'Islamic' can be applied in theory to the entire period from 622 till the present day, but is usually used to describe the literary activity of the lifetime of the Prophet Muḥammad and the first four caliphs. Following this, a new principle takes over, that of the period during which a particular dynasty held actual or nominal sway: firstly, the Umawī, for which Western scholarship has retained the term 'Umayyad' (complete with its Westernised Greek suffix); and then the ʿAbbāsī, similarly termed 'Abbasid'. Even before the end of the era termed 'Abbasid', the areas reckoned to be within the 'Dār al-Islām' (region of Islamic dominion) had fragmented into a large number of smaller hegemonies, each controlled by a succession of dynasties that provided sources of patronage for littérateurs. In the context of an examination of various approaches to the organisation of literary historical writing, the case of al-Andalus (as the Iberian Peninsula was called during the period of Islamic (Moorish) rule) and the fact that its literary riches have mostly failed to be integrated into a collective vision of the Arabic literary tradition may be considered emblematic of the problems raised by methods that place more emphasis on non-literary criteria (such as geography and dynastic history). The issues become even more difficult when it comes to addressing the period which roughly spans the thirteenth to eighteenth centuries, an era designated by yet another kind of title, 'the period of decadence'. Here a combination of factors, among them the rule of large parts of the region by non-Arabic speakers and a perceived preference among the implied audience for Arabic literary works for aesthetic norms considerably at variance with our own, has led – at least until relatively recently – to a widespread ignorance of five centuries of creativity in Arabic aptly reflected in the title generally applied to the period. Beyond the clear problem of our lack of knowledge about such a substantial time-period, there is also the fact that any assessment about the nature of the changes that occurred during the nineteenth century, generally gathered together under the heading of 'modernisation' – involving an encounter with the West and a revival of the heritage of the past, is rendered difficult, or even impossible, by the fact that the real circumstances of the 'pre-modern' remain unclear. Thus, while renewed contacts with the Western world have clearly played a major role in the developments that have taken place in the Arabic literary tradition during the 'modern period' and the 'revival' that brought it about, there is still room for a good deal of discussion about the relative importance of different factors during its earliest phases.

The principal point to be made following this discussion of traditional modes of periodisation of Arabic literature is that they have no internal consistency. Even so, I have to note that the majority of previous surveys, penned by distinguished scholars such as Goldziher, Nicholson, Gibb,

Blachère, Huart, Brockelmann, and Nallino, make use of these principles, and acknowledge with gratitude that such works often brought important Arabic literary texts to the attention of Western readers for the first time and, with their wealth of information about writers and trends, clearly illustrated the central role that literature played and continues to play in Arab society.

As we consider the issues involved in different approaches, there is one crucial and enormous gap in our knowledge of Arabic and Islamic studies in general that needs to be identified from the outset: a sizeable and by definition unquantifiable percentage of Arabic manuscripts on all topics from the early periods of Islamic history remains unpublished and, in some cases, uncatalogued. It is such a context that the shelf-lists of a Baghdādī book-seller, ibn al-Nadīm (*d.* 990), collected into his famous book, *al-Fihrist*, offer us, through listings of titles that we do not possess, a clue as to the extent of what we are missing. Beyond such regrettable realities as these that stem from a variety of causes (not the least of which is that the field has so few practitioners), we can point out that these earlier accounts of Arabic literature are predominantly concerned with the writings of a literate élite that was almost exclusively male. Recent research into women's writings during the last two centuries suggests that a lively tradition of literature existed behind the closed curtains of the women's quarters, but that, at lcast till now, the products of such exchanges have not entered the public domain.

A concentration on the writings of this same élite has led to another interesting circumstance involving attitudes, namely the entire question of the significance of popular literature. For, while the Western world became completely fascinated by the narratives of the *Thousand and One Nights* and the fantastic worlds that they invoked following the publication of Galland's translation into French at the beginning of the eighteenth century, most Arab critics have ignored not only them but also the many other collections of popular narrative since they are not considered to be part of the literary canon. The situation has been changing more recently, however, with the advent to the educational and cultural institutions in the region of social scientific studies and especially folklore.

An Introduction to Arabic Literature should thus be seen as an attempt to present an alternative approach to the production of a survey of Arabic literature. It begins with the text that holds an especially privileged position within Islam and Arabic, namely the Qurʾān. In giving prominence to the Qur'ān, as divinely inspired text, as linguistic yardstick, and as motivation for the need to record the pre-Islamic poetic tradition in written form, we acknowledge its central place in almost every aspect of the development of Arabic language and literature.

The three chapters that follow are surveys of the development of the genres of poetry, belletristic prose and narrative, and drama. As noted above, the linkages between the genres of Arabic literature, the concept of *adab*, and the terms used to describe their analogues in Western literary traditions, are rarely exact. To cite just a single example: within the realm of narrative, the concept of *adab* admits of categories (travel narratives and biographies, for example) that have not generally attracted the attention of literary critics in the Western world.

The final chapter moves away from the literary texts themselves to consider the tradition of criticism that has existed alongside them from the outset. The distinction between the two may seem relatively clear in a modern context, but in earlier times the linkages between them, and indeed between the analysis of the Qur'ānic text and the development of criticism, are particularly close.

In recent years several nations have attempted to reflect the political and economic ramifications of what is often termed a 'global vision' in new or revised national educational curricula. A frequent component of such plans and their reception is the inclusion of more materials that deal with non-Western cultures. It is with a conscious awareness of the need for an introductory work for a general, non-specialist readership that I have written this book. I have tried to stress the continuity of the Arabic literary tradition and thus have sought as many occasions as possible to provide illustrations of the linkages that connect present and past; this is particularly the case in the introductory section to the chapters on specific genres where features of the great tradition of the past are mirrored in a present-day instance or debate. I might add that, in several of the chapters, I have deliberately made use of the introductory section to recount some of my own experiences with Arabic literature and littérateurs in the region itself; my hope is that those accounts may exemplify the considerable increase in contact with Arab littérateurs and critics which, in my view, is a major and desirable feature of recent Western scholarship. In the interests of readability, I have restricted such academic conventions as footnotes to the very minimum, listing references – where necessary – in parentheses within the text itself. The Guide to Further Reading lists only the most significant works in the field and concentrates on studies in English; sources in other European languages are included only when none is available in English (a not infrequent occurrence in many subfields).

But clearly the greatest difference lies in the fact that *An Introduction to Arabic Literature* is intended as an introductory survey. In trying to capture the riches of so vast a literary tradition in so restricted a space, I have been aware that the risks are considerable, since what is left out will always exceed what is included by a large margin. However, if readers of this work find themselves tempted to explore the literary heritage of Arabic in more detail and, dare one hope, in the original language, then this work's task of 'translation' will have been achieved.

CHAPTER 2

The contexts of the literary tradition

INTRODUCTION

The Arab League, Arab nationalism; Arabic numerals, Arabic literature; the Arabian Peninsula, the *Arabian Nights*. The English language makes use of several epithets to describe the people, language, and region whose literary creativity is the topic of this book. The Arabic language itself, by contrast, has a single word, *ʿarabī*, an adjective derived from what must be one of the earliest words in the history of the language, *ʿarab*, originally used to describe the nomadic peoples in the central regions of what is now termed the Arabian Peninsula. Quite how far back the existence of the *ʿarab* can be traced is difficult to say, but a group called the *ar-ba-a-a* are cited as components of an army in cuneiform inscriptions dating from as early as 853 BC. At the end of the 1950s the same word, *ʿarab*, was used by Jamāl ʿAbd al-Nāṣir (Nasser), the President of Egypt, when he proclaimed in a speech that 'from the Atlantic Ocean to the Arabian Gulf we are Arabs'.

In this chapter I will provide a series of contexts that are intended to serve as background for the investigations of the genres of Arabic literature that follow. Firstly I will discuss two particular contexts within which the literary tradition has been created, developed, and recorded: the physical and the linguistic. A more diachronic approach will then be used for an overview of the historical background against which the literary texts were produced; it will be subdivided into two parts, a first that looks at rulers and the changing patterns of authority, and a second that examines some of the intellectual debates against the background of which Arabic literature has been composed.

THE PHYSICAL CONTEXT

The pre-Islamic poet, Labīd, includes the following lines in the opening section of his famous *Muʿallaqah* poem:

Sites dung-stained and long abandoned after times of frequentation,
with their changing seasons of peace and war,
Fed with spring rains of the stars, hit by the thunder of a heavy
rainstorm or fine drizzle,
Falling from every passing cloud, looming dark in the daytime and with
thunder resounding at eventide.

The effect of rain on a desert environment is truly remarkable; the transformations that it brings about are immediate. While water – its presence or absence – was a very practical aspect of life within the desert existence of the earliest poets, it has been a potent image for the modern poet as well, one of fertility, of potential, of revolution. Labīd's twentieth-century successor, the Iraqi poet, Badr Shākir al-Sayyāb (*d.*1964), devotes a poem to rain ('*Unshūdat al-maṭar*') which evokes the imagery of the earliest poetry in the cause of his country's liberation:

On the night of departure how many tears have we shed,
and then, for fear of reproach, pretended it was rain . . .
Rain . . .
Rain . . .
Since our childhood, the skies
were always cloudy in wintertime,
and rain poured down,
but every year, as the earth blossomed, we stayed hungry,
Never a year went by but there was hunger in Iraq.
Rain . . .
Rain . . .
Rain . . .

And, as desert-dwellers know only too well, water, this same essential, life-giving resource, can also have a potent destructive force. The flash-floods of the *wādī* (stream-valley) can bring sudden death, a fate that is depicted with telling effect both at the conclusion of another *Mu'allaqah* poem from the earliest period of poetry, that of Imru' al-Qays, and in the fate of the hero's mother in the novel, *Nazīf al-ḥajar* (The Rocks Bleed, 1990) by the Libyan writer, Ibrāhīm al-Kūnī (*b.* 1948).

The tension between these dualities of aridity and moisture, of death and birth, has been a constant in the Arab world for the entire period represented within these pages. The text of the Qur'ān itself shows an obvious concern with the rigours of daily life in the way it depicts Paradise as a well-watered garden. This struggle to survive in such a delicate ecological balance continues to affect the lives of people who live in large areas of the Middle East and has a substantial effect on patterns of homogeneity within particular areas and nations. Thus, a nation such as Egypt, whose people cling to the fertile Nile Valley region, will tend to possess a greater sense of identity than one like the Sudan or Algeria, where geographical factors and sheer distances will serve to create real and psychological barriers.

While the coastal regions of the Mediterranean, the Red Sea, the Indian Ocean, and the Gulf, have always served as a base for wide-scale regional commerce, reflected in the famous Sindbad cycle from the *Thousand and One Nights*, the seas of the Middle East do not appear to have roused the interest of Arab littérateurs to any great extent. Perhaps as is the case with English literature, it needed the concern of an islander, the Sicilian ibn Ḥamdīs (*d.* 1132) who later travelled to Spain, to produce Arabic poetry depicting the sea. In the main, however, it is the land that has served as a major means of identity for the Arab people; the fate of the Palestinians, with their annual 'Day of the Land', is a potent contemporary symbol of that sentiment of long vintage.

The other primary geographical feature of the region is mountains. Northern Iraq, Yemen, Lebanon, and the Maghrib, for example, possess mountain ranges that have played a major role in the cultural life of their people. Mountains are often akin to cultural breakwaters, in that they can afford refuge to minority groups. The Atlas Mountains of the Maghrib have served to create a large divide between those living on the coastal plain and the mountain dwellers; in this case differences of language – Berber, French, and Arabic – only compound attitudinal differences created by different means of subsistence (animal herding and agriculture) and widely variant types of education and culture. In Yemen and Lebanon, they have provided lines of separation between different religious and political groupings, as twentieth-century conflicts in both regions have convincingly demonstrated.

This wide expanse of territory that constitutes the Arab world, with its variety of geographical and climatic features, is peopled by citizens of many nations who speak Arabic and thus trace their linguistic and cultural origins back to the Arabian Peninsula. Many of the predominant themes depicted in the literature of the pre-Islamic period – the power of community, encampments, travels, horses, camels, palm-trees – continue to resonate in the minds of Arab littérateurs. The texts of the Qur'ān and prophetic tradition (*ḥadīth*) are filled with references to the image of the palm-tree; the latter source enjoins mankind to 'honour the palm-tree which was created from Adam's own clay'. Relics of this aspect of the pre-Islamic way of life endure in colourful ways: the system of metrics devised by the great scholar of al-Baṣrah, al-Khalīl ibn

Aḥmad (*d.* 791), uses the term *bayt* (tent) for the line of poetry, and *sabab* (tent-rope) and *watad* (tent-peg) for the segments of an individual foot. The ancient virtue of *ṣabr* (tolerance of adversity, endurance) was often invoked by the vagabond (*ṣuʿlūk*) poets of the pre-Islamic period in their taunts levelled at the 'soft' life of the tribe, and has since been cited often to explain a willingness to 'bide one's time': in the case of the Crusaders, for example, who were eventually ejected after centuries of occupation. Yet another such traditional virtue is that of hospitality, a quality that, as any visitor to the Arab world knows, remains as prevalent and forceful as ever.

When the great social historian, Ibn Khaldun (*d.* 1406), wrote the Introduction (*Muqaddimah*) to his book of history, he proceeded to develop a cyclical theory of civilisation that was based on the traditional tribal virtues of the Bedouin, some of which we have just mentioned: courage, endurance, and, above all, group solidarity. His model at the time envisaged two elements – desert culture and civilisation, with the former continually replacing and invigorating the latter. The growth of cities in the Arab world, and especially the emergence of the great Islamic centres – al-Baṣrah, Baghdād, Cairo, Qayrawān, Fez, and Cordoba, for example – as sources of religious debate and intellectual dynamism, was to have a major impact on both urban and provincial life, frequently to the detriment of both. Cairo, the capital city of Egypt, is perhaps the most extreme example of this, in that fully one quarter of the inhabitants of the entire country live within the city's boundaries. But people still leave the countryside and pour into the cities; and this is just one type of migration. The discovery of oil and the vast wealth that it has brought to the countries of the Gulf region has led to the migration of huge numbers of workers in search of a living wage.

There are two particular 'lenses' through which the Western world examines the Middle East that need to be identified; not so much to avoid their use as to admit the limitations that they impose. The first involves treating 'the Arabs' and 'Islam' as monoliths, and indeed often to fuse the two into one. To be sure, the majority of Arabs are Muslims, but there are significant communities of Arabs who are not – the Maronites of Lebanon and the Copts of Egypt, for example. On the other hand, many Muslims are not Arabs; Iranians, for example (whose Persian language is a member of the Indo-European family), Pakistanis, and large communities in Malaysia, Indonesia, and China. But, beyond these points of information, there lies the assumption that the peoples of a region as diverse in history and culture as the one that we have just outlined can be described as a single, unified whole on the basis of their being linked by a common language (in itself a problematic notion, as we shall see below). The same principle can be applied to Islam, an entity which the Western world has always found it convenient to treat as a monolith in order to compensate for a failure to investigate its variety. Perhaps we might suggest, adopting de Saussure's well-known categories, that Islam, like other faith systems, clearly stipulates what constitutes its *langue* – the canonical texts that lay down the basis for its principles, but that the *parole*, the actual application in such areas as the difference between the tenets of the Sunnī and Shīʿī communities and the practices of Sufism and popular Islam, present us with a staggering variety of beliefs and rituals which reflect the world-wide scope of the faith.

The second 'lens' that I have been using is the term 'Middle East', an American term that, along with the European 'Near East', reflects the geographical location of those who coined it. Numerous scholars have addressed themselves to the precise designation of this 'region', pointing out as they do so that very few of the borders in the region were drawn by its inhabitants. For some the Middle East is coterminous with 'the Fertile Crescent', the 'central lands' of the region – Lebanon, Syria, Jordan, Israel, Egypt. However, in academic terms departments that carry the name 'Middle East' will teach not only Arabic, but also Persian and Turkish (and often other languages as well), thus including within their purview the broader definition of the Arab world represented by not only ʿAbd al-Nāṣir's Ocean-to-Gulf phrase, but also the Arab nations represented at the United Nations and the Arab League. It is this broader definition of the world of Arabic literature that will be intended when the phrase 'Middle East' is used in this book; indeed, the need to examine the literature of al-Andalus in the West and, on occasion, the lands 'beyond the river' in the East require an even broader definition.

THE LINGUISTIC CONTEXT

Arabic is a Semitic language, and is regarded by historical linguists as the member of that family of languages that has preserved the largest number of features of postulated proto-Semitic. It is the official language of a large number of nations in Africa and Asia: Morocco, Algeria, Tunisia, Libya, Egypt, the Sudan, Jordan, Lebanon, Syria, Palestine, Iraq, Saudi Arabia, Kuwait, Bahrain, Qatar, Oman, the United Arab Emirates, and Yemen. These nations make up what is known as the 'Arab world'. The Arabic language also has official status in Israel, and, because of continuing contacts across the desert regions of North Africa, is used for communication in such states as Senegal, Mauritania, and Chad. If we include within our purview the use of Arabic as the canonical language of Islam, then the spread of nations and peoples becomes enormous, incorporating Iran, Pakistan, Bangladesh, Malaysia, Afghanistan, and Indonesia as Muslim countries, and sizeable communities in many other countries, of which Tadjhikistan, India, the Philippines, China, France, Britain, and the United States are merely a representative sample. Arabic is also the official language of the League of Arab States founded in Cairo in 1945, and is one of the official languages of the United Nations.

Linguists term Arabic one of those languages that are 'diglossic', by which they imply that its native-speakers will use different registers of language according to the requirements of the social situation involved. The first language of every native-speaker of Arabic will be one of a number of colloquial dialects. That language will be used in the home and in day-to-day communication between inhabitants of the dialect area in question. As is the case with any language, there are of course many sub-dialects within each country and region, but one may begin by making a distinction on the broadest scale between the dialects of the Maghrib (Libya and westward) and those of the Eastern countries. Within the latter group the dialect of Cairo has, by dint of population size and the widespread popularity of contemporary Egyptian media, come to be regarded in the region (and among Western Arabists) as the colloquial that is at least understood (if not spoken) by the largest number of people. Other clusters of dialects include the 'Levantine' (Israel, Jordan, Lebanon, Palestine, Syria) and the Gulf (Saudi Arabia, Iraq and the Arab Emirates).

The emergence of these dialects seems to have begun with the early conquests of Islam. As the Muslim soldiers from different tribes of the Arabian Peninsula congregated in the garrison cities of the border regions (such as al-Kūfah, Fusṭāṭ, and Qayrawān), the practicalities of day-to-day – not to mention, military – living demanded that their different language systems be fused into a common medium of communication. To these changes implicit in the geographical diversity of the Muslim community in the classical period has been added in the past century and a half a further differentiating factor in the form of neologisms and technical terms culled from the lexica of Western languages, initially Italian as a result of trade with Genoa and Venice, but later

French and English. Thus, the Lebanese word for a lorry or truck is *kamiyon* while in Jordan the word is *lūrī*.

For the many inhabitants of the Arab world who receive little or no education the colloquial dialect will be the only language they use to communicate. While a number of television programmes will be broadcast in the colloquial dialect of the region, newspapers and televised news bulletins use the 'standard' language which we will discuss below. Because of the predominantly oral nature of the colloquial dialects we possess little historical record either of their use in daily communication or of the various types of entertainment that may have been performed in them, but the demands of modern drama for realism on stage have led not only to the performance of plays in the colloquial language but also to the publication of some of the texts of those plays in printed form.

The colloquial dialect is then the first language of all native-speakers of Arabic. Those who attend school and even proceed on to university acquire as a second kind of Arabic language the written form of Arabic that is standard throughout the Arab world and thus a major expression of the Arab individual's sense of identity and unity with his fellow Arabs. While very early examples of the language are to be found in Assyrian, Nabatean (first century BC to fourth century AD), and Palmyrene (first to third centuries AD) sources, the great ideal for this standard Arabic language is provided by the Qur'ān, regarded as the supreme and inimitable masterpiece of Arabic. The Qur'ān's clear statement that it is 'an Arabic Qur'ān' and that every sacred revelation comes to its people in their own language initiated a movement of standardisation that, to a remarkable degree, has preserved the classical patterns of standard Arabic morphology and syntax. In the eighth and ninth centuries the grammarians of al-Kūfah and al-Basṛah set about sifting and recording the principles of the language, and local variants that fell outside the framework of such a system of 'regularity' were scrupulously noted, presumably so as to be avoided at all costs.

However, in spite of the availability and application of such powerful conservative forces, the written Arabic language did undergo the natural process of linguistic change. From the outset, some regions adopted the language as their own mode of written communication: Egypt, Syria, and Iraq, for example. Others adopted Arabic as part of the process of conversion to Islam, but indigenous regional languages remained a powerful source of social cohesion – as with Berber in the Maghrib, for example. Persian and Turkish later reassumed their positions as the primary mode of cultural expression for their native speakers while Arabic maintained its canonical status within those spheres (such as the law) where the role of Islam retained its significance. Those inhabitants of the conquered territories who converted to Islam brought to Arabic several features of their own native languages, and this gradual process of adaptation and change was accelerated by the translation movement of the eighth and ninth centuries (discussed in more detail below) whereby works from the Indo-Persian and Greek traditions were rendered into Arabic. As the intellectual centres of the expanding Islamic community now became the bases for scholarship in a huge variety of disciplines – for example, grammar, law, mathematics, astronomy, music, philosophy, medicine, and literature – so did the Arabic language become a clear, subtle and adaptive medium for recording a truly remarkable tradition of learning.

While the great canonical Islamic works of the classical period of Arabic learning show a remarkable degree of unanimity regarding the appropriate level of discourse to be used, the different cultures gathered together within the framework of Islam, the wide variety of subjects that were the object of scholarly research, and the sheer passage of time made it inevitable that elements of difference would also emerge in the written language. However, the very regularising instincts of the grammatical tradition and our less than complete knowledge of some six centuries (twelfth to eighteenth) of Arabic linguistic history combine to make it difficult to comment in detail on the effects on written Arabic discourse of a period in which the dominance of other languages (particularly Ottoman Turkish) and the political fragmentation of the Arabic-speaking regions seem to have served in several spheres to narrow the gap separating the structures of the written language from those of the colloquial dialects.

Whatever the case may be, the movement of cultural revival that followed contacts with the Western world in the eighteenth and nineteenth centuries found itself able to revive the classical tradition of language and to reassert the primacy of its principles in the face of yet another process of cultural and linguistic interchange, this time with the forces of European colonialism. Such is the continuing immense prestige of the standard language – the language of the Qur'ān and the classical heritage of Arab-Islamic culture – that the morphology and syntax of modern written Arabic show remarkably little change from those of the classical written language. Organisations such as the Language Academies of Damascus (founded in 1919) and Cairo (founded in 1932) have met with the somewhat equivocal success that characterises such institutions everywhere in monitoring language change, most particularly in the lexical realm. Even so, the hallowed place accorded the standard written form of the language within the cultural mindset of the vast majority of Arabic speakers today, whatever their nation, race, or religion, makes it a principal symbol of stability in a context of continual change.

Combining our discussion of these two types of language, the colloquial and the standard, we may suggest that a native-speaker of Arabic operates along a spectrum that starts from a pole represented by the colloquial language. Those people who enter the educational system will move along that spectrum towards the achievement of the status of an educated person. Here the linguistic yardstick is the classical Arabic language and its current manifestation, often termed modern standard Arabic. Quite apart from the chronological distinction implied by the 'classical' language of the cultural heritage and the 'current' (or 'modern'), there are other distinct levels of language at this end of the spectrum also: from discussions among educated people on the media, to news bulletins, to official speeches and sermons, and to some types of drama.

While linguists specialising in the study of Arabic may endeavour to describe the language as it is used by its native-speakers, religion and cultural heritage combine to assign widely variant degrees of prestige to the different types. We can begin by considering the terms themselves. *Al-fuṣḥā* (or *Al-lughah al-fuṣḥā*) is in the form of a comparative adjective: it implies 'the language that is more correct'. The dialects by contrast are called *ʿāmmiyyāt* (languages of the populace) or the less pejorative *lughāt dārijah* (current languages). The attitudes implicit in these terms colour the discussion of the cultural value of many modern literary genres, most especially drama and fiction. They have also served to consign surviving texts of earlier popular literature to the realm of non-literature; this includes the *Thousand and One Nights* itself, a work that was recorded in a form of the written language that reflects the discourse practices of story-telling rather than those of élite literature.

One of the features of Arabic which links it to the other Semitic languages is the basis of its lexicon on a series of consonantal patterns usually called 'roots'. Thus, the triconsonantal pattern K-T-B denotes the semantic field of 'writing'. KaTaBa means 'he wrote', *KāTiBun* (the active participle) means 'a writer, scribe, secretary', *maKTūBun* (the passive participle) means 'written, fated', *maKTaBun* (the noun of place) means 'desk, office', *Kitābun* means 'book', *KuTTāBun* means 'Qur'ān school', and so on.

This algebraic approach to language analysis also makes its way into morphology. The consonantal structure of the verb *F-ʿ-L* (to do) becomes the framework which can be used to illustrate the forms of verbs and nouns; they being two of the three categories in Arabic grammar, while the third is 'particles' – whatever is not a noun or verb. Using once again the root pattern K-T-B I can say that *KaTaBa* ('he wrote', also the basic morphological pattern for the verb) is of the pattern *Faʿ aLa* while *KāTiBun* is of the pattern *Fāʿ iLun*. When we turn to the verb, we find that each example will have two basic time frames – complete and incomplete, active and passive participles, and a gerund (for example, *QaTaLa*, 'he killed'; *yaQTuLu*, 'he kills'; *QāTiLun*, 'killer'; *maQTūLun*, 'killed'; *QaTLun*, 'murder').

Arabic has two types of sentence structure: the nominal sentence which begins with a noun, and the verbal sentence which begins with a verb. Using the two 'stars' of Arabic grammar sentences, ʿAmr and Zayd, and their preferred verb, 'to strike', I can say: *ʿAmrun ḌaRaBa Zaydan* and *ḌaRaBa ʿAmrun Zaydan*, where the English translation of both is 'ʿAmr struck Zayd'. The former is a nominal sentence; the assumption behind the choice of this kind of sentence structure over a verbal sentence is that ʿAmr is to be the topic about whom a particular piece of information is to be imparted.

The features of the Arabic language, its huge lexicon with a concomitant potential for enrichment and obfuscation, its repertoire of morphological transformations, its exultation in the sheer beauty of the sound of words, these elements have served as the inspiration for generations of littérateurs who have made virtuoso use of the potential it offers.

THE HISTORICAL CONTEXT

Introduction

The breadth of the geographical space into which the Islamic dominions expanded is matched by the length of their recorded history. If we adopt the year AD 622 – the beginning of the *hijrah* era marked by the Prophet Muḥammad's 'emigration' from Mecca to Medina – as a point of reference, then we are talking of some thirteen centuries. However, this time frame also has to be extended backwards. In Chapter 1 I noted the primary historical division that is created by the revelation of the Qurʾān to Muḥammad: between an Islamic period and a pre-Islamic one, termed *al-jāhiliyyah* (the period of ignorance). However, as the Muslim community began to realise the need to codify the Arabic language and to assess the accuracy of the memories of transmitters (the Arabic term is 'carriers') of the Qurʾānic text, the pre-Islamic period came to be regarded as a repository of information that was of extreme value to the emerging scholarly communities in the fields of the Islamic sciences. One of the most illustrious of the early historians, al-Ṭabarī (*d.* 923), begins his account with the story of the Creation and the Fall and then uses a combination of biblical, pre-Islamic Arabian and Iranian myths as a means of linking together received wisdom concerning the earliest periods in the region that was brought together under the aegis of Islam.

Pre-Islamic Arabia

The Arabian city of Mecca (Makkah) is set in the mountains to the east of the Red Sea coast at approximately the halfway point between South Arabia and the lands of the Fertile Crescent to the north. Mecca was a thriving mercantile community, but it was also renowned for other reasons. Close by were Mount ʿArafāt, a traditional place of pilgrimage, and the town of ʿUkāẓ which was the venue of a celebrated annual poetry festival at which tribal poets would compete. Within the city of Mecca itself was the Kaʿbah, a remarkable sanctuary enclosure that served as the focus for the worship of a number of pagan deities. The guardians of this shrine in the sixth century were the tribe of Quraysh. Apart from cities such as Mecca, another kind of venue at which the more sedentary tribes would cluster was the oasis, which, needless to say, provided other opportunities for commercial activity. One such was the town of Yathrib, some two hundred miles due north of Mecca. It was to this town that Muḥammad travelled in secret in 622. As it became the centre of the new Muslim community, so did its name change to Madīnat al-nabī (the city of the Prophet), abbreviated to al-Madīnah or Medina.

The harsh terrain and climate of the central regions of the Peninsula seem to have served for the most part as effective barriers to incursions from the outside. To the north and east two tribal confederations served as buffers between the peoples of the Peninsula and the two major empires of the region. The Banū Ghassān fulfilled this function vis-à-vis the Byzantine authorities based in Constantinople (now Istanbul), while the Banū Lakhm operated from a capital at al-Ḥīrah in Southern Iraq in their dealings with the Sasanian rulers of Persia.

THE PROPHET MUḤAMMAD AND THE FIRST CALIPHS

It was in the city of Mecca that Muḥammad received his first revelation in about AD 610. Following the death of his father, he had been taken under the protection of his uncle, Abū Ṭālib, and had successfully engaged in trade on behalf of a wealthy widow, Khadījah, whose offer of marriage he accepted. Following his custom of contemplating as he wandered the hills near the city, he heard a voice that told him: 'Recite in the name of your Lord who created, created mankind from a blood-clot' (Sūra 96). This was to be the first of the revelations that he received for the rest of his life and that were gathered together after his death as the Qur'ān. When Muḥammad began to preach his message – of a transcendent God who passes judgement on sinners and of his own role as a prophet – the reaction of the Meccans was one of antipathy to both the content of the message and its implications for their way of life. Following the death of both Abū Ṭālib and Khadījah in 619, the situation of Muḥammad and his followers became progressively more difficult, and in 622 he accepted the invitation of a group of tribal leaders in the oasis of Yathrib to serve as arbiter in their dispute with each other. This emigration (*hijrah*) is a major event in Islamic history in that Muḥammad's arrival in Medina marks the beginning of the formation of the Muslim community that was soon to burst out of the Arabian Peninsula and establish itself as a major world religion.

The ten years that Muḥammad spent in Medina laid the groundwork for the emergence of Islam as a community and system of belief. The revelations of that period were to form the basis for many of the institutions, laws, and societal norms that were to govern the behaviour of Muslims. As the new religious community began to establish its guidelines in this way, some of the groups who had initially welcomed Muḥammad's arrival began to dissociate themselves. At this time Muḥammad was inspired to change the direction of prayer for the new community from Jerusalem to Mecca. Meanwhile, relations with the Meccan community remained antagonistic, particularly when the Muslims launched attacks on the Meccan caravan trade. However, after a series of battles that displayed the strength of the new community, an agreement was reached between the two sides in 628 that permitted

Muḥammad to lead a large group on a pilgrimage to Mecca in the following year. In 632 Muḥammad again travelled from Medina to Mecca to perform the pilgrimage (*ḥajj*), but died suddenly in June of that year.

At the time of Muḥammad's death no arrangements had been made concerning the authority structure of the community of believers that he had brought together. However, he did bequeath to his successors two sets of sources that were of enormous importance to the development of Islam. The first was, of course, the revelations of the Qurʾān that are regarded by Muslims as God's word to His community conveyed to them in Arabic by one of His 'messengers' or Prophets; and Muḥammad is in fact designated as the 'seal of the Prophets'. The second important source that Muḥammad created was his personal practice during his lifetime (*sunnah*) which was regarded as providing a model of behaviour for the community in those many particular situations for which the corpus of Qurʾānic revelations provided no guidance. The process of collecting, organising, and assessing the 'traditions' (*ḥadīth*) concerning the Prophet's activities became, along with the analysis of the text of the Qurʾān itself, one of the most urgent tasks of scholars within the Muslim community.

After the unexpected death of Muḥammad, the elders of the Muslim community convened a meeting at which Abū Bakr, one of the very first converts to the faith, was chosen as the first holder of the position of 'successor of the Prophet of God' (*khalīfat rasūl al-lāh*) or caliph. Abū Bakr found himself placed at the head of a religious community (*ummah*) that was to be based on principles that had yet to be codified. Furthermore, the ties that had bound together the various groups attracted to the community during Muḥammad's lifetime were now shown to be not a little ambiguous; much of Abū Bakr's brief period as caliph (*r.* 632–4) was spent in the so-called 'Riddah' (restoration) wars, the process of bringing the Arabian tribes back into the fold by force. It was the decision of Abū Bakr's shrewd successor, ʿUmar ibn al-Khaṭṭāb (*r.* 634–44), to channel much of this tribal recalcitrance to the benefit of the community by initiating a process of expansion which is one of the most remarkable in world history. In 634 Khālid ibn al-Walīd defeated a Byzantine force in Syria; Damascus fell in 636 and Jerusalem in 638. By 643 ʿAmr ibn al-ʿĀṣ had captured the whole of Egypt. The armies of the Sasanian empire were defeated in the major battle of Qādisiyyah in 637, resulting in the occupation of the entire region of Iraq.

This first wave of conquests was accomplished within little more than a decade of Muḥammad's death. In a second era of expansion, Muslim armies moved across North Africa. The governor of the region, Mūsā ibn Nuṣayr, dispatched a party headed by his Berber commander, Ṭāriq, that reached the Straits separating Africa from the Iberian Peninsula in 710. Crossing the water (during which he passed by Jabal Ṭāriq (Tariq's mountain, Gibraltar), he initiated the conquest of the Iberian Peninsula. By 732 Muslim armies had crossed the Pyrenees and reached the city of Tours in France where, in a memorable battle against the forces of Charles Martel that has been much fêted in Western historical sources, they were defeated and gradually forced back across the Pyrenees. The Muslim forces also moved against the Byzantine borders in Anatolia, and the repertoire of Arabic panegyric records the many occasions in the eighth, ninth and tenth centuries when the two armies were ranged against each other in this region. Further to the east the lands of Transoxania became part of the Muslim dominions by 713.

While the first phase of these campaigns succeeded in uniting the tribes of the Arabian Peninsula in a common purpose, questions regarding legitimacy and authority and specifically the mode of succession to the caliphate continued to beset the community in Medina. When ʿUmar was assassinated in 644, the caliphate was passed to another early convert to Islam, ʿUthmān ibn ʿAffān (*r.* 644–56), a member of the Banī Umayyah clan; the claims of ʿAlī, Muḥammad's cousin and son-in-law, were thus overlooked. When ʿUthmān was assassinated in 656, ʿAlī assumed the caliphate, but objections were immediately raised to the legitimacy of his succession. ʿAlī left Medina in order to bolster his claims in Iraq, but near al-Baṣrah he was challenged by two of Muḥammad's former companions and the Prophet's wife, ʿĀʾishah. The Battle of the Camel, so-called because fighting raged around ʿĀʾishah's riding beast, was the first one to bring the Muslim community into conflict with itself. ʿUthmān's cousin, Muʿāwiyah ibn Abī Sufyān (whom he had appointed governor of Syria), now entered the continuing struggle for power, and the inevitable confrontation between the rival claims and interests took place at Ṣiffīn on the River Euphrates in 657. After some skirmishes between the two sides, ʿAmr ibn al-ʿĀṣ, the renowned army commander, suggested an arbitration process. Some of ʿAlī's supporters were disgusted by his acceptance of the proposed resolution and abandoned him, becoming known as 'those who left' (*al-khawārij*, sing. *khārijī*). The angry opposition of these former colleagues, coupled with the arbitrators' decision to request that ʿAlī renounce the caliphate, weakened his support. In 660 Muʿāwiyah proclaimed himself caliph, and in 661 a Khārijite assassinated ʿAlī in al-Kūfah.

While Muʿāwiyah was able to consolidate his power as leader of the Muslim community from Damascus, al-Ḥasan and al-Ḥusayn, the two sons of ʿAlī, became a rallying-point for forces who believed in the right of Muḥammad's own descendants to the position of caliph. When Muʿawiyah died in 680 and his son, Yazīd, was designated his successor by heredity, al-Ḥusayn refused to acknowledge the new caliph. In a battle at Karbalāʾ in Iraq al-Ḥusayn's small force of followers was defeated by a much larger group of Yazīd's army, and al-Ḥusayn himself, the grandson of Muḥammad, was killed. *Shīʿat ʿAlī* (ʿAlī's party, usually abbreviated to Shīʿah and its adherents to Shīʿīs) would become a vigorous, yet separate, part of Islam, with its own beliefs, codes of law, and rituals.

The caliphate

The Banū Umayyah

Once in power, the Banū Umayyah faced a formidable set of problems resulting from a number of factors. The task of establishing the procedures that would produce order within the Islamic community was begun by the caliph ʿAbd al-Malik (*r.* 685–705), who, among many other things, ordered the construction of the Dome of the Rock in Jerusalem, a site as revered in Islam as in the faith of Jews and Christians, described in the Qurʾān as 'the people of the book'. The domains of Islamic authority had expanded as more sections of the '*dār al-ḥarb*' (the haven of conflict) were added to '*dār al-Islām*' (the haven of Islam). The pace of these conquests severely taxed the military and administrative resources of the young community. To control the outlying regions, garrison cities (*amṣār*) were set up: Fusṭāṭ to the south of present-day Cairo, Qayrawān in Tunisia, and both al-Kūfah and al-Baṣrah in Iraq. Lines of communication between these cities and the central administration in Damascus were long, and it is therefore hardly surprising that these garrisons became the focal points of much debate and unrest. As the Islamic communal structure began to take shape, the dissidence of these two Iraqi cities was converted to more intellectual pursuits, and they became primary centres of learning and intellectual controversy.

The area now under Muslim control incorporated within its boundaries a variety of ethnic types, languages, and religious beliefs. The society, and especially that in the garrison towns of the outlying areas, found themselves overwhelmed with converts to Islam (*mawālī*). These people did not command the communal respect accorded to the Arab Muslims who had brought Islam from the Peninsula to this larger area, but they were Muslims and had to be accommodated within the community. As these converts flocked to the garrison towns, the countryside became severely depopulated (especially in the fertile regions of Mesopotamia). It was the function of another administrator-caliph, ʿUmar ibn ʿAbd al-ʿazīz (*r.* 717–20), to begin the process of establishing a community in which the status of Muslim was of primary importance and other modes of identity were secondary. Meanwhile, those who did not wish to convert to Islam were given a contract of protection (*dhimmah*) and were thus known as *dhimmīs*.

The problems that needed to be addressed by the caliph as head of the Muslim community were enormous, and the measures taken by the Umawī holders of the office were not sufficient to quell increasing feelings of resentment. The Banū Umayyah were viewed by the new converts to Islam as tribal chieftains, as secular monarchs, who continued to indulge in their tribal rivalries and to assert a superiority based on their desert origins in the Arabian Peninsula. In 747 these feelings among the *mawālī* burst into a full-scale revolt. From a centre in al-Kūfah, the Banū ʿAbbās – descendants of al-ʿAbbās, Muḥammad's uncle – sent Abū Muslim to the distant province of Khurāsān, where he raised the black flags of rebellion against the Banū Umayyah. Gathering support as they proceeded towards Iraq, the leaders of this revolt against the Banū Umayyah claimed the caliphate for Abū al-ʿAbbās (nicknamed 'al-Saffāḥ' (blood-letter)) in al-Kūfah in 749. The forces of the Banū Umayyah were defeated at the Battle of the River Zāb in 750, and all the members of the Banū Umayyah were systematically killed, apart from a certain ʿAbd al-raḥmān (nicknamed 'Ṣaqr Quraysh' (the falcon of the Quraysh)) who managed to escape detection and made his way to Spain. In 755 he was acknowledged as *Amīr* in Cordoba. When his successor, ʿAbd al-raḥmān III, was acknowledged as caliph in 925, the era of a single caliphate – albeit a focus of both support and opposition – was at an end.

The Banū al-ʿAbbās

The caliphs of the Banū al-ʿAbbās served as heads of the Muslim community for a period of five centuries, from 750 till the sack of Baghdād by the Mongols in 1258, an era during which the geographic spread of the 'haven of Islam' continued – extending eastward to the borders of India and establishing contacts far beyond that. This lengthy era is usually subdivided into an initial stage when the caliph, as spiritual leader of a community based on the faith of Islam, managed to maintain some form of control over the region, and a second stage – a period of some three centuries – when the caliph was essentially a symbolic figure at the head of the Muslim community, while secular authority was vested in other offices and the separate regions of the Islamic dominions enjoyed substantial amounts of autonomy.

One of the first gestures of al-Saffāḥ's brother and successor, al-Manṣūr (*r.* 754–75), was to order the construction of a new city at a point where the Tigris and Euphrates rivers come closest to each other. The establishment of the capital in Baghdād – with its Persian name – in 762 marks an acknowledgement of the expansion of the Islamic dominions and the need to move beyond the region and trappings of a purely Arab power centre. As the bureaucracy began to expand and to organise itself into separate divisions of records, taxes, and military matters, so did an increasing number of Persian administrators come forward to fill the new positions. The caliphs al-Mahdī (*r.* 775–85) and Hārūn al-Rashīd (*r.* 786–809) formalised the recognition of this administrative apparatus by appointing members of the Barmak family (of Persian origin) to the post of *wazīr* (the current term in the Middle East for minister), a decision that set in motion a gradual but continuing process whereby the functions of caliphal authority were subdivided and alternative power centres came into existence.

Following the death of al-Rashīd the tensions aroused by this new Persian influence led to conflict. His Arab wife had produced a son, al-Amīn, while a Persian concubine had given birth to another son, al-Maʾmūn. The struggle for succession between the two sons involved the Muslim community in yet another period of civil war that concluded with al-Maʾmūn's victory over his half-brother in 813. This war, needless to say, wreaked havoc not only on the civilian population of the region but also on the loyalties of the army. The practice was now developed of importing Turkish youths into service in order to create a trained and loyal military force. By the time of the caliph al-Muʿtaṣim (*r.* 833–42), this new category of soldiers had become such a disruptive element in the life of Baghdād that the caliph decided in 836 to move them to the purpose-built city of Samarrāʾ further up the River Tigris, and to establish his centre of authority there. In 892 the caliph al-Muʿtaḍid decided to return to Baghdād, but the new patterns of authority had now been firmly established.

By this time, several regions within the larger area of Islamic dominion were already politically independent. Al-Andalus had been governed by a separate dynasty of the Banū Umayyah since their fall from power in the east. As the ʿAbbāsī authorities in Baghdād dispatched governors to the different areas of the region, several of them established themselves as local potentates and passed on their position through hereditary succession. The Aghlabī dynasty in Tunis dates from as early as 800 and managed to cause considerable consternation in Europe through its conquest of the island of Sicily that was finally completed in 878. In Egypt Aḥmad ibn Ṭulūn, the builder of one of Cairo's most glorious mosques, was to establish his own dynasty in 868. Other family dynasties also controlled large segments of the Iranian region. The year 945 sees the completion of a process that put an end to effective caliphal power. In the blunt but accurate phrase of Shawqī Ḍayf, the caliph was now like a parrot in a cage.

The steady diminution of caliphal authority during the three centuries that precede the sack of Baghdād by the Mongols in 1258 served to amplify still further the already immense variety of the political and cultural landscape. The Shīʿah community had split into a number of groupings according to their beliefs regarding the legitimacy of the Imams who were ʿAlī's successors. One group, called the Ismāʿīlīs after the eldest son of the sixth Imām, were particularly vigorous in their missionary activity. In 910, one of their number, ʿUbaydallāh, arrived in Tunis and succeeded in wresting power from the Aghlabī ruler. Proclaiming himself Shīʿī caliph, he named the dynasty that he established Fāṭimī after Fāṭimah, the Prophet's daughter and ʿAlī's wife. In 969 Fāṭimī forces captured the capital city of Egypt and established their rule there. Work started immediately on the building of a new city, named 'the victorious' (Al-Qāhirah, later rendered by Italian travellers who visited the region as 'Cairo'), and in 972 a seat of Shīʿī learning, the al-Azhar Mosque, was established at its centre. Further to the west, the cities of Qayrawān in Tunisia and Fāṣ (Fez) in Morocco continue their process of development as intellectual centres around their great mosques. In al-Andalus, the Umawī dynasty reaches its zenith of power when ʿAbd al-rahmān III (*r.* 912–61) proclaims himself as caliph. At this period, the capital city of Cordoba is one of the major intellectual centres of Europe, and Andalusian society is an admixture of races, religions, and languages, living alongside each other in a fertile atmosphere of intercultural exchange that is of incalculable importance in the intellectual history of Europe. The pattern of decentralisation that we have already seen in the east is replicated in the Iberian Peninsula. The Umawī dominions break up into a number of petty states that almost immediately begin to lose territory to the Christian kingdoms to the north. By 1085 Toledo was in Christian hands, part of the process of '*reconquista*' that was not completed until 1492 when the forces of the redoubtable Isabella of Castille and her husband, Fernando of Aragon, captured Granada and expelled the Arab and Jewish communities to North Africa.

Spain was not the only venue where Christian forces were advancing southward. The Normans overran Sicily, completing its conquest by 1091. The region of Syria had witnessed a succession of conflicts and was divided into areas controlled by the Fāṭimī dynasty of Egypt, the Orthodox Christian Emperor of Byzantium, and the Turkish dynasty of the Saljūqs which had taken over the secular administrative authority in Baghdād (with the connivance of the ʿAbbāsī caliph, al-Qāʾim) in 1055. By the end of the eleventh century the Saljūqs had seized control of much of the region, including the Holy Places in Jerusalem, a situation that led the Byzantine Emperor to appeal to the Pope in Rome for aid. In 1096 Pope Urban II gave a speech in France that called for a crusade that would lead to the recovery of the Holy Places from the hands of the 'infidels'. The First Crusade set out at once, and Jerusalem was captured in 1099 amid gruesome scenes of pillage, slaughter, and bounty hunting. Several decades later (in 1144) Muslim forces, led by Zanjī, the governor of the Iraqi city of Mawṣil, launched a counter-attack. Zanjī's son, Nūr al-dīn, took over the task of ousting the Crusaders and was soon in control of much of Syria. He was followed by the renowned Ṣalāḥ al-dīn (Saladin), who managed to seize power in Egypt following the death of the last Fāṭimī caliph, al-ʿĀḍid in 1171, and, following the death of his uncle, he undertook the conquest of Syria, first overcoming the almost legendary branch of the Ismāʿīlī Shīʿah known as the Assassins (*ḥashīshiyyūn*) and then capturing Jerusalem in 1191.

Upon Ṣalāḥ al-dīn's death in 1193, his successors – the Ayyūbī dynasty – countered numerous attempts by Christian forces to capture both Jerusalem and Egypt. The last Ayyūbī ruler of Egypt, Tūrān Shāh, was overthrown and killed in 1250 by a most unusual and interesting social group, one of the slave regiments of the army called Mamlūks. These slaves, mostly Turks or Circassians purchased as boys, proceeded to establish a dynasty based in Cairo in which the Sultan had to be a manumitted slave, a regime that lasted until the Ottoman conquest of Egypt in 1516–17. Even then, the Mamlūks retained authority within Egypt under the overall suzerainty of the Ottoman Sultan in Istanbul, and it was not until 1811 that Mamlūk power was finally eliminated when an

Albanian Turkish soldier in the Ottoman army named Muḥammad ʿAlī engineered a spectacular massacre following a banquet in the citadel of Cairo that Ṣalāḥ al-dīn had built on the Muqaṭṭam Hills overlooking the city.

From 1218 the easternmost regions of the Islamic dominions – Transoxania and Khurāsān – began to encounter a new and mighty military force, the armies of the Mongol ruler, Jinkiz (Gengis) Khān. In 1256, Hūlāgū Khān, Jinkiz's grandson, moved into Iraq, and the ʿAbbāsī capital fell in February 1258. The city and its inhabitants were subjected to a brutal assault: libraries and mosques were destroyed and the entire ʿAbbāsī family was killed by being trampled to death by horses. The Mongols did not pause to celebrate their triumph, but continued to Syria where they captured Aleppo. However, the advance of the Mongol army, its lines of communication and supply stretched perilously thin, was finally halted at the battle of ʿAyn Jālūt in 1260. The great victory of the Mamlūk army and the military feats of their general, Baybars, are the topic of one of the Arab world's favourite popular epics. Retreating to the east, the Mongols established a dynasty – named Ilkhan after the title of their leaders – converted to Islam, and ruled parts of Persia, Iraq and Anatolia into the fourteenth century.

The Mamlūk and Ottoman periods

As we have already noted, the process of fragmentation within the Islamic dominions was well under way long before 1258, and the tenth century had witnessed no fewer than three caliphates – in Iraq, Egypt, and Spain. Thus, even as we acknowledge the cataclysmic effect of the Mongol invasion in the regions of Persia, Iraq, and Syria, we must wonder whether the more distant regions within the Islamic dominions – the Maghrib and Spain, for example – were affected in any significant way. The inhabitants of al-Andalus, for example, had seen their 'petty kingdoms' replaced by two waves of Muslim zealots from Morocco, the Almoravids in the eleventh century and the Almohads in the twelfth. In 1232 Muḥammad ibn al-Aḥmar announced his independence and declared himself Sultan. Six years later he entered the city of Granada and established the dynasty that survived until 1492. While the Mongols were moving through Persia and Iraq towards Baghdād, Ibn al-Aḥmar's successors were in the process of building one of al-Andalus's most spectacular monuments, the Alhambra Palace in Granada (named after the dynasty's founder).

During the fourteenth century, the suzerainty of the dynasties that held sway in Persia and Iraq was challenged by a new figure whose reputation for brutality rivalled that of the Mongols: Tīmūr Lang (Tīmūr 'the Lame', usually known in English – as in Marlowe's play – as Tamburlaine). From his capital of Samarqand he first subdued the lands of Khurāsān and the Caucasus, destroying cities and farmlands as he went. After a foray into India (where one of his descendants, Bābūr (*d.* 1530), was to found the Mughal dynasty) he moved against the Mamlūk territories of Syria, capturing Damascus in 1403. However, Tīmūr died suddenly in 1405 while planning yet another campaign to China.

One of the groups that Tīmūr confronted and overcame during his march to the west was the army of the incipient Ottoman dynasty which traced its origins back to ʿUthmān (Turkish Osman), the son of a tribal leader who in the thirteenth century had assisted the Saljūqs in their ongoing conflict against the forces of Byzantium. Having established a base at Būrsa in Anatolia, the Ottomans took their attack to the Balkans, beginning a process of transformation in the region, the results of which continue to make themselves evident in the break-up of the former Yugoslavia in the 1990s. Bāyezīd I (*r.* 1389–1402) brought most of the Balkans under Ottoman control, and in 1453 his great-grandson, Muḥammad (Mehmet) Fātiḥ ('the conqueror'), managed to achieve a long-standing goal of the Ottomans when the city of Constantinople, the seat of Eastern Christendom, was captured. The city was renamed Istanbul and for four and a half centuries was to be the centre of a huge empire and bureaucracy.

The campaigns undertaken during the reign of the Ottoman Sultan Selīm (dubbed 'the Grim' (*r.* 1512–20)) were of a pace and sweep to rival those of the early Muslim conquests. In 1514 he set out to subdue a rival force that had come to prominence in the regions of Iran, the Ṣafavī dynasty which assumed power after the downfall of Tīmūr's successors and, most significantly, had become a vigorous centre of Shīʿīte belief. However, while Selīm succeeded in driving the Ṣafavī forces from Anatolia, the Ṣafavī ruler, Ismāʿīl, who had proclaimed himself Shāh in 1501, consolidated his authority in the region which now constitutes Iran (where Shīʿah Islam remains the national religion). Under Ismāʿīl's successor, Shāh ʿAbbās I (*r.* 1588–1629), the city of Iṣfahān became a major centre of learning and culture. Sultan Selīm now turned his attention southward, and by 1517 he had also defeated the Mamlūk armies and entered the city of Cairo. When Selīm died in 1520, the Ottoman Empire included Anatolia, Syria, Egypt, and the western part of the

Arabian Peninsula; the Sultan was 'the guardian of the two holy places [Mecca and Medina]', a title that has in more recent times been adopted by the Saudi monarchs. Under his successor, Sulaymān (*r.* 1520–66) – known as 'the lawgiver' and 'the magnificent', North Africa was brought under Ottoman control. In Europe the armies of the Sultan moved beyond their possessions in the Balkans and besieged the Austrian capital of Vienna.

When we bear in mind the sheer scope of the empire that was administered from Istanbul and the length of time that it held sway over the Middle East region, it should not surprise us that the process of decline, which – as ibn Khaldūn had noted – would involve both inside and outside forces, was a gradual one. Among outside factors we should note the discovery of the Cape route to the Far East, and the commercial destabilisation brought about by the tremendous wealth that Spain was bringing to Europe as a result of its conquests in the Americas. Within the Ottoman system itself the huge size of the ruling family frequently led to destructive feuds at the time of succession. Equally damaging to stability and authority was the fact that the tight organisation of the armed forces, most especially the much feared janissary infantrymen and the navy, was allowed to slacken. In the seventeenth and eighteenth centuries Ottoman forays into Europe became less and less successful, and the peace agreements that brought them to an end were increasingly detrimental to Ottoman interests. With the Treaty of Karlowitz in 1699 the Ottomans were forced to hand over Hungary to Austria, while in 1774 the Treaty of Kutchuk Kainardji assigned to the ruler of Russia the right to protect Christians living within Ottoman dominions.

The Middle East and the West

In 1826 the Ottoman Sultan, Maḥmūd II (*r.* 1808–39), seized the opportunity afforded by the unpopularity of the janissary corps to carry out long-needed reforms to the Ottoman armed forces. Under Maḥmūd's successor, ʿAbd al-Majīd (*r.* 1839–61), these initial gestures were expanded into a wide-scale process of reform, known under the general title of *tanẓīmāt* (reorganisations): included were such concepts as subjects' rights, freedom of religion, fair assessment of taxes, and the right of all nations to indulge in free commerce.

Elsewhere in the Middle East, contacts with Europe took a different form. In Lebanon, for example, the Maronite community had maintained ties with the Vatican in Rome since at least the sixteenth century;

a Maronite College had been established by the Pope in 1584. By contrast, the Ottoman authorities elsewhere – in Syria, Iraq, and the Maghrib, for example – exercised a tight degree of control over the intellectual community and its modes of communication with the outside world.

It was in Egypt that the meeting of cultures was most abrupt. Napoleon launched an invasion of Egypt in 1798, bringing with him not only an army and navy but also a substantial group of scientists. The Egyptian army, even though bolstered by Ottoman reinforcements, was roundly defeated at the Battle of the Pyramids. An Albanian Turkish commander of the Ottoman contingent sent to resist the French, Muḥammad ʿAlī, regarded the invasion and occupation as an obvious demonstration of the extent to which the force that he had commanded could be no match for a well-trained army equipped with modern weaponry. It was Muḥammad ʿAlī who stepped into the power vacuum that was left following the withdrawal of French forces, establishing his family as a dynasty that ruled the country until the revolution of 1952.

Beginning in 1809 Muḥammad ʿAlī began sending missions of young men to Europe – to Italy initially and later to France – to study European languages and to learn about military technology. A translation school was established, headed by the *imām* of one of these missions, Rifāʿah al-Ṭahṭāwī (*d.* 1873). Manuals on warfare and weaponry were translated, and a new cadre of officers and administrators began to take shape. Such initiatives had obvious benefits beyond the purely military sphere, not least through the educational opportunities that were made available to young Egyptians and the expansion in contacts with European commercial concerns that was the result of the country's need for technology and financial assistance. This applied most notably in the agricultural sector where, after wresting control of much productive land from its traditional owners, Muḥammad ʿAlī considerably expanded the production and export of cotton through the construction of a variety of irrigation projects. The process that began in Muḥammad ʿAlī's reign was continued by his successors, most notably the Khedive Ismāʿīl whose declared intention it was to make Egypt part of Europe. In 1869 his most grandiose project, the Suez Canal, was opened amid the greatest possible splendour. The Egyptian capital was rapidly becoming a bustling cosmopolitan city, and the liveliness of the Egyptian commercial and cultural scene was further enhanced in the 1850s and 1860s when, as a consequence of intercommunal conflict in Syria, large numbers of Christians – including many of the most prominent contributors to the earliest phases in the cultural revival – left their homeland and emigrated to Egypt.

The French occupation of Egypt in 1798 was the first, albeit short-lived, example of a pattern of Western incursions into the Middle East region that was to be a principal feature of the next century and a half. The French invaded Algeria in 1830 and gained control over a small coastal area from which their authority was gradually expanded during following decades. A pattern was established whereby the administration and educational system of the countries of the Maghrib were thoroughly gallicised. The British meanwhile were also protecting their interests in India by seizing the port of Aden in Yemen for use as a way station in 1839. As these strategic interests came to be joined by others that were of a more commercial nature, governments found themselves drawn still further into the complex web of relationships and motivations in the Middle East region. In 1881 France occupied Tunisia in order to protect its interests there, and in the following year, Britain – initially supported by France but later on its own – used the state of Egypt's finances following the conspicuous spending of the Khedive Ismāʿīl as a pretext for occupying the country. In 1904, an agreement was reached between France, Britain, and Spain acknowledging Morocco as a sphere of French influence in exchange for a similar understanding of the British role in Egypt.

Many of the seeds of the conflicts that have continued to affect the Middle East to the present day were sown during and immediately after the First World War; in this connection it needs to be borne in mind that the majority of the borders on any current map of the Middle East are the result of agreements among Western powers and not of indigenous factors. The tribes of the Arabian Peninsula had been given undertakings (in the so-called Ḥusayn–McMahon correspondence) about independence following the conclusion of the conflict in the region. Meanwhile, 1917 saw the publication of the famous Balfour Declaration in which the British government announced its support for the idea of a homeland for the Jewish people in Palestine, with the additional proviso that the interests of the current population not be affected by the implementation of such a plan. With the end of the First World War, the Ottoman Empire was no more. To all extents and purposes, Egypt and Tunisia had been separate entities for some time, but, as the secular state of Turkey now turned inwards under the rule of Muṣṭafā Kamāl (Atatürk), the remaining areas of the Middle East came to be viewed by the Western powers as 'spheres of influence'. Britain and France avoided the need to resolve the many ambiguities contained in the various understandings that they had reached by agreeing to implement the terms of a secret pact that they had drawn up with Russia in 1916, the Sykes–Picot agreement. In 1920, France was assigned control of Syria (including Lebanon), while Britain assumed control of Palestine (including Transjordan) and Iraq. The French control of the Maghrib and the British of Egypt remained as they had been.

The years 1919 and 1920 saw popular nationalist uprisings against the policies of British occupying forces in Egypt and Iraq. The years between the two World Wars were to be a period of constant confrontation between the increasingly strident demands of pan-Arab and local nationalisms and the maintenance of the status quo by the mandate powers. In Palestine the British found themselves bogged down in a political quagmire largely of their own making. In 1943 an agreement between Sunnīs and Maronites in Lebanon led to the foundation of a Lebanese state, one that was based on a tragically fragile balance between the different communities – as the events of the 1970s and 1980s showed all too clearly. The Saudi family consolidated its control in the Arabian Peninsula, while Western oil interests were permitted to explore the extent of the reserves lying beneath its soil. However, any moves in the direction of 'independence' that may have been granted by the mandate powers during the inter-war period were abruptly swept aside when, in the early 1940s, the armies of the Axis Powers and the Allies fought their way across North Africa.

The aftermath of the Second World War produced changes in hegemonic patterns on both the international and local scale. The emergence of two superpowers, the United States and the Soviet Union, led to a radical shift in the balance of global influence and its effects on the Middle East region. On a more local plane, high levels of cynicism regarding the motives of the mandate powers and resentment towards the sheer corruption of the existing governmental systems produced a volatile political mixture that was to lead to a series of revolutions in the 1950s, beginning with the overthrow of Muḥammad ʿAlī's dynasty in Egypt – represented by the corpulent figure of King Fārūq [Farouk] – in 1952. The continuing aspirations of Arab nationalists were reflected in the decision to establish a League of Arab States in Cairo in 1945. Within a year, however, this body found itself presented with a major crisis, as the United Nations – the new international body that had emerged from the ashes of the Second World War – announced a partition plan for Palestine and Britain announced a date for its withdrawal.

The War of 1948 was the first of many conflicts between the new state of Israel and its Arab neighbours.

During the 1950s Iraq, Morocco, the Sudan, and Tunisia became independent. Following a prolonged and vicious struggle – called the 'war of a million martyrs', Algeria gained its independence in 1962. The idea of Arab unity, fostered by many writers since the beginnings of the nineteenth-century revival and enshrined in the founding of the League of Arab States, took actual form in the the United Arab Republic (1958–61) between Egypt and Syria. For the Arab world the 1950s was a period of release and of growing optimism. Projects like the reapportionment of land and property through Agricultural Reform Laws were a frequent and popular choice for early implementation, but other changes that would create the bases for the new independent and secular society were more difficult to bring about.

This complex process of adaptation and change continued into the 1960s. As the United Arab Republic broke up in some bitterness, the plight of the Palestinian people continued to weigh on the conscience of the Arab world and served as a primary unifying factor. It was this cause that led the Egyptian President and the Arab world as a whole into its biggest disaster, the June War of 1967. Quite apart from the loss of Jerusalem, the West Bank, the Golan Heights, and Sinai, there was the fact that, throughout the initial days of the conflict, the leaders of the Arab world lied to their peoples. All the pretensions of previous decades were swept away, and what ensued was a moral crisis on the broadest scale.

The three decades since the 'setback' (*al-naksah*) of 1967 witnessed little change in the situation of the Palestinians. When many members of the younger generation decided to resort to a more systematic use of force against Israel by joining the fedayeen (*fidā'iyyīn*, those who sacrifice themselves), they were expelled from Jordan in a bloody conflict known as 'Black September'. Moving to Lebanon, they became one of the many catalysts in the protracted civil war that erupted in 1975. Even though the Palestinians withdrew from the country following the Israeli invasion of 1982, the Lebanese civil war between the various religious and political factions continued with barbaric ferocity until 1988. Alongside these much reported conflicts, others in different regions of the Arab world have continued off and on for decades: in the south of the Sudan, for example, in the Kurdish regions of Syria, Turkey, and Iraq, in Chad, and in the former Spanish Sahara. When coupled with the Iranian Revolution (1979), the assassination of Anwar al-Sādāt

(1981), the Iran–Iraq War of the 1980s, and the Gulf War of 1991, these events do indeed reveal what Albert Hourani terms 'a disturbance of spirits'.

Alongside these significant global events other issues have also had a major effect on Arab society. As many of the most highly populated Arab nations with secular and mostly socialist regimes have endeavoured to promote a sense of national welfare and progress in the course of feeding, clothing, housing, and educating their peoples, they have been forced to establish economic and political alignments, both local and international, within a global context that seems to condemn all but the very richest Arab states to an apparently endless client status as importer of Western goods and trends. The situation has led to some truly enormous disparities. Thus, at the end of the 1990s we see a region deeply divided, as the customary balance in each of the Arab nations – between the Arab and Islamic, the traditional heritage and modern development – continues to be disturbed by factors beyond the control of the majority of the region's inhabitants.

THE INTELLECTUAL CONTEXT

The Qur'ān and the foundation of the Islamic sciences

The text that resulted from the transcription and collation of God's revelations to Muḥammad – the Qur'ān – presented the incipient Islamic community with an enormous challenge. Perhaps the most profound of the changes was that a society which had relied for centuries on oral communication and memory as its favoured medium of record soon found it necessary to disambiguate the different versions of Muḥammad's utterances by establishing a single written version of them as the canonical source and declaring other versions non-canonical. This decision automatically led to a need to record in written form and to authenticate a wide variety of other sources and to develop modes for prioritising them. The demands of the rapidly expanding Islamic community accelerated the move to a more literate culture in specific areas of concern, but the incorporation into it of converts from the conquered areas guaranteed that the transformation process, once set in motion, would gather momentum. The introduction of paper from Asia towards the end of the eighth century clearly expanded the availability of resources and contributed further to the use of writing as a medium for both creativity and the preservation of learning. All this said however, it would appear that, alongside the emerging written tradition of literature and its criticism, the oral modes of expression and transmission have retained their hold on the public ear throughout the period covered by this volume.

The status of the Qurʾān as a canonical text served as the basis for the initiation of a series of fields of study that were to develop into the Islamic sciences and therefrom into Arabic literary scholarship. The very act of recording the sound of the utterances in written form required that the alphabetic system be refined in order not only to clarify the distinctions between sets of similar graphemes but also to incorporate symbols for vowels, elisions, and stops. The text itself contained numerous individual words and phrases that reflected the linguistic and religious environment of the Arabian Peninsula in the pre-Islamic era. Such words had to be codified, and their meanings and origins had to be investigated. Thus did Arabic lexicography begin, and with it the search for precedents to the language of the Qurʾān; among principal sources were the sayings of the pre-Islamic soothsayers couched in an ornate variety of the language known as *sajʿ* (rhyming prose) and the highly elaborate poems of an oral tradition that was the most recent manifestation of a process of creativity and transmission that could be traced back for many generations. In all three of these areas – alphabet systematisation, lexicography, and poetry – al-Khalīl ibn Aḥmad of al-Baṣrah (*d.* 791) was an important pioneer: he devised the system of symbols that identify and govern the sounds of the text of the Qurʾān and that has been used ever since in the teaching of the Arabic alphabet and morphology; he composed a dictionary, *Kitāb al-ʿayn* (Book of ʿAyn), which is arranged on phonetic principles; and he codified the metrical patterns of the pre-Islamic tradition of poetry into a prosodic system that was declared canonical by later generations of critics and remained as a pillar of Arabic poetics till well into the twentieth century. Alongside these concerns with the recording and analysis of texts there arose a desire to ensure that the principles of the language be systematised. A tradition has it that the caliph ʿAlī himself was sufficiently dismayed by errors in reading the Qurʾānic text that he instructed Abū al-aswad al-Duʾalī (*d.* 668) to prepare a work that would summarise Arabic grammar, thus commencing a process of codification and debate that was greatly expanded during the eighth and ninth centuries among the intellectual communities in the rival Iraqi cities of al-Baṣrah and al-Kūfah.

Once the revelations of the Qurʾān had been committed to writing, the process of studying and interpreting the text intensified. Regarding a number of issues – family law, debt, and inheritance, for example – the text was explicit. The Qurʾān's injunctions concerning God's will also contributed to the process of formulating the five 'pillars' of Islam: the statement of belief (*shahādah*); the five daily prayers (*ṣalāt*); almsgiving (*zakāt*): fasting during the holy month of Ramaḍān (*ṣawm*); and pilgrimage to Mecca (*ḥajj*). To these were added a further obligation, that of *jihād*, a much misunderstood concept that implies 'effort' on an individual and communal level, including the process of spreading the word of Islam to other peoples and defending the religion against its opponents. However, beyond these rituals and obligations there were many areas on which the Qurʾān remains silent; in such cases the community resorted to another source: records of the Prophet's own conduct during his lifetime, the *sunnah*. This in turn initiated another process of gathering information, as accounts of Muḥammad's acts (the Arabic term is *ḥadīth*) were collected and organised by category. As the role that these *ḥadīth* played in providing information to corroborate or establish tenets and modes of conduct came to be more fully appreciated, there developed a tradition of *ḥadīth* criticism that was designed to check on the authenticity of the reports. At a later date, the reports that were deemed the most reliable were collected into volumes called *Ṣaḥīḥ* (genuine); the two most famous collections were those of al-Bukhārī (*d.* 870) and Muslim (*d.* 875). Beyond such potential evidentiary functions the process of collecting and sifting these *ḥadīth* also marks the initial stages in the tradition of Qurʾānic exegesis (*tafsīr*), since the accounts often included discussions of problematic passages that had been recorded from earliest times. It was the great historian, al-Ṭabarī, who was the first to compile a commentary on the Qurʾān that incorporated within it the labours of his predecessors.

The processes of sifting accounts and authenticating sources that we have just described also revealed a need for detailed information on the reliability of individuals, and therefrom on the history of family groups and tribes. Genealogy was thus added to the list of fields with which the Islamic community concerned itself, as scholars investigated the histories of prominent families and their tribal affiliations. All this retrospective searching for details of tribal histories, for linguistic precedents to the lexicon and style of the Qurʾān, and for details regarding customs and beliefs in pre-Islamic times, inevitably led scholars to the greatest repository of such information: the huge corpus of poetry stored in the memories of generations of tribal and professional bards. Collections of the poems were made according to a variety of criteria: the most well known was that of length, leading to the compilation of *al-Muʿallaqāt* – elaborate, polythematic celebrations of tribal values, and *al-Mufaḍḍaliyyāt*, a collection of shorter poems gathered by the famous bard and transmitter, al-Mufaḍḍal al-Ḍabbī (*d.* 876).

From the outset the Islamic community assigned great value to the scholarly contributions of individuals who devoted themselves to knowledge of the religion; the Arabic word for such people is *ʿālim* (a learned person), and the plural of that word – *ʿulamā*ʾ (religious scholars) – came to represent a cogent force within the community, in that the people so named represented the collectivity of its learning on matters of significance for the maintenance and propagation of Islam.

The changing intellectual environment

While religious scholars devoted themselves to the urgent tasks connected with the demands of the incipient religious community, their researches stimulated other scholars to expand their interests in different directions. Much of this initial activity occurred during the period of the Umawī caliphs, when, as was noted above, the rapid expansion of the Arabian peninsular forces over a wide area brought Islam and its tenets into contact with a wide variety of cultures. The new converts assimilated many of the values advocated by the carriers of their adopted faith, but they also retained many aspects of their own indigenous cultures. It was only in 697, for example, during the reign of the caliph ʿAbd al-malik that Arabic was designated the official language of administration (substituting for the Greek and Persian of numerous functionaries who continued to work in many areas of the caliph's chancery).

As the functions of the administrative sector (known as *kuttāb*, sing. *kātib* – secretary, scribe) grew in complexity, there came the need to develop codes of conduct and appropriate models of style by which the chanceries at the various levels of authority within the Islamic dominions would facilitate the transfer and exchange of goods, information, and ideas. Pioneers like ʿAbd al-ḥamīd al-Kātib (*d.* 750) and ibn al-Muqaffaʿ (*d.* 757) – whose works will be examined in detail in the chapter on narratives below – established through their writings and the style in which they were couched an environment and tradition that came to be known by the designation *adab*, the literal translation of which is 'manners'. The person who practised, studied, and taught within this cultural realm was known as an *adīb* (pl. *udabā*ʾ), and, as the term *adab* itself came to change meaning and incorporate additional areas of interest, its best definition became 'what *udabā'* consider part of their area of interest'.

Ibn al-Muqaffaʿ was just one among many scholars and writers of Persian origin who began to make major contributions to Arabic literature and its study. In the crucial ancillary field of grammar, for example, Sibawayh (*d. c.* 794), a pupil of al-Khalīl ibn Aḥmad, wrote a comprehensive study of the written Arabic language that is still revered as a major source on the subject. Another major influence on the development of Islamic thought was that of Hellenistic Greek culture. The fruits of the schools of Athens and Alexandria had been carried to centres in Western Asia; the Nestorian Church played a particularly important role in the process of preserving and transmitting Greek learning through their schools in Nasibin in Syria and at Jundishapur in Persia. The large-scale translation movement that was sparked by the curiosity of the dynamic intellectual community that we have just described spanned a period of at least two centuries. The translations that were undertaken reveal the concerns of a community interested in acquainting itself with a huge variety of topics and in the modes of organising and discussing them: from philosophy to astronomy, from music to pharmacology. The pace of translation activity was greatly accelerated by the personal interest of some of the ʿAbbāsī caliphs. In particular, al-Ma'mūn is remembered in this connection for establishing an institution in Baghdād, *Bayt al-ḥikmah* (The House of Wisdom), that provided a wonderful library and research facility to receive the fruits of such translation activity.

Given the variety of cultures that were represented within this intellectual milieu, certain biases were bound to make themselves evident. One that has attracted the particular attention of intellectual historians is the movement known in Arabic as the *Shuʿūbiyyah*, which is often regarded as an argument between Persian and Arab secretaries and littérateurs over the relative merits of their respective cultural heritages, as illustrated by the following lines of poetry of Bashshār ibn Burd (*d.* 783):

> Where is there an emissary to chant to all Arabs? . . .
> I am a person of high class, raised above others;
> Chosroes is the grandfather through whom I claim precedence, and
> Sāsān was my father . . .
> Never did he sing camel songs behind a scabby beast,
> nor pierce the bitter colocynth out of sheer hunger . . .
> nor dig a lizard out of the ground and eat it . . .

However, the *Shuʿūbiyyah* movement needs to be viewed as not so much an expression of nationalist pride in an era in which primary modes of self-identification within the community tended to focus more on adherence to Islam and the use of Arabic as its language, but rather more an attempt to forge the bases for a multicultural intelligentsia.

Within the côteries of religious scholars and secretary-bureaucrats, elaborate systems of education emerged whereby scholarship in the various fields of learning was passed on to the next generation. The systematisation of jurisprudence (*fiqh*), for example, led to the foundation by prominent figures of colleges (*madāris*, sing. *madrasah*) at which the various fields of study connected with the *Sharīʿah* would be taught. The college itself was established by attaching a hostel to a mosque so that students who came to study in the 'circle' of the master could remain with him until they had 'read' with him all the major texts germane to the field, whereupon they would be granted a 'licence' in those subjects in which they had gained mastery.

The major debates

The development of discrete 'schools' of law (*madhāhib*) and the formalisation of a system of education in jurisprudence indicate the central role that the *Sharīʿah* occupied in a community as a law code that was not limited to certain specific requirements of faith but governed every aspect of the life of the individual. The *ʿulamāʾ* studied the text of the Qurʾān and produced commentaries (*tafsīr*) that explicated the text of God's revelation to His people. They advocated the primacy of the Qurʾān as a source of legislation and went on to note that the *sunnah* of the Prophet collected in *ḥadīth* was an equally valid basis for the codification of Islamic practice. The distinctions and tensions that existed between the two tendencies within the legislative community are visible in the early codes of Abū Ḥanīfah (*d.* 767) and Mālik ibn Anas (*d.* 795). It was the important role of al-Shāfiʿī (*d.* 820) to codify and prioritise the relationships between the various sources of law. Both the Qurʾān and the *sunnah* were declared primary in the process of formulating legislation, but to them was added the process of reason that would need to be applied in those situations where interpretation was needed. The *ʿulamāʾ*, those schooled in the doctrine of Islam, were enjoined to make use of analogy (*qiyās*) in order to assess the validity of incorporating new and unfamiliar circumstances into the corpus of law regarding issues that had already been determined.

The codification and study of the 'principles of jurisprudence' (*uṣūl al- fiqh*) and their elaboration into a huge library of works concerning *Sharīʿah* now gathered momentum. As this corpus of scholarship was collected, examined, and elaborated within the legal colleges (*madāris*), orthodox scholars came to declare that, since all possible circumstances had been elaborated in the legal codes that were available, the 'gate of independent judgement' (*bāb al-ijtihād*) should be considered closed. The principle to be followed was that of adherence to past practice (*taqlīd*).

The development of codes of law that has just been outlined served as a major impetus for the study and explication of the text of the Qurʾān and the elaboration of a system of *ḥadīth* criticism. Beyond such issues lay deeper questions of a theological nature. How was Allāh represented in the Qurʾān, and what was His relationship with human beings? The investigation of the nature of God's word to His people as transmitted by His Prophet, Muḥammad, began from a vigorously unitarian position that categorically denied the possibility of God having any associate, so that the very term 'association' (*shirk*) was synonymous with heresy. God is transcendent and all-powerful, and His revelation to His people takes the form of a 'recitation', the Qurʾān.

The text of the Qurʾān underscores God's oneness, His power, and His control over human beings, but it also enjoins them to turn away from sin and live a virtuous life. As theologians considered the question of responsibility for sin within such a context, a number of schools of thought emerged. In the eighth century, the issue was taken up by a movement termed *al-Muʿtazilah* (literally 'those who retire', but coming to imply 'those who take a neutral position'). Since God is One, they reasoned, He can have no attributes, including that of speech; from this they deduced that the Qurʾān cannot be uncreated. A central belief of Islam, that God is just, implies that He cannot ordain evil; sin results from the freedom of will that is an attribute of humanity. During the reign of the caliph al-Maʾmūn (*d.* 833), the beliefs of the Muʿtazilah became part of official doctrine. Officials were subjected to a 'test' (*miḥnah*) during which they were asked if God was the Creator of all things; a positive answer – thus including the Qurʾān – implied that such persons believed in the doctrine of the Muʿtazilah. A negative response could lead to unpleasant results. One of the primary opponents of the Muʿtazilah was Aḥmad ibn Ḥanbal, founder of one of the four major schools of law, who, rejecting the Muʿtazilah's reliance on speculative dogmatics, insisted on a return to the primary sources of Islam. His patience and endurance were rewarded when the caliph al-Mutawakkil (*d.* 861) abandoned the doctrine of the createdness of the Qurʾān.

The task of finding a compromise between the two poles of the speculative reason of the Muʿtazilah and the literalism of the traditionalist followers of Aḥmad ibn Ḥanbal was taken up by al-Ashʿarī (*d.* 935). Regarding God's attributes, he was prepared to acknowledge the value of the application of reason up to a point, but suggested that true faith required that such issues should be accepted 'without asking how'. By reconciling the basic tenets of Islamic tradition with the application of reason in this way, al-Ashʿarī laid the foundations for the further development of an orthodox theology. Through his many pupils and their successors, among the more famous of whom are al-Bāqillānī (*d.* 1013), al-Qushayrī (*d.* 1074), and al-Juwaynī (*d.* 1085), his views came to be the most widely accepted within Sunnī Islam. One of the students of al-Juwaynī was al-Ghazālī (*d.* 1111), widely acknowledged as 'the proof of Islam' and as one of the most significant figures in the whole of Islamic thought. Through his writings, and especially his monumental work, *Iḥyāʾ ʿulūm al-dīn* (The Revival of the Religious Sciences), al-Ghazālī succeeded in exemplifying the methods and limits of al-Ashʿarī's doctrines, showing how the application of reason could be used to defend the status of the Qurʾān and *ḥadīth* while at the same time quashing the worst speculative excesses of the philosophers. Against this latter group he wrote a notable treatise, *Tahāfut al-falāsifah* (The Incoherence of Philosophers), in which he explored the incompatibilities between the concerns of philosophy and the belief in a divinely revealed system of faith.

The response to al-Ghazālī's attack was written by the great Andalusian philosopher (and Mālikī judge), ibn Rushd (*d.* 1198). In his direct retort, *Tahāfut al-tahāfut* (The Incoherence of 'the Incoherence') and in other works of which the most significant is *Faṣl al-maqāl* (The Decisive Treatise), he was at some pains to show that any incompatibility that was seen to exist between philosophical investigations and the lessons of the Qurʾān could only result from literalist readings of the divinely revealed text. It is a sign of the significant role that Arab philosophers were to play in the elaboration of transmission of ideas inherited from the Greek tradition that the names of ibn Rushd and his predecessor, ibn Sīnā (*d.* 1037), Europeanised as Averroes and Avicenna, hold honoured places in the history of European philosophy. Ibn Sīnā's most prominent predecessors were al-Kindī (*d.* 865) and al-Fārābī (*d.* 950). The former maintained the primacy of revelation but insisted that the application of reason was also appropriate. Al-Fārābī, known as 'the second teacher' (*al- muʿallim al-thānī* – Aristotle himself being the first), sought a role for the philosopher within the Islamic community by challenging the former's modes of argumentation.

Ibn Sīnā's own masterwork on medicine, *al-Qānūn fī al-ṭibb* (The

Canon on Medicine), renowned for its accurate observation and clarity of expression, was to remain a prominent source in Europe till the seventeenth century. In the realm of philosophy itself ibn Sīnā composed a series of works that endeavour to reconcile the tenets of Islam with the principles of Aristotelian logic and Neo-Platonist explorations on the nature of the soul; the most famous is *al-Shifāʾ* (The Cure [of the Soul]), but his works also include a number of fascinating allegories.

Alongside the more public and communal aspects of the Islamic faith and the community that it fostered, the text of the Qurʾān also enjoins believers to read and reflect. Studying the text of the Qurʾān and engaging in acts of private devotion and piety were encouraged alongside the more corporate rituals of public worship. These particular aspects of the message of the Qurʾān were among the factors that led to the emergence of another major trend in the life of the Islamic community, one that has continued to play a significant role in the propagation of Islam: mysticism (*taṣawwuf*, whence the English word, Sufism), the development of mystical sects, and the search for a 'way' (*ṭarīqah*, path) to achieve 'a closer walk with God'.

As with so many other intellectual currents in early Islamic history, the earliest beginnings of Ṣūfī ideas are traced to the twin Iraqi cities of al-Kūfah and al-Baṣrah. Al-Ḥasan al-Baṣrī, revered by Ṣūfīs and the Muʿtazilah alike as a founding figure, practised a personal life of asceticism and private devotion. As Sufism began to assume an identity of its own, it developed particular rituals and, most significant from the literary point of view, an awareness of the allegorical potential of language. Mystics began to move from a literal interpretation of the text of the Qurʾān to one which suggested levels of meaning, from the most direct to hidden symbolic significances only attainable through spiritual experience. The combination of extreme self-denial and a desire for communion with the transcendent produced some of the remarkable utterances of mystics such as Rābiʿah al-ʿAdawiyyah (*d.* 801), Abū Yazīd al-Bisṭāmī (*d.* 874), and Manṣūr al-Ḥallāj (*d.* 922), who in an ecstatic moment declared 'I am the Truth' and was later executed for heresy. The dangers inherent in the use of language in this extremely allegorical fashion to reflect and comment on the experience of an individual knowledge of God can be seen also in the execution of another prominent mystic, al-Suhrawardī, in 1191 and in the accusations of heresy levelled against the great Andalusian mystical writer, ibn al-ʿArabī (*d.* 1240), by a number of traditionalist authorities, including ibn Taymiyyah (*d.* 1328) in the fourteenth century and the Egyptian censor in the twentieth.

The extreme emphasis of mystics on the role of the individual conscience in assessing personal conduct towards God and other people led to opposition from traditionalist theologians who were anxious to codify proper behaviour on a more communal level. The process of reconciling these different views, undertaken by al-Ḥarith al-Muḥāsibī (*d.* 857), al-Junayd (*d.* 910), and al-Qushayrī (*d.* 1072), reached its crowning point in the writings of al-Ghazālī. His monumental opus, *Iḥyā' ʿulūm al-dīn* (The Revival of the Religious Sciences), succeeded in integrating the various aspects of revelation, canon law, and personal devotion into a single statement of faith.

Al-Ghazālī's achievement in incorporating Sufism into the mainstream of Islamic belief led to a palpable increase in popular interest in the more personal approach to God that the mystical path appeared to offer. An immediate consequence was a growth in Ṣūfī orders, which were, more often than not, named after their founders: thus, the Qādiriyyah order named after ʿAbd al-qādir al-Jīlānī (*d.* 1166) and the Rifāʿiyyah order after Aḥmad al-Rifāʿī (*d.* 1183). The rapid expansion of these orders was to lead to a considerable diversification of religious ritual, as local customs that were even remotely adaptable to an Islamic framework were incorporated into the litanies of particular groups and regions.

This expansion and elaboration of popular Islamic belief aroused considerable opposition among conservative theologians. The negative aspects of these Ṣūfī practices to which ibn Taymiyyah and others objected and the extent to which they have continued to exert a major influence on the life of the populace are illustrated by the great twentieth century intellectual, Ṭāhā Ḥusayn (*d.* 1973), in his famous autobiography, *al-Ayyām* (The Days, 1925). With undisguised contempt, he describes the impact of a visit by a famous mystical 'shaykh' on a poor family that has to provide the best possible entertainment for him, and then goes on to note the shaykh's virtually total ignorance of the basic doctrines of Islam.

It may be reasonable perhaps to expect that, following several centuries of theoretical and empirical research in so many areas (of which we have only touched on a few above), certain scholars felt a need to draw breath, as it were; to collate and elaborate on what was already available. The principle of adherence to already established norms (*taqlīd*), while not considered binding by all schools of law and theology, certainly encouraged efforts at explication, commentary, and elaboration. We have also suggested above that, given the breadth of the area in which Islam was the dominant religious system, the impact of the fall of Baghdād in 1258 – traditionally regarded as a turning-point in the chronology of Arab-Islamic history, needs to be seen in a broader context. The destruction of the ʿAbbāsī capital, with its libraries and colleges, was clearly an enormous loss to the world of Arabic scholarship, but it was an accumulation of 'falls', those of Baghdād, of Constantinople in 1453, of Granada in 1492, and of Cairo in 1516, that transformed the map of the Middle East and its cultural life. For example, the advent of Ottoman rule to large parts of the region introduced the Turkish language as the primary medium of administration. The cultured élite that had been the principal locus and sponsor of literary activity was now constrained to conduct official transactions in a language other than Arabic. If the poetry and belles-lettres of the time (to the rather limited extent that they have been studied) appear to be replete with the rhetorical flourishes that were being so carefully recorded and illustrated by the critical tradition and if much of the society's store of originality seemed to be invested in the more popular literary genres (which are still in need of much more research), then we should perhaps not be unduly surprised.

While the series of events (the 'falls') mentioned above clearly represent major shifts in the nature of political power in the region, the processes of change within the cultural environment of literary texts are less obviously identified. In fact much of that environment changed rather little. In the realm of travel literature, for example, ibn Baṭṭūtah (*d.* 1377) continues the tradition established earlier by al-Idrīsī (*d.* 1165) and ibn Jubayr (*d.* 1217) of Granada. The writing of economic and urban history, and especially descriptions of the prominent citizens and quarters of the Islamic world's great cities, is further developed by al-Maqrīzī (*d.* 1441), who served as the supervisor of weights and measures (*muḥtasib*) in Mamlūk Cairo. His monumental study of the city, *al-Mawāʿiẓ wa-al-iʿtibār fī dhikr al-khiṭaṭ wa-al-āthār* (Admonitions and Lessons Regarding the Mention of Districts and Monuments), established a model for the analysis of the topography of cities (this title, incidentally, is the first example in this work of a trend that we will notice in many titles of Arabic books, a deliberate process of elaboration through the use of rhyming patterns in the title; the topic of the work in question will be in the second phrase – in al-Maqrīzī's case above 'the topography of cities' – while the first phrase provides an appropriate rhyming phrase to precede it). Ibn Khaldūn (*d.* 1406), one of the world's most illustrious historians, surveyed the disarming frequency with which ruling dynasties changed in the North-West Africa region in which he himself lived and penned a theoretical Introduction (*al- Muqaddimah*) to his work of history that is universally acknowledged as marking a fresh approach to the study of human societies and their processes of change.

The desire to collate and organise materials into useful forms remained a constant. The earliest known version of the *Thousand and One Nights* as a collection of popular tales dates from about the fourteenth century. Encyclopaedias and compilations of fact and anecdote continue to appear in ever more elaborate and varied form (as we will see in Chapter 5 below). This predilection for the gathering and analysis of information found a particularly conducive field in lexicography; during the first half of this long period work was begun on the compilation of the two great dictionaries of the Arabic language, *Lisān al-ʿarab* (Language of the Arabs) completed by ibn Manẓūr (*d.* 1311) and *Tāj al-ʿarūs min jawāhir al-qāmūs* (The Bride's Crown Taken from the Jewels of the 'Qāmūs') begun by al-Fayrūzābādī (*d.* 1414) and completed by al-Zabīdī (*d.* 1790).

Coinciding with the halfway point in this much neglected period is the career of the renowned Egyptian polygraph, Jalāl al-dīn al-Suyūṭī (*d.* 1505); no single figure, we might suggest, illustrates so well the concerns and priorities of an era whose engagement with the forces of continuity and change has yet to be properly understood. He wrote on an enormous variety of subjects (some scholars put the total of his works at well over five hundred). To the study of religion, for example, he contributed works on the exegesis of the Qurʾān, on *ḥadīth*, and on Sufism; he wrote biographies and works of general history; to philology and grammar he contributed *al-Muẓhir fī ʿulūm al-lughah* (The Brilliant [Work] Regarding the Sciences of Language); and he also composed poetry and a set of *maqāmāt*.

The Egyptian historian, ibn Iyās (*d.* 1523), has left us an account of the panic that gripped Cairo in 1516 after the defeat of the army of the Mamlūk Sultan al-Ghawrī and of the subsequent arrival in Cairo of the victorious Ottoman troops. The impact that this and other Ottoman conquests had on the political, economic, and social life of the Arabic-speaking world was, of course, enormous, but, as we have noted above, the cultural ramifications – among them the change in administrative language and, in many regions, the tight control over the dissemination of information – were no less significant. Literary production in Arabic continued during the seventeenth and eighteenth centuries, but such is the exiguous state of our knowledge of its fruits throughout the Arabic-speaking region that references in the chapters that follow to authors and works from what might be termed the 'pre-modern' period will be few and far between.

The challenge of modernity: the relationship to present and past

The incompleteness of our understanding of the cultural forces at work in the Arabic-speaking world in what I will term the 'pre-modern period' clearly makes any discussion of the factors involved in the cultural revival of the nineteenth century (*al-nahḍah*) more difficult. For, while increased contact with the West was clearly a very important part of the process, contacts both within and without the broad compass of the Middle East region were ongoing. Beyond issues of cultural contact, there is the further question as to whether the indigenous cultural tradition was quite as moribund as previous scholarship has tended to suggest. In Egypt, the French scientists who came to Egypt with Napoleon's army at the end of the eighteenth century and compiled the *Description de l'Egypte* found themselves debating issues with intellectuals who were thoroughly acquainted with the riches of the Arabic literary heritage.

In 1826 Muḥammad ʿAlī, the ruler of Egypt, sent Rifāʿah al-Ṭahṭāwī (*d.* 1873), to France as *imām* of a mission of Egyptian students. Al-Ṭahṭāwī's famous account of his time in Paris, *Takhlīṣ al-ibrīz fī talkhīṣ Bārīz* (The Purification of Gold Regarding Paris in Brief, 1834) is full of observations regarding issues that are exotic in their peculiarity: for example, the institution of parliament and the appearance of women in public. In the transfer of these and other ideas – the Western concept of 'nation', for example – to the intellectual community of the Arab world two institutions were to play a crucial role. The first was the Translation School that Muḥammad ʿAlī established in 1835 with al-Ṭahṭāwī himself as its director. The second institution was the press. In 1828 Muḥammad ʿAlī founded an official gazette, *al-Waqāʾiʿ al-Miṣriyyah* (Egyptian Events), and al-Ṭahṭāwī became its editor in 1841. During the reign of the Khedive Ismāʿīl, who was bent on westernising his country to the maximum extent possible, these two institutions provided a ready vehicle for an increasingly rapid introduction of Western ideas into Egyptian intellectual life. The very atmosphere that Ismāʿīl's policies engendered was also a major factor in the decision of many Syro-Lebanese Christian families to come to Egypt following the civil disturbances of the 1850s. With its large population, central geographical position, and lively cultural environment now quickened by the new arrivals from Syria, Egypt became the fullest and most often cited example of intellectual developments in the early decades of the twentieth century.

The imported and the indigenous, the modern and the traditional, the Western and Middle Eastern, the non-Islamic and the Islamic, these pairs and many others became the focus of lively debate in the last decades of the nineteenth century and into the twentieth. During the 1870s and 1880s in Egypt we find, on the one hand, an ever-expanding number of newspapers and specialist journals publishing serialised novels, both translations of European works and initial efforts in Arabic such as *Dhāt al-khidr* (Lady of the Boudoir, 1884) by Saʿīd al-Bustānī, and, on the other, a scholar such as Ḥusayn al-Marṣafī (*d.* 1890) writing a two-volume work, *al-Wasīlah al-adabiyyah* (The Literary Method, 1872, 1875), in which he expresses his clear admiration for the models provided by the 'classical' poetic tradition. In such a context Muḥammad al-Muwayliḥī's acerbicly witty analysis of an Egyptian society in cultural turmoil at the turn of the century, *Ḥadīth ʿĪsā ibn Hishām* (ʿĪsā ibn Hishām's Tale, 1898 in newspaper form; 1907 as a book) attempts a kind of synthesis of old genre and modern topic.

Al-Muwayliḥī was a student of Muḥammad ʿAbduh (*d.* 1905), one of the most significant figures in the debate concerning the role of Islam within a society trying to find a balance between the traditional and the modern. As was the case with many other intellectuals of the time, ʿAbduh was much influenced by the ideas of Jamāl al-dīn al-Asadābādī (*d.* 1897), an Iranian Shīʿī scholar generally known by the name 'al-Afghānī' who was determined to modernise Islam and to make full use of reason to reformulate the faith as a cogent basis for resisting the threat posed by European domination of the Middle East. Muḥammad ʿAbduh was as anxious as his mentor to protect Islamic principles; for him, the Qur'ān and *ḥadīth* remained the principal sources of guidance, but, as his pronouncements on matters of legal interpretation make clear, he did not base his judgements on the principle of *taqlīd* (adherence to past practice). If Islam was to survive and remain strong, he argued, it needed to be adaptive.

The teachings of ʿAbduh had an enormous impact on his numerous pupils and acquaintances in Egypt and elsewhere in the Arab world. This is most obvious perhaps in the career of his most famous pupil, Rashīd Riḍā (*d.* 1935), a Syrian scholar who supported the notion of an Islamic faith based on the Qur'ān and the views of the great authorities of the past (the *salaf*). The ideas of ʿAbduh and Riḍā, termed the *salafiyyah* movement, were particularly influential in North Africa (most especially at the hands of ʿAbd al-ḥamīd ibn Bādīs in Algeria) and in the East reached as far as Indonesia.

Among those who were much influenced by ʿAbduh's ideas was Qāsim Amīn. In 1899 he aroused a storm of controversy by publishing *Taḥrīr al-marʾah* (The Emancipation of Women); in this book and a second, *Al-Marʾah al-jadīdah* (Modern Woman, 1900), he follows the method of ʿAbduh by resorting to the basic tenets of Islam as a means of justifying the need to provide education for women, for not only their benefit but also that of society as a whole. The reaction to his published books shows clearly enough that his views reached a broad public, but the existence of the literary salons of Princess Nāzlī and of Mayy Ziyādah (*d.* 1941), the famous Palestinian writer resident for many years in Cairo, and the writings of Zaynab Fawwāz (*d.* 1914), Malak Ḥifnī Nāṣīf (*d.* 1918), and Labībah Hāshim (*d.* 1947) – much of which has yet to be published in book form – provide equally clear evidence that, while women's voices may not have commanded as much attention in the public domain, they were no less insistent in raising these same issues.

These often intense debates regarding the role of Islam within a process of cultural revival and change occurred within a political and social context in which other forces were tending to marginalise the role of religion. As banks, stocks exchanges, the press, and international commerce stimulated the appearance of a new class of Western-educated bureaucrats and professionals, the diminution of the traditional power of the *ʿulamāʾ* and the emergence of more secular voices and priorities that reflected an increasing awareness of Western political theories were almost inevitable. The concept of an Arab nation, one based on an awareness of a shared language and culture, began to gather momentum. Fostered by such pioneers as ʿAbd al-raḥmān al-Kawākibī (*d.* 1903) and Najīb ʿAzūrī (*d.* 1916), who in 1904 founded in Paris a group known as 'Ligue de la patrie arabe', the movement was given considerable impetus by the Western powers during the First World War.

The half-century from 1919 till the June War of 1967 sees the debate on nationalism elaborated in both pan-Arab and local contexts. Arab nationalism in its widest and most ambitious dimensions is developed primarily among the intelligentsia of Iraq and Syria. Two among many prominent contributors to the literature on the subject are Qusṭanṭīn Zurayq (*b.* 1909) and Ṣātiʿ al-Ḥuṣrī (*d.* 1964); both stress that, if the larger Arab cause is to thrive, more local concerns need to be sacrificed. These goals took a more ideological form in the writings of Michel ʿAflaq (*d.* 1989), a Syrian Christian who invoked the notion of revival (*baʿth*) as a rallying cry for Arab national unity and social justice. More local nationalist movements and parties have existed alongside the broader agenda of a pan-Arab movement, catering to particular classes and groups within each society. In Syria, for example, Anṭūn Saʿādah (*d.* 1949) established a National Syrian Party in 1932 that was organised along militia lines and became a vigorous advocate of Syrian nationalism. In Egypt, the dashed expectations of the Arabs at the end of the First World War and the popular uprising in Egypt that followed in 1919 brought to the fore the country's great nationalist leader, Saʿd Zaghlūl (*d.* 1927) – yet another member of ʿAbduh's circle who had been particularly influenced by the writings of one of the primary expounders of Egyptian nationalist principles, Aḥmad Luṭfī al-Sayyid (*d.* 1963).

Any progress that may have been made in the 1920s and 1930s towards the goal of independence was immediately lost in 1939. The whole of North Africa became a primary theatre of war, and the strategic imperatives of Britain and France tended to shove aside the negotiated agreements of peacetime. The foundation in the Egyptian capital of *Jāmiʿat al-duwal al-ʿArab* (The Arab League) in 1945 was intended to represent and implement the long-awaited aspirations of the Arab nation, but since its foundation it has come to symbolise all the complexities of international politics in the Middle East. Indeed, it was immediately faced with the problem that, since the conclusion of the Second World War, has become, in the words of the Moroccan historian, Abdallah Laroui, '*the* Arab issue': the fate of the Palestinian people.

During the 1950s a number of Arab nations gained their independence and set themselves to establish social agenda in a post-colonial era. In the aftermath of revolution many political groups discovered that the changes they had hoped and fought for were not to be realised. In Egypt, a broad spectrum of interests had participated in the concerted campaign against the British occupation and governmental corruption in the late 1940s, most notably the Communists and the Muslim Brethren. However, in the uneasy atmosphere of the early years of the Egyptian revolution both were ruthlessly suppressed. Many Communist intellectuals were to spend much of their life in jail, and among them are a number of prominent littérateurs who have provided accounts of their experiences. The Muslim Brethren, a group that had been founded by Ḥasan al-Bannā (*d.* 1949), a student of Rashīd Riḍā, in 1928, also lent its support (and highly organised underground network) to the anticolonial cause, but it was precisely the breadth and efficiency of its organisation that almost immediately brought it into conflict with the new revolutionary government. In 1954, an attempt was made on (then Colonel) ʿAbd al-nāṣir's life, and many Muslim Brethren were imprisoned, among them Sayyid Quṭb (*d.* 1966), who had officially joined the Brethren just one year earlier.

The intellectual life in most countries of the Arab world during the 1950s and 1960s was a patchwork of complexities and contradictions. On the international level there were the triumphs of the Bandung Conference (1955) at which the concept of a new Third World non-alignment was formulated, the nationalisation of the Suez Canal in 1956, the creation of the United Arab Republic between Syria and Egypt (1958–61), the conclusion of the Algerian Revolution (1962), all of which led to significant changes in local and international alignments. Within the societies themselves however the debates and controversies of the intellectual community were closely monitored by an elaborate security apparatus, and expression was subject to the tightest control. Those many intellectuals who espoused the goals of the revolution, whether on a broader or more local scale, and who felt themselves able to function within prescribed guidelines eagerly adopted commitment (*iltizām*) as the organising principle of their writing; it was part of the motto of what remains the most widely circulated Arabic literary journal, *Al-Ādāb*, founded in 1953 by Suhayl Idrīs (*b.* 1923) in Beirut. Palestinian writers, and especially their poets, found a direct incentive for this literary credo within their own particular circumstances, but elsewhere too fiction, drama, and poetry were drawn into an approach to the portrayal of the new societies that was predominantly committed and social realist. Those writers who chose to explore the darker side of the image so carefully constructed by the government-controlled media found themselves imprisoned or worse; for them the most frequent resorts were to silence or exile.

The bitter aftermath of the June 1967 War led many contemporary Arab intellectuals to undertake a profound re-examination of the foundations upon which their societies are assumed to be based. Many stopped writing altogether, while others sought solace and reaffirmation through an investigation of the classical heritage of the Arabs and of the bases of cultural authenticity (*aṣālah*). During the 1980s and 1990s one of the principal arenas of both action and debate in the Arab world (and elsewhere) has focused on Islamic revival and especially a major increase in popular Islamic movements which, in several countries, have become a prominent political force. In such a context, the Iranian Revolution of 1979 assumes a major importance, in that Iran's active bolstering of self-identity among Shīʿī communities in the Arab world (most notably in Iraq, the Gulf States and Southern Lebanon) has not only galvanised those communities into action – as subsequent events in Iraq, Lebanon, and the Gulf have shown, but has also led Sunnī governments in the Gulf region (and particularly that of Saudi Arabia) to counter the threat posed by their assertive Shīʿī neighbour by encouraging and fostering popular Islamic movements elsewhere in the region. The political and social problems of such countries as Algeria, Palestine, Egypt, and the Sudan have provided fertile ground for the growth of increasingly activist popular Islamic movements.

Another area of discussion that has enriched debate among the intelligentsia of the Arab world in the post-1967 period and thus been reflected in literary production is that of the status of women in Arab and Islamic society. One of the pioneers in this movement is Zaynab al-Ghazālī, an Egyptian writer who worked with Ḥasan al-Bannā and later with Sayyid Quṭb on an organisation of Sisters alongside the Muslim Brethren. In her writings she advocates the need for an Islamic state, basing her position on an understanding that, since Islam has provided women with all the rights they need, there is no need to talk in terms of liberation. Al-Ghazālī's fellow countrywoman, Nawāl al-Saʿdāwi (*b.* 1931), clearly does not share her views. Al-Saʿdāwī has made use of her prominence as both a medical doctor and a writer of fiction to challenge societal norms regarding gender roles and the tendency to keep the open discussion of sexual mores under wraps. Another Arab feminist whose works are known in the West is the Moroccan sociologist, Fāṭimah al-Marnīsī (*b.* 1940), who discusses the issue of gender in its contemporary Islamic framework from a rather more scholarly and historical viewpoint. For her, it is not so much the status of women themselves that needs to be reconsidered, but rather the relationship between the sexes in marriage and the provisions of Islam that perpetuate male domination.

CONCLUSION

When an English television company made a film series about the Arabs in the 1980s and devoted a programme to the role of literature in society, it was entitled *The Power of the Word*. The choice is entirely appropriate. From the beginnings of the Arabic tradition, literature has been an immensely influential force in society. We might illustrate what appears to be one point of contrast by invoking the old English proverb of uncertain provenance which runs: 'Sticks and stones may break my bones, but names can never hurt me'. No sentiment could be further from the realities of the situation in the world of Arabic literature. Names and words could not merely hurt; they could be the verbal triggers that would start wars. Words do indeed have the power to lift up and to crush; '*Hādhā huwa-smī*' (This is My Name) is the modern poet Adūnīs's defiant proclamation of the writer's sense of his own identity and significance. Littérateurs in Arab society continue to have at their disposal a formidable mode of expression in order to uplift, persuade, criticise, and entertain. Most significantly, the tremendous emphasis that Islamic scholarship was to place on the creation of a written record of reports, opinions, and ideas did nothing to lessen the prevalence of the oral and public dimension that have been part of the literary heritage from the very outset.

CHAPTER 3

The Qur'ān: sacred text and cultural yardstick

INTRODUCTION

In the previous chapter I discussed the revelation of the Qur'ān to the incipient Islamic community and then explored the multifarious ways in which that event had an impact on the course of Middle Eastern history and the development of the Islamic sciences. For the Muslim believer the Qur'ān is the primary source on matters theological and legal, but in addition to that it is a daily presence in the life of the community and its individual members. Beyond these aspects of its message, however, the recorded text of the Qur'ān is a work of sacred 'scripture', and the miraculous qualities attributed to its style (termed *i'jāz*) have long been the object of scrutiny by the critical community.

The opening verses of *Sūrat al-'alaq* (Sūrah 96, The Blood-clot) are believed to represent the first of God's revelations to His messenger, the Prophet Muḥammad. Their structure and style serve as an excellent illustration of many of the features of Qur'ānic discourse.

> Recite: in the name of your Lord who created (1)
> created mankind from a clot of blood. (2)
>
> Recite: and your Lord is most generous, (3)
> He who instructed with the pen, (4)
> instructed mankind what he knew not. (5)

This passage illustrates the primary mode of communication found in the Qur'ān: God, the speaker, addresses His messenger in the second person and instructs him to recite to his listeners, the initially small but ever-expanding community of Muslims. The messages that Muḥammad's early audience heard in Mecca were couched in short rhyming phrases; in the example above the final word in each verse of the two sections (1–2 and 3–5) ends with a rhyming syllable; in 1 and 2, for example, it is *khalaq* and *'alaq*. The repetition of the word 'recite' (in Arabic, *iqra'*) is a further structuring device. The word *iqra'* is the imperative form of the verbal root Q-R-ʾ, a noun derivative of which is the word *Qurʾān* itself. The original meaning of this verbal root was 'to recite'; thus the Qurʾān is a 'recitation', a series of utterances, the word of God, transmitted orally by Muḥammad to his listeners. I use the adjective 'original' because the root has since added a further meaning to that of 'to recite', namely 'to read'. That very shift in predominant meaning may be seen as a reflection of firstly the text's own acknowledgement of the function and power of writing (that God 'instructed with the pen') and secondly the juxtaposition within the developing Islamic tradition of the written and the oral. Just as the root Q-R-ʾ has never lost its implicit sense of 'to recite (out loud)', so have Islamic societies throughout the world continued to pay the greatest respect to the oral traditions of their heritage even as they compiled an enormous and varied corpus of textual scholarship.

STRUCTURES

The Qurʾān is subdivided into 114 chapters called *sūrah*s. Each *sūrah* has a title; for example, the 96th, the opening of which we cited above, is called *Sūrat al-ʿalaq*. The title is a word that is mentioned within the text of the *sūrah* itself. While in many cases the word in question will occur near the beginning of the *sūrah*, that is not always the case; in *Sūrat al-shuʿarāʾ* (26, The Poets), for example, the word 'poets' occurs in the 224th verse of a *sūrah* with 226 in total. The first *sūrah*, called '*al-Fātiḥah*' (The Opening), is in the form of a prayer; its privileged position within the ordering of the text is a recognition of its special status: within Islamic societies the process of 'reading the *al-Fātiḥah*' is a requirement in completing contracts, most especially that of marriage. Apart from the *Fātiḥah*, the *sūrah*s are arranged by length, starting with the longest, *Sūrat al-baqarah* (2, The Cow) which has 286 verses and finishing with a number of extremely short *sūrah*s; *Sūrat al-kawthar* (108, Abundance), for example, and *Sūrat al-naṣr* (110, Help) each have three verses, and *Sūrat al-nās* (114, The People) has six.

The public recitation of the Qurʾān is considered a meritorious act, most especially during the month of Ramaḍān which is devoted to fasting and meditation. For this and similar purposes, the text is divided up into thirty equal parts (*ajzāʾ*), one for each day of the month, and each 'part' is also subdivided into halves called *aḥzāb* (sing. *ḥizb*).

Each *sūrah* is prefaced by a section that states its number and title, the place – Mecca or Medina – where the majority of revelations cited in the *sūrah* were first recited, the number of verses it contains, and its place in the sequence of revelations; *Sūrat al-zalzalah* (99, The Earthquake), for example, 'was revealed after [*Sūrat*] *al-Ṭalāq*' (65, The Divorce). In addition, twenty-nine of the *sūrahs* begin with a sequence of letters, the function of which remains a mystery. Some of these sequences, *ALIF-LĀM-RĀ'*, for example, and *ALIF-LĀM-MĪM*, are to be found at the beginning of several *sūrahs*, while others occur only once. Two of them, TĀ-HĀ (verse 1 of *Sūrat Ṭāhā*, Sūrah 20) and *YĀ-SĪN* (verse 1 of *Sūrat Yāsīn*, Sūrah 36) are regularly used as names for male children.

We have already noted that the *sūrahs* are arranged in order of length; in other words, the *sūrahs* placed later in the order consist of fewer revelations than the earlier ones. In the earliest period, when Muḥammad wished to draw the attention of the people of Mecca to the implications of his message, his revelations show very particular structural features. Here, for example, is the beginning of *Sūrat al-Mursalāt* (77, Those Sent Forth):

wa-al-murasalāti ʿurf-an	(1)	By the ones sent forth in droves
f-al-ʿāṣifāti ʿasf-an	(2)	storming in tempest,
wa-al-nāshirāti nashr-an	(3)	by the scatterers scattering
f-al-fāriqāti farq-an	(4)	cleaving a cleavage
f-al-mulqiyāti dhikr-an	(5)	tossing a reminder,
ʿudhr-an aw nudhr-an	(6)	excuse or warning,
inna-ma tuʿadūna la-wāqiʿun	(7)	what you are promised will happen!
fa-idhā n-nujūmu ṭumisat	(8)	When the stars are snuffed out,
wa-idhā s-samā'u furijat	(9)	when the heavens are cleft,
wa-idhā al-jibālu nusifat	(10)	when the mountains are pulverised,
wa-idhā r-rusulu uqqitat	(11)	when the messengers are assigned a time,
li-ayyi yawmin ujjilat	(12)	to what day will they be delayed?
li-yawm il-faṣli	(13)	to the Day of Decision.
ma adrāka ma yawm ul-faṣli	(14)	What will inform you about the Day of Decision?
waylun yawma'idhin li-l-mukadhdhibīna	(15)	On that day woe to the liars!

These sections – with their references to natural phenomena, their remarkable parallelisms, and their final and internal rhyme schemes – are a typical feature of many of the *sūrahs* from the Meccan period. This particular *sūrah* is remarkable, in that it begins with a sequence of invocations – an oath-preposition (*wa-* or *fa-*) followed by a participial form in the feminine plural and a noun in the indefinite singular (repeated with exactly the same sound-structure at the beginning of *sūrahs* 37, 51, 79, and 100, and with different sound-patterns in a number of others, 52 and 53, for example). It then continues with a second segment (vv. 8–11) that replicates the series of 'when' clauses which serve as the opening for several other Meccan *sūrahs* (56, 82, and 84, for example); the opening of *Sūrat al-takwīr* (81, The Enshrouding) contains fully fourteen of these phrases. Sequences such as these were apparently similar in structure to the pronouncements of other types of preacher and 'warner' to be encountered in sixth-century Mecca, particularly soothsayers (*kuhhān*, sing. *kāhin*). However, the crescendo of images and sounds that marked the beginning of several of these early revelations recited by Muḥammad to the people of his native city were followed by a new and disturbing message, often preceded by a question ('What will inform you about . . . ?'), which contained clear warnings concerning the inevitability of God's judgement that awaited sinners.

In the imagery and sounds of these invocations of nature and the elements we can see the message of the Qur'ān being revealed to the people of Mecca in not only their own language ('an Arabic Qur'ān', as *Sūrat Yūsuf* (12, Joseph) declares in verse 2) but also a formal structure that they would recognise. That this process of 'recognition' became problematic for Muḥammad in his prophetic mission is clear from the text of the Qur'ān itself: it was necessary to distinguish the revelations of God to His Prophet from these other types of homiletic utterance, and verses 41 and 42 of *Sūrat al-ḥāqqah* (69, The Indubitable) are unequivocal on the subject:

> It is the saying of a noble Messenger,
> not that of a poet; how little you believe!
> nor of a soothsayer; how little you remember!
> a revelation from the Lord of the worlds.

Part of the problem in the association that the people of Mecca made between Muḥammad's recitations and those of poets and soothsayers lies in the fact that they all sought to exploit the sound-qualities of Arabic by resorting to the cadential rhythms of *saj'* (lit. 'the cooing of a dove', but thereafter 'rhymed and cadenced discourse'), a style and structure that makes full use of the morphological potential of Arabic (described in the previous chapter and amply illustrated by the transliteration of the Arabic text just provided). The traditional English 'translation' of the

Arabic word has been 'rhymed prose', a reflection of the later use of *sajʿ* in prose writing and especially the narrative genre known as the *maqāmah* (discussed in Chapter 5). However, even though the early development of the style is not known to us, several features suggest the possibility of a link to the very earliest stages of Arabic poetry. While the presence in the above quotation from *Sūrah* 77 of rhyme, parallelism, and imagery – and the 'different' discourse that characterises many modern definitions of poetry – are more than sufficient for a modern reader to declare segments from many *sūrahs* 'poetic', the quotation from the text of 'The Indubitable' reminds us that, in Mecca before the *hijrah*, any such generic similarities had to be disavowed. The Qur'ān was unique: it was neither prose nor poetry, but the revelation of God to His people.

Sūrat al-baqarah (2, The Cow), the longest in the Qur'ān, contains a number of different types of discourse. One of the most remarkable is in the form of a direct address from God to His messenger (v. 186):

> If My servants ask you about Me, indeed I am near;
> I answer the call of the caller when he calls Me.
> So may they respond to Me and believe in Me.
> Perhaps they will be rightly guided.

The *sūrah* also contains injunctions and homiletic narratives couched in verses that are considerably longer than those of the early Meccan period. Specific obligations incumbent upon the community of believers are presented in the form of a series of imperatives that begin with the phrase: 'O you who believe . . .' These segments provide instructions on such matters as food, retaliation, wills, fasting, divorce and its consequences, and – at the very end of the sūrah – debt. A single verse (196), detailing some of the obligations connected with the pilgrimage and visitation (*ʿumrah*) to the holy cities of Mecca and Medina, serves as an excellent illustration of both the length and tone of the verses from the Medinan phase of Muḥammad's mission:

> Complete the pilgrimage and visitation to God; if you are prevented, then such offerings as are feasible. Do not shave your heads until the offerings reach their place. If any of you is sick or has a pain in his head, then redemption comes through fasting, alms, or sacrifice. When you are safe, whoever enjoys the visitation up to the pilgrimage, then such offerings as are feasible. Anyone who can find none, then for you a three-day fast during the pilgrimage and a seven-day fast following your return, making ten in all. That is for those whose family is not present in the Holy Mosque. Fear God and know that God is dire in retribution.

The dynamic nature of the process of revelation and its reception by the community can be gauged by the implied questioners who are reflected in a further set of segments beginning with the phrase 'They will ask you about . . .', and which provide clarification on such matters as drinking and gambling, the treatment of orphans, the direction of prayer, and fighting during the holy month; the response to the inquiry is prefaced with the word 'say' (*qul*):

They will ask you about orphans. Say: The best is to do well by them. If you mingle with them, they are your brethren. God knows the corrupter from the doer of good. Had God so willed, He would have harried you. He is mighty and wise. (v. 220)

The narratives invoke the careers of Moses, Abraham, Saul, and David, and references to Jesus and Mary, as a means of addressing the message of the revelations to the 'People of the Book' (Jews and Christians) and of showing the way in which the new calling to which Muḥammad's audience was being summoned incorporated the Judeo-Christian prophetic tradition within it, and at the same time placing the mission of Muḥammad to his people within the same prophetic framework.

The sections created by these different types of address are set off by verses that draw attention to God's power and generosity; verse 164 may serve as an example of the language of such statements and of the increased length of the rhyming unit:

Indeed in the creation of the heavens and the earth, the difference of night and day, the ship that plies the seas to people's profit, and the water that God releases from the heavens, thus reviving the soil after it has died and placing all kinds of beast in it, in the turning of the wind, and the clouds employed between heaven and earth, in these things are signs for the intelligent.

Sūrat al-nisā' (4, Women) is another lengthy *sūrah* from the period in Medina, and shows many of the same structuring features that we have just described: detailed instructions to the community in imperative form concerning points of doctrine and law (and particularly, as the title implies, concerning the status of women); and responses to points that have been raised regarding the revelations, now introduced by the specific verb 'They will ask you for an opinion [*istaftaw*]'. Believers are enjoined to obey God and His messenger (v. 59), and particular wrath is reserved for those people who, having joined the faithful, began to have doubts when conflicts arose between the small community of Muslims in Medina and the people of Mecca; these doubters were termed 'hypocrites' (*munāfiqun*), and verse 138 shows a certain grim humour in proclaiming their fate:

Give the hypocrites the good news: they will have a gruesome punishment.

The features that, within the tradition of Islamic scholarship, have been considered as contributors to the Qur'ān's unique textual qualities have served to bemuse and frustrate many Western readers of the Qur'ān. This, no doubt, helps to explain at least in part why the authors of the relatively few studies of the literary aspects of the Qur'ān in Western languages have tended to concentrate on those *sūrah*s and segments that conform with criteria recognisable to Western readers. The *sūrah* that has attracted much attention in both Arabic and other languages for its unusual structural unity and narrative qualities is *Sūrat Yūsuf* (12, Joseph). The elements of the narrative – Joseph's dream and its interpretation, the duplicity of his brothers, the attempted seduction of Joseph by Potiphar's wife, the imprisonment and recognition scenes – these are all well known from the account in Genesis (chs. 37–50).

The Qur'ānic version of the narrative opens with a passage that provides a framework for the text as a whole: after a set of the 'opening letters' – ALIF-LĀM-RĀ' (discussed above) – the text declares that the recitation is 'an Arabic Qur'ān', a statement the implications of which have had a vast impact upon ritual practice throughout the Islamic world. The third verse of the *sūrah* then provides confirmation of the very qualities to which we have just alluded: it announces that 'We will tell you the best of stories'. The perfect chiastic symmetry of the Joseph narrative gives the central portion – his imprisonment and the homily that he delivers (vv. 37–42) – a tremendous importance. And, just as aspects of the narrative, especially the betrayal of Joseph by his brothers, possessed a powerful symbolic resonance within the Christian tradition, so are the words of Joseph to his fellow-prisoners clearly intended to convey a powerful and important message to the hearers of Muḥammad's recitation in Mecca:

It is not for us to make any association with God; that is part of His bounty to us and all people, but most of them show no gratitude. (38)

O my prison-companions, which is better: to have a number of different gods or God the One and All-powerful? (39)

The entities you worship other than Him are mere names that you and your ancestors have named, and God has not revealed to them any authority. Judgement belongs to God alone; you should worship no other god than Him; that is the proper religion, but most people do not know. (40)

The elaborate way in which the narrative establishes a web of situations – the telling of the dream, the plotting of the brothers, the resigned patience of Jacob (the quality of '*ṣabr*' (v. 18) that has been highly regarded as an Arab trait since pre-Islamic times), the betrayal, the attempted seduction, and the imprisonment, and then proceeds to resolve them in reverse order – the discovery of the 'trickery' (*kayd*) of Potiphar's wife and companions (which in turn becomes a common motif in Arabic writing), the encounter with the brothers, their confession of guilt, the reuniting of Jacob with his long-lost son, and the fulfilment of the dream – all this serves as a wonderfully appropriate framework for the message that Muḥammad conveyed to the people of Mecca concerning the power of the One God and the authority that He gives to His chosen prophets.

As we noted above, the Qur'ān includes a number of other homiletic narratives and parables, some of them scattered in different *sūrah*s. A particularly rich source of somewhat shorter narratives is *Sūrat al-Kahf* (18, The Cave). In it we find firstly the story of the seven sleepers of Ephesus (vv. 9–26) which tells the legend of a group of Christians persecuted during the reign of the emperor Decius (249–51) who resort to a cave (whence the *sūrah*'s title) and fall into a profound and lengthy sleep; verse 25 says that the period involved is 309 years. When they wake up, they find themselves in a new era in which Christians are no longer persecuted. At the hands of the modern Egyptian playwright, Tawfīq al-Ḥakīm (*d.* 1987), this legend is turned into a five-act play, *Ahl al-kahf* (The People of the Cave). At verse 60 of *Sūrat al-Kahf* begins one of the Qur'ān's most fascinating tales, that of Moses and his encounter with a figure called al-Khaḍir. With a young companion Moses embarks on a quest to find the 'meeting place of the two seas', during the course of which the two encounter 'one of Our servants' (v. 65). Moses is set a challenge: not to ask any questions concerning this person's deeds, however odd they may seem. The series of seemingly violent and illogical actions that this person perpetrates are eventually explained to the all too humanly impatient Moses.

LANGUAGE AND IMAGERY

The tradition of pre-Islamic poetry (to be discussed in Chapter 4) serves as a clear historical precedent for the language of the Qur'ān; the language of the Bedouin of the Peninsula became an authoritative source for 'correctness' during the period when Muslim scholars began the process of codifying Arabic grammar. However, we possess little information about the status of the language of the Qur'ān in the context of the general linguistic situation in the Arabian Peninsula at the time of its revelation. The entire topic is still the subject of considerable debate.

In several verses the text of the Qur'ān notes that it is couched in 'a clear Arabic language' (*lisān ʿarabī mubīn*; see *Sūrat al-Naḥl* (16, The Bee), v. 103, for example, and *Sūrat al-Shuʿarā'* (26, The Poets), v. 195). Furthermore, the root of the word *mubīn* is found in another significant passage regarding language: *Sūrat Ibrāhīm* (14, Abraham) v. 4 declares that 'We have never sent down a prophet with anything but his own people's language so that he may make things clear [*yubayyin*] to them'. The statements, reports, and implied questions ('They will ask you about . . .') that are included in the *sūrah*s of the Qur'ān make it clear that God's message was indeed recited by Muḥammad in a language that was comprehensible to his listeners.

Concordances of the Qur'ān list a number of words that appear to be of non-Arabian provenance; in his *The Foreign Vocabulary of the Qur'ān* Arthur Jeffrey lists some 275 such items. It needs to be said from the outset that the very notion of 'foreignness', when dealing with the necessarily adaptive language situation in a commercial centre such as that of Mecca, is somewhat problematic. While the Arabic language of the desert nomads may have been less subject to linguistic change than its northern Semitic cousins, the various towns, oases, and tribal confederations were far from being isolated from social and commercial contacts with regions to the north and south.

As many of the examples we have already cited show clearly, the language of the Qur'ān is often used with excellent figurative effect, providing further illustration of the close linkage between metaphor and the homiletic. The Qur'ān uses the metaphors of blindness and deafness to convey unbelief: 'God has removed their light and left them in darkness, not seeing; deaf, dumb, blind; they shall not return' (*Sūrat al-Baqarah* (2, The Cow), vv. 17–18). Those who follow other gods have 'gone astray', and just as those who do not believe have had the light removed, so do those whom God has guided to belief have the light, a metaphor which provides one of the Qur'ān's most extended and beautiful images:

> God is the light of the heavens and the earth; the likeness of His light is as a niche with a lamp in it; the lamp is in a glass, and the glass is like a pearly star kindled from a blessed tree, an olive from neither East nor West, its oil almost giving light even though no fire has touched it; light upon light. God guides to His light whomever he wishes (*Sūrat al-Nur* (24, The Light), v. 35).

These features of the discourse of the Qur'ān are encapsulated into the religious and critical doctrine of *iʿjāz*, the 'inimitability' of God's revelation to Muḥammad. It is enshrined in the 'challenge' (*taḥaddī*) verses, such as 'If you have doubts concerning what we have sent down to our servant, then produce a sūrah like it' (*Sūrat al-Baqarah* (2, The Cow), v. 24), and 'If mankind and the jinn got together to produce the like of this Qur'ān, they would not produce its like' (*Sūrat al-Isrā'* (17, The Night-Journey), v. 88). The existence of this doctrine has deterred most writers from attempting to take up the implicit challenge; one who did was Arabic's most famous poet, who thereby earned himself the name by which he is generally known, 'al-Mutanabbi' (he who claimed to be a prophet). Such exceptions aside, however, the language and style of the Qur'ān endure as yardsticks of Arabic eloquence, to be admired, cited, and, in particular, recited.

THE ROLE OF SOUND

Once the Qur'ān was established and canonised in textual form, the overwhelming bulk of learning devoted to its study was concerned with the written dimension – with the Qur'ān as text, and that has been reflected in the contents of this chapter. However, the oral dimension continues to exert its enduring influence on society. The ability of a devout Muslim to memorise the entire text and to recite it at will remains today what it has always been, a sign of a complete Islamic education, starting at the Qur'ān school (*kuttābi*) where the text is taught by rote. The 'recitation' of the Qur'ān (its original meaning, it will be recalled) remains a daily phenomenon, enjoined upon the faithful: 'chant the Qur'ān [a chanting]' (*Sūrat al-Muzzammil* (73, The Enwrapped), v. 4). Indeed, the advent of powerful modern means of communication has served to amplify this effect: not only is the traditional craft of chanting the text of the Qur'ān (*tajwīd*) readily available on radio and television as a celebration of the sounds of the sacred text that may be heard and watched several times a day, but also at the mosques of Middle Eastern cities the often heavily amplified voice of '*mu'adhdhin*' fills the air with his elaborate intonations as he summons the faithful to prayer five times daily.

In discussing the structure of some of the shorter *sūrah*s in the Qur'ān, I drew attention to the shortness and parallelism of phrases, and to repetition and rhyme, most especially those connected with the style known as *sajʿ*. If such features are transferred from the purely textual to the acoustic realm, their impact is, needless to say, even greater: words and chant, message and sound, combine to carry the significance of the revelation to even higher levels of understanding and emotional response. The practitioner of *tajwīd* is required to possess a beautiful voice; emphasis can be given to specific consonants and vowels through elongation, and 'n' and 'm' are singled out for 'nasalisation' (*ghunnah*). When the chanter uses these techniques to accentuate the assonantal features of passages such as verse 17 of *Sūrat al-Baqarah* (2, The Cow) noted above – 'ṣummun bukmun ʿumyun' – or the opening verse of *Sūrat al-Qadr* (97, Power) – '*inna anzalnāhu fī laylati l-qadri*' – and then blends this technical repertoire into the rise and fall of traditional chant, the effect on the listener transcends that of words alone.

As with any linkage between sacred text and musical setting, the ritual chanting of the Qurʾān clearly has a powerful effect on listeners. As numerous accounts show, that effect will often assume an enhanced form in the rituals of the Ṣūfī community; the gathering of a brotherhood (termed *ḥaḍrah*) will include not only recitations from the Qurʾān but also texts in praise of God (*dhikr*) and mystical poems such as the *Burdah* of al-Būṣīrī (*d.* 1296). It is the heightened intensity brought about by this particular kind of experience and in particular the prevalence in many regions of Ṣūfī orders whose rituals make full use of it that have led to an uneasy tension between popular practice in many Muslim communities and the orthodoxy espoused by conservative scholars who have always viewed the impact of music on believers with suspicion.

QURʾĀN AND ARABIC LITERATURE

The doctrine of *iʿjāz*, confirming the Qurʾān's miraculous nature, demanded its severance from the statements of humans couched in such forms as poetry and *sajʿ*; its revelation may be associated with a period and a language, but it is by definition unique. In spite of the clearly oral nature of its original revelation, its form as canonical text and the role that it plays within the Islamic community turns it into *al-kitāb* (*the* book). It becomes the paradigmatic text, and its language, structures, and images pervade the whole of Arabic discourse.

In the realm of poetry the language of the Qurʾān and particularly its imagery became a rich source for allusion and citation. When the caliph-poet, ibn al-Muʿtazz (*d.* 908), wrote his *Kitāb al-badīʿ* (Book of Figures of Speech) with the purpose of codifying poetic devices, the Qurʾān was a principal source in providing him with examples of the use of imagery. The poets' resort to the Qur'ān as a source of imagery and allusion is not limited to the more obvious genres such as poems of asceticism (*zuhdiyyah*) and the inspirational odes of Ṣūfīs, but can also be seen in the more overtly 'political' poetry, for example odes in praise of the caliph – as leader of the community of faithful – and his entourage. The quest for forgiveness and the depiction of paradise provide thematic links between the message of the Qur'ān and the tradition of love poetry (*ghazal*) that emerged as an independent genre in the early decades of Islam; many of the stock images of this genre and of the *khamriyyah* (wine poem) were adopted by Ṣūfī poets as means of providing a symbolic representation of the believer's aspiration for closer contact with the Almighty.

In modern times the Qur'ānic themes of divine retribution against sinful peoples and the ephemerality of human existence have provided fertile images through which poets can express their political opinions: in his famous poem, '*Unshūdat al-maṭar*' (Hymn to the Rain), Badr Shākir al-Sayyāb (*d.* 1964) invokes the fate of the ancient Arabian people of Thamud as a warning to modern oppressors.

While poetry in Arabic antedates the revelation of the Qur'ān, the emergence of a belletristic prose tradition (the topic of Chapter 5) can also be considered a consequence of the revelations to Muḥammad, in that it reflects both the needs of the bureaucratic class within the growing Islamic community and the expanding fields of scholarly interest. ʿAbd al-ḥamīd al-kātib (*d.* 750), whose writings are generally recognised as being among the earliest monuments of this tradition, shows a complete familiarity with the Qur'ān and makes copious citations from it in his epistles which were to serve as models of polite discourse. The predilection of this bureaucracy for compendia of information about an amazing variety of topics sees its most sophisticated realisation in the works of ʿAmr ibn Baḥr, nicknamed al-Jāḥiẓ (*c.* 776–869); in an anecdote from his *Kitāb al-bukhalā'* (Book of Misers) we follow the increasing despair of the narrator as he listens with ever-increasing incredulity and exasperation to the lengths a miser from Marw in Khurāsān will go to in order to preserve oil in a lamp, but, even in such a context, the conclusion takes the form of the famous 'light' verse from the Qur'ān that we cited earlier (*Sūrat al-Nūr* (24, The Light), v. 35).

The genre of the *maqāmah* which retained its popularity well into the twentieth century is linked to the Qur'ān in both direct and indirect ways: directly through the use of *sajʿ* structures that inevitably provoke echoes of the cadences of the sacred text; indirectly through the homiletic message that can be inferred from the often nefarious antics of the picaresque characters who people the vignettes. Another source of narratives that provides a direct link to the Qurʾān is the *Thousand and One Nights*. The gloomy tale of the 'City of Brass', for example, can be seen as an elaborate homily on a predominant theme in God's message in the Qurʾān, the ephemerality of the life in this world: its narrative and especially its many *zuhdiyyah* poems are intended to provide 'warnings' and 'lessons' to the prudent.

In more recent times Najīb Maḥfūẓ's controversial novel, *Awlād ḥāratinā* (1959/1967; *Children of Gebelawi*, 1981) provides us with an example of not only a modern narrative genre being used to invoke themes, images, and language found in the Qurʾān but also the continuing confrontation between creative writers and religious orthodoxy regarding the interpretation of such works. Maḥfūẓ uses allegory as a vehicle for narratives of the careers of four Qurʾānic prophets, Adam, Moses, Jesus, and Muḥammad, and their attempts to bring God's message to a human community ever prone to violence.

CONCLUSION

The above examples are intended as a small sample of the myriad ways in which the text of the Qurʾān has been a continuing influence on every aspect of the Arabic literary tradition. Quotations from and allusions to the Qurʾān – prayers, phrases, individual words – are as much a given in the Arabic literary tradition as themes and citations from the biblical text are in English literature and the societies of its publics.

Having now examined its status as the founding monument of the Muslim community and explored some of the more literary aspects of the text itself, we will now turn to consider the genres that emerged and developed within the framework of that community. Our survey begins with poetry, considered from the outset as the great repository of Arab creativity and values.

CHAPTER 4

Poetry

INTRODUCTION

In November 1988 I attended the Mirbad Festival of Poetry in Iraq. On one of the evenings the attendees were all gathered in the town hall of al-Baṣrah in Southern Iraq, a city renowned in earlier times for the Mirbad Square where, as we will see below, poets (such as the redoubtable lampoonists, al-Farazdaq (*d. c.* 729) and Jarīr (*d.* 732)) would gather and more recently for the statue of one of Southern Iraq's most illustrious modern poetic sons, Badr Shākir al-Sayyāb (*d.* 1964). Sitting next to me on this occasion was another invited guest, the French novelist, Alain Robbe-Grillet. After listening patiently for a while to the ringing tones of several poets, he asked me if any of them had changed the theme from the predominant topic of the last several days, the successful conclusion of a prolonged conflict with Iran. I responded in the negative and went on to point out that these poets were all faithfully replicating the role of their predecessors, eulogising the ruler and celebrating his glorious victories. The opening ceremonies in Baghdād had produced new odes from Nizār Qabbānī from Syria, Muḥammad Faytūrī from the Sudan, and Suʿād al-Ṣabāḥ from Kuwait, and on this particular evening in al-Baṣrah the theme was being re-echoed in a welter of imagery and bombast.

Just two years later, the army of Iraq invaded Suʿād al-Ṣabāḥ's homeland of Kuwait, and Arabic poetry was again called upon to fulfil one of its traditional roles. In a wonderful revival of ancient traditions, each side in this most conservative part of the Arab world unleashed not merely its contemporary military might but also the literary heritage's ultimate poetic weapon, the lampoon (*hijāʾ*), as the media carried stinging attacks against the rulers of the other side in the conflict.

Arabic poetry has always been regarded as the *dīwān al-ʿarab* (the repository of the Arabs), a resort in times of sorrow and happiness, of defeat and victory, an expression of the Arab people's cultural ideals and greatest aspirations. It continues to be called upon to fulfil the visible public function it has upheld through the centuries. As we suggested in Chapter 2, words in the Arabic-speaking world are powerful and effective weapons; contrary to the English adage, names can indeed hurt. As a result, poetry – society's most highly effective projector of words and names – matters.

POETRY

As just noted, poetry is indeed 'the record of the Arabs'. A good deal of what has been preserved of the heritage of the past consists of what can be termed occasional poetry. We learn, for example, through the famous *Muʿallaqah* of Zuhayr ibn Abī Sulmā (*d. c.* 607) of the means by which tribal conflicts in pre-Islamic Arabia could be resolved, while the poetry of al-Ṭirimmāḥ (*d. c.* 730) reflects the religious fervour of the Khawārij, the group that 'went away' from the other divisions within the Muslim community after the arbitration at the Battle of Ṣiffīn in 657. The odes of Abū Nuwās (*d. c.* 815) and Bashshār ibn Burd (*d.* 784) give us insight into the tensions that arose when new converts to Islam brought with them many of the values of their own cultural traditions and sought to challenge the hallowed norms of the earlier poetry. Abū Tammām (*d.* 846) and al-Mutanabbī (*d.* 965) are two of many poets who bequeathed to later generations ringing odes in praise of a ruler whose forces have just won a great battle for the cause of Islam. Within a very different political and strategic balance modern Arab poets such as Ḥāfiẓ Ibrāhīm (*d.* 1932) and Abū al-qāsim al-Shābbī (*d.* 1934) compose poems in support of nationalist causes, while at a point of the most extreme adversity – the June War of 1967 – Nizār Qabbānī (*d.* 1998) reflects savagely 'On the margins of defeat'.

For the critic, Qudāmah ibn Jaʿfar (*d.* 948), poetry is 'discourse that is metred, rhymed, and conveys meaning', a set of what appear to be definitional minima that came to be adopted as a prescriptive device; the formula was used to exclude types of writing that did not match those criteria. Qudāmah's definition is still being cited in 1898 by an Egyptian critic like Muḥammad al-Muwayliḥī (*d.* 1930), but with an interesting elaboration: poetry, he says, is 'one of the conditions of the soul'. His colleague, the poet Ḥāfiẓ Ibrāhīm, suggests that poetry is 'a science to be found along with the sun'. Rather than sticking with Qudāmah's pedantic definition, he suggests, critics should regard poetry as being anything that has an effect on the soul. In what may be seen as a prescient statement he suggests that, while metrical discourse provides many wonderful examples of the poetic, it is not out of the question to consider some prose writers as showing similar qualities.

The Syro-Lebanese poet, Adūnīs (a pseudonym of ʿAlī Aḥmad Saʿīd, *b.* 1928?), has discussed the nature of poetry in a number of his works. For him, poetry has a distinct purpose, that of renewing language, of changing the meaning of words by using them in striking new combinations. Through his own poetic creativity and critical writings, Adūnīs has underlined the completeness of the shift from a time when poems that did not conform with a set of prescriptive formal norms were thereby excluded from the very category of poetry to one in which it is the poet who chooses the subject matter and language of the poem and thereby determines anew in each case what the nature of the poem will be.

In what follows we will try to trace some of the major features of this lengthy and varied process of development, beginning with role and status of the poet as the practitioner of the art, and then considering the structures and themes of the poems themselves.

THE POET

Person and persona

The poet in Arabic is one who senses, *shāʿir*; in the more elaborate version of the eleventh-century poet-critic, ibn Rashīq (to be discussed in Chapter 7), the poet is someone who perceives things that other people cannot. Such a view of the poet encouraged the notion that such people were born, not made; that the poetic gift was the consequence of innate rather than acquired qualities; not that certain skills did not have to be learned, but that the spark of intangible genius had to be already present for a poet to become really great. These assumptions concerning the nature of poetic talent led early Arab critics to assign greater credit to 'natural' poetry (*maṭbūʿ*) than to 'artificial, contrived' (*maṣnūʿ*); the breaking down of such categories, which, almost by definition, accorded greater credit to earlier poetry rather than contemporary, was to occasion much critical debate (also discussed in Chapter 7).

This designation of poets as those who have unique qualities of perception assigns them a function that transcends that of composing in a particular way, a role in society that is akin to that of a shaman. Poets within pre-Islamic Arabian society were believed to be gifted with insight, and their utterances possessed special power. With this in mind, the clash between poets and Muḥammad that is reflected in the revelations of the Qurʾān (and particularly in the *sūrah* on Poets (26), where poets are said to be followed by the deluded and to say things they do not do) can be placed into a different context. What is being addressed in the revelations of the Qurʾān is the power that poets continued to exert at a time when Muḥammad was endeavouring to introduce the new message of the Qurʾān into a society which detected similarities between the two types of expression.

The Arab poet then possesses 'the power of the word'; as Caton notes with reference to the poetic tradition in Yemen today, 'the poet has power over men, and poetry is a deeply political act' (*Peaks of Yemen I Summon,* 40). In the earliest stages of the literary tradition the emergence within a tribe of the Arabian Peninsula of a truly gifted poet was a cause for great rejoicing. The poet could rouse the tribe with eulogies (*madīḥ*) extolling the chivalry and generosity of its leaders and men; could remind them of the qualities of fallen heroes in elegies (*marthiyah*), a category in which women poets seem to have played a prominent role; and, deadliest of verbal weapons, could cast aspersions on the qualities of enemy tribes, their leaders and womenfolk, in vicious lampoons (*hijāʾ*). In an interesting reversal that only serves to underline the significance of these functions, poetic personae were created to reflect the anti-tribal scenario, the so-called vagabond (*ṣuʿlūk*) poets such as Taʾabbaṭa Sharran (a nickname meaning 'he who has put evil under his armpit'), ʿUrwah ibn al-Ward, and al-Shanfarā. Their scoffing at the need for tribal solidarity and their glorification of deprivation, solitude, and the company of wild animals only serve to emphasise for poetry's audience the benefits that affiliation could provide. That there was also a class of itinerant 'professional' poets who would earn their living by proceeding from one court and occasion to another seems confirmed by the accounts of the life of a poet such as al-Aʿshā (literally, 'night-blind', *d. c.* 630), renowned for his wine and hunt descriptions, whose search for a livelihood seems to have taken him across the length and breadth of Arabia.

With the advent of Islam some aspects of the poetic function changed. Clearly, the establishment of new cultural centres outside the Arabian Peninsula – Damascus, Baghdād, Cairo, Qayrawān, Marrakesh, Fez, and Cordoba, to name just a few – and the vibrant cultural admixture that populated them created new and expanded opportunities for the patronage of littérateurs and, given the predominant position of poetry, of poets in particular. The poet is now an important court functionary, and poetic careers are made or broken according to the extent that talent is recognised. The negative side is shown in the career of ibn al-Rūmī (*d.* 896) who complains bitterly in some of his poems about a lack of recognition. On the other hand, poets like al-Buḥturī (*d.* 897) and al-Mutanabbī feel sufficiently confident of their status to drop unsubtle hints about the lack of appreciation they feel from their patrons. 'When I am dealt with badly', says the former in his famous ode contemplating the Persian ruins at Ctesiphon, 'I'm liable to spend the morning in a different place from the night before'.

We still encounter vestiges of this tradition of the patronised poet, habitué of court and literary salon, during the earlier phases of modern Arabic literature. Criticisms of the Egyptian court poet, Aḥmad Shawqī, tend to harp on his close ties to the royal household. Gradually, however, the emergence of new modes of publication, expanded educational opportunities, and changing local and international configurations provided the basis for a different readership and focus for literary texts. Nationalisms, pan-Arab and local, served as a major standard under which the Arab poet sought to express sentiments both corporate and individual, and no more so than in the odes of the Tunisian, Abū al-qāsim al-Shabbī, composed in the 1920s and 1930s. The period following the Second World War saw this poetic role intensified. The rallying cry was now 'commitment', and many poets addressed themselves to the urgent issues of the time: for Palestinians like Maḥmūd Darwīsh and Samīḥ al-Qāsim, the topics were both obvious and immediate – loss of land and of human rights. For other poets as varied as Nizār Qabbānī, ʿAbd al-wahhāb al-Bayātī (*b.* 1926), and Ṣalāḥ ʿAbd al-Ṣabūr (*d.* 1981), the topics to which their poems were addressed were the concerns and aspirations of an educated and mostly middle-class readership that found itself confronting the injustices and complexities of life in the newly independent societies of the Middle East.

The shift away from the patronage of an influential individual or office towards that of the broader societal community has led the poet to a new sense of individual responsibility, something that has not been without its risks for the modern Arab poet in the latter half of the twentieth century. It is now the task of the individual modern poet alone to select those inspirational moments and occasions, both public and private, for celebration in poetic form; the consequences of doing so – whether they be recognition, imprisonment, exile, or death – are the poet's also. We have already suggested that a poet such as al-Mutanabbī and the noisy critical controversy that surrounded his poetic career give us some insight into the motivations of the individual voice found within his poetry; the poetic persona is certainly a major one, but we also seem to catch a glimpse of the person behind it. With many other poets, the linkage between the individual voice and the public persona remains pleasingly, indeed poetically, ambiguous. When ʿUmar ibn Abī Rabīʿah (*d.* 711) composes poems that describe his Don Juanesque encounters with the ladies of Meccan society, we are given an intimate glimpse into the society of his time that many commentators have chosen to link closely to the poet's own lifestyle; at all events, it creates a poetic vision that is considerably different from the traditional love poetry associated with the tribal life of the desert (both to be discussed below). At a later stage, the verses of Abū Nuwās (*d. c.* 815), Arabic's ribald poet *par excellence* and, at least in the *Thousand and One Nights*, a regular member of Hārūn al-Rashīd's night-time côterie, seem to reflect a richly complex persona's quest for meaning, at one moment indulging to the utmost in all the sins of the flesh and boasting of his 'heroic' exploits, and then recognising the essential frivolity and ephemerality of life and the inevitability of judgement:

> Lo! Grey-haired old age has surprised me by its appearance;
> how evil and ill-starred it is!
> I have repented of my mistakes and of missing the designated
> times [of prayer].
> So I pray You, God – all praise to You! – to forgive, just as
> You did, Almighty One, with Jonah!

Viewing the status of the Arab poet from a contemporary perspective, one thing that may seem somewhat striking is the extent to which the balance of poets during the earlier centuries of the Arabic heritage – at least those whose works have come down to us – is overwhelmingly male. That is not to say, of course, that there is a complete lack of female poets: among the more famous names in that category are al-Khansāʾ (*d. c.* 640), renowned for her elegies on her brother; Rābiʿah al-ʿAdawiyyah (*d.* 801), the famous Ṣūfī poetess; and Wallādah (*d. c.* 1077), Umawī princess of al-Andalus. While research is insufficient to make any firm judgements, it seems plausible to posit the notion that the process of recording women's poetry was directly linked to levels of education and literacy; thus the contents of their poetic heritage which were stored in the memory and passed on through successive generations were for the most part not committed to written form. This situation has, needless to say, changed considerably in the modern period due to enhanced educational opportunities and different attitudes to publication.

Training

By the tenth century poetry had been subsumed within the syllabus that was part of the formation of a littérateur (*adīb*), a term to be discussed in detail in Chapter 5). The aspiring poet, ibn Rashīq tells us, needs to memorise the poetry of the ancients, study grammar, tropes, rhyme, and meter, and then familiarise himself with genealogy.

The trainee phase was that of the 'bard' (*rāwī*); it involved learning the rudiments of the craft by memorising the poetry of a senior poet, performing the odes of the master and others, and perfecting the various aspects of the creative process. Once these tasks had been successfully completed, the aspiring poet would gradually be invited to imitate the best examples of other poets, and finally achieve a level of competence which would permit him to create his own compositions. The efficacy of the system is well illustrated by a chain of illustrious names from the earliest period provided for us by Ṭāhā Ḥusayn: Ṭufayl had ʿAws ibn Ḥajar as his bard; ʿAws had Zuhayr ibn Abī Sulmā; Zuhayr had his son, Kaʿb ibn Zuhayr; Kaʿb had al-Ḥuṭayʾah; al-Ḥuṭayʾah had Jamīl Buthaynah; and Jamīl had Kuthayyir ʿAzzah – thus over successive generations did bard-trainee become illustrious contributor to the poetic tradition.

The modern poet who is encouraged to cultivate such gifts is now able to find inspiration from a number of sources and especially through readings of the treasures of his own and other traditions: first and foremost, the collections (*dawāwīn*, sing. *dīwān*) of the renowned poets of earlier centuries collected and preserved within the highly elaborate system of Islamic education, but also through engagement with the works of the great poets of world literature. Some of the greatest among the modern Arab poets – one thinks of Badr Shākir al-Sayyāb and Adūnīs – are notable for the extent to which their poems, for all their modernity, show a familiarity with the language and imagery of the poetic heritage. Meanwhile, it is in those areas where the cultural norms of the past remain strongest – among the Bedouin of the desert and in the Arabian Peninsula – that we continue to find clear echoes of the training processes that have been responsible for turning the truly gifted from apprentice poets into masters.

Performance

The performance of Arabic poetry has been a constant from the outset. One of the earliest accounts that we possess finds the illustrious poet, al-Nābighah (*d. c.* 604), adjudicating a poetry competition as part of the annual fair held at the Arabian market-town of ʿUkāẓ. This tradition of poetic competitions, jousts, and duels continues today; an example is found in the *zajal* tradition in Lebanon, in which two poets (and their choruses) will pass the evening hours exchanging verses on the qualities of an oppositional pair of topics such as black and white.

Alongside somewhat spontaneous and local types of occasion which lie at the more popular end of the performance spectrum, there have always been, of course, more official events at which the poet has been expected to fulfil a more ceremonial function, whether the venue was a tribal gathering, court ceremony, or day of national remembrance. Such occasions would include celebrations of victory in battle, prominent events in the lives of the ruling dynasty – births, weddings, and funerals, and religious festivals. For the most formal gatherings (for which the Arabic term is *majlis*) the subject matter of these poems would be a matter of court protocol. Later in the evening when the ruler gathered with his boon-companions (*nudamāʾ*) and slave-girls (*jawārī*), the *majlis* would have a more intimate atmosphere and the topics for poetic performance were considerably less constrained, at least if we are to credit some of the accounts concerning the poet, Abū Nuwās. Abū al-faraj al-Iṣfahānī's (*d.* 967) famous anthology of poets and poetry, *Kitāb al-aghānī* (The Book of Songs) is replete with accounts of both formal and less formal occasions for musical and poetic performances by such illustrious singers as Ibrāhīm al-Mawṣilī (*d.* 804), Ibrāhīm ibn al-Mahdī (*d.* 839 – as his name implies, the son of the caliph, al-Mahdī), and, most virtuoso of all, Isḥāq al-Mawṣilī (*d.* 849, son of Ibrāhīm).

In earliest times the occasion for poetic performance would have been a tribal gathering, whether it involved the members of a single grouping around a campfire in the evening or a larger annual gathering of tribal confederacies. Current practice in countries like Yemen may not be an entirely accurate guide to earlier times, but, in the almost total absence of recorded information on the topic, it may provide some clues. Coffee is being served, and there is much noise as the group converses. When the poet is ready to begin, he will clear his throat to request silence and then start declaiming. The two halves of the first verse of the poem will both end with the rhyming syllable, and the poet will repeat the first line so that the audience has a clear sense of both rhyme and metre. The audience listening to the performance is thoroughly familiar with the occasions, motifs, and facets that make up the poetic craft and will be quick to express its approval of excellent lines (often requesting their repetition) and criticism of less satisfactory efforts through silence or bodily gestures of disapproval.

THE POEM

Collections

A collection of Arabic poems is usually called a *dīwān*. The early philologists who gathered poems into collections used a variety of organisational criteria. Some were named after the tribe under whose protective umbrella the works had been conceived and performed: thus the poems of the Banū Hudhayl. Others were named after their compilers: the *Mufaḍḍaliyyāt* of al-Mufaḍḍal al-Ḍabbī, for example, and the *Aṣmaʿiyyāt* of al-Aṣmaʿī. Still others were clustered around particular motifs; one of the most cherished was heroism, *ḥamāsah*, providing the title for a number of collections of which the most renowned is that of the poet, Abū Tammām. However, the most favoured organising principle for collections of Arabic poetry has been and remains the gathering of the works of a single poet (the *Dīwān* of al-Mutanabbī, for example).

Until relatively recently it was not the practice to give Arabic poems descriptive titles. The majority of collections by early poets frame the poems themselves within a series of short statements that recount the occasion for which the poem was composed and/or performed: upon the death of a prominent person, for example, or in celebration of a significant event in the life of the community (occasions and categories that will be explored in more detail below). A preferred mode of sequence for the collected poems was an alphabetical one based on their end-rhymes. The most famous poems were often referred to in this way: thus, the vagabond-poet al-Shanfarā's most famous ode is known as 'the L-poem of the Arabs' (*lāmiyyat al-ʿArab*). Another method of identification is through the opening of the poem: thus, Imru' al-Qays's *muʿallaqah* poem is instantly recognisable through its renowned beginning: 'Halt, you two companions, and let us weep . . .' (*qifā nabki*). As the Arabic poetic tradition developed and particular genres came to be recognised as separate entities, the *dīwān* of the poet was often subdivided into categories. Abū Nuwās's collected poetry, for example, contains large separate sections of love poems addressed to males and females (*ghazal*) and wine poems (*khamriyyah*); in addition to anticipated sections on eulogy, lampoon and elegy, there are also others gathered around the themes of hunting, asceticism, and reprimand. With Abū Tammām's *Dīwān* we find separate sections on eulogy, lampoon, elegy, love, chiding, description, boasting, and asceticism.

Political and social developments in the Arab world during the twentieth century have led to significant changes in the status and role of the poet. Thus, in addition to the new creative environment within which poets sense a need to speak with a more individual voice, there is also a marked transformation in modes of communication with their public, in that the advent of modern print technology provides a broader, swifter, and readier means of contact. Journals, magazines, and newspapers regularly publish poems, and, given the right political circumstances (admittedly a large proviso in certain regions), such works can be gathered into publishable collections. With a poet like Badr Shākir al-Sayyāb, for example, whose early death allows us to assess the collected poems of a contemporary writer, each *dīwān* published separately comes to be regarded as a representative of the poet's art at a particular phase in his career. The Arab world's most popular poet in the latter half of the twentieth century, Nizār Qabbānī (*d.* 1998), garnered a sufficient following to be able to found his own publishing house.

Rhyme and metre

The form of the pre-modern Arabic poem on a printed page suggests symmetry. The lines are laid out so as to emphasise the end-rhyme of each line. The gap that separates the two halves of the line indicates the point at which the metrical pattern (according to the prosodic system of al-Khalīl ibn Aḥmad) is repeated; while this space will often also mark the division between two distinct segments of syntax, the sense of the line may be carried over from the first half to the second. In the case of the *qaṣīdah* the resulting columns of neatly margined print are a primary characteristic of printed editions, and the lack of such patterning is a distinct feature of modern poetry.

Rhyme in Arabic is based on sound; there is no concept of visual rhyme. In the majority of poems the rhyming element is the final consonant in the line, although a poet such as al-Maʿarrī (*d.* 1058) set himself in his collection *Luzūm mā lā yalzam* a greater challenge of incorporating the vowel-sound of the previous syllable as well. While some of the categories of poem that will be discussed below exhibit different rhyming patterns, the scheme of the predominant form – the *qaṣīdah* – is that of the monorhyme at the end of each line of the poem. While this monorhyme scheme is the most predominant within the poetic tradition, there are a number of other patterns: one such is the 'doublet' (*muzdawijah*), which may well have entered the Arabic tradition in imitation of the Persian *mathnawī*; the pattern involved is that the two halves of each line rhyme: aa, bb, cc, and so on.

Following the Second World War, Arabic poetry moved beyond earlier experiments with different types of rhyming scheme and even with blank verse (a short-lived trend which had little success) and abandoned rhyme as a defining element. After an initial phase of explorations in *shiʿr ḥurr* (an Arabic translation of *vers libre* (free verse) that subsumed under its name a number of different experiments), many poets moved on to experiment with the prose poem. In contemporary poetry the sound-elements traditionally associated with rhyme have been replaced by such features as assonance and repetition.

By the time of Qudāmah ibn Jaʿfar (*d.* 948) the mention of metrics had come to imply an adherence to the system developed by al-Khalīl ibn Aḥmad of al-Baṣrah. The system was one that quantified sound-patterns into two categories: one that was fixed, termed *watad* (the Arabic word for 'tent-peg'); and one that was variable, *sabab* (meaning 'tent-rope'). The different sequences of pulses that he recorded were formed into five continuous chains in the form of circles; by starting the chain at different points on the circle, he identified fifteen independent metres.

The metrics of a sizeable percentage of Arabic poetry can be analysed using al-Khalīl's system; it is just one of the remarkable achievements of a scholar who contributed much to the study of Arabic language, literature, and music. However, within this context we need to keep al-Khalīl's account of his procedure in mind: that he had recorded what he heard. The process of converting his description into a prescriptive metrical system for the identification of what constituted poetry (and what did not) was not without its problems. Quite apart from the fact that certain lines and categories of poem do not seem to conform with this system, it is in connection with the subject of music and accompaniment that a strict adherence to al-Khalīl's system as sole criterion in this area becomes problematic.

We noted above that in the aftermath of the Second World War Arabic poetry went through a period of profound change. In addition to the abandonment of rhyme as a *sine qua non* of poetry, the metrics of al-Khalīl were initially adapted as part of a movement known under the general heading of 'free verse', but, in the revolutionary atmosphere of the late 1940s and 1950s, Arab poets were not inclined to replace one set of rules with another. With the advent of the prose poem all ties to the requirements regarding rhyme and metre as defining elements of poetry were severed.

Categories

Qiṭʿah *and* Qaṣīdah

Since the corpus of pre-Islamic poetry emerged as the Qurʾān's most ready and obvious linguistic precedent, philologists set out to collect as much of the poetic heritage as possible, using as their primary source the bards and poets of the Arabian tribes and urban centres who had learned the poetry of the desert. Many of the texts that were recorded through this process clearly represented the most prized products of the poetic tradition, poems varying in both length and structural complexity that constitute the most recent versions of a performance practice going back through many generations of bards. Alongside these types of poem were other shorter examples, some of which seem complete in their own right while others appear to represent fragments of lengthier structures, perhaps favourite parts of longer poems selected from the memory of a particular bard in order to illustrate a theme, image, or section of the poem.

It is possible that the shorter of the two primary types, called the *qiṭʿah*, is antecedent to the lengthier, the *qaṣīdah*, but the process referred to above, whereby several centuries of poetic creativity were recorded in an intensely concentrated manner, served to obscure the stages in the development of the poetic genres themselves. The shorter form often served as a monothematic poem for a particular occasion, a brief elegy on a fallen hero or an account of a raid or encounter.

The early *qaṣīdah* was a poem intended to convey a message. Examples of the genre from different periods display a degree of variation on the apparent structural principles of the initial segments of the poem, but the arrival at the crux is, more often than not, clearly marked within the poem's textual form and was presumably even more so in public performance. Here, for example, are some lines from a *qaṣīdah* by the elder of two poets called al-Muraqqish (sixth century) taken from Sir Charles Lyall's still affecting version of the collection of al-Mufaḍḍal al-Ḍabbī (*d. c.* 786), *al-Mufaḍḍaliyyāt*:

> O camel-rider, whoever thou mayst be, bear this message, if
> thou lightest on them, to Anas son of Saʿd, and Harmalah:
> 'Great will be the virtue of you twain and your father, if the
> man of Ghufailah escapes being slain!'

In the introduction to his *Kitāb al-shiʿr wa-al-shurʿarāʾ* (Book of Poetry and Poets), ibn Qutaybah (*d.* 889) attempts a summary of the *qaṣīdah*'s structure, prefaced with a cautionary phrase, 'Some literary folk say . . .': the *qaṣīdah* is a tripartite structure, consisting of a nostalgic opening (*nasīb*), leading through a 'release' (*takhalluṣ*) to a travel section (*raḥīl*), and finishing with the message of the poem in the form of praise of tribal attributes (*fakhr*), lampooning the enemy (*hijā'*), and moral aphorisms (*ḥikam*). This is a convenient summary of the primary features of a number of Arabic *qaṣā'id* (convenience being a primary principle of ibn Qutaybah's writing). Thus, for example, the opening of the *qaṣīdah* does indeed often take the form of an invocation of the beloved's name; ʿAmr ibn Qamī'ah begins a poem:

> Umāmah is gone far from thee, and there is left for thee
> only to ask after her the place where she dwelt, and the
> vision of her that comes when thou dreamest –
> Its appointed time is when night closes in, and as soon as
> dawn breaks it refuses to stay any longer,

The same ode also provides a succinct illustration of ibn Qutaybah's model; the fourth and fifth lines provide a wonderful example of the transfer to the travel section:

> Sooth, fear seized my heart when they proclaimed their purposes,
> and men said, 'Our comrades are preparing for an early
> departure';
> And the two captains of the caravan hurried her swiftly away at
> earliest dawn, after stirring up the male camels to rise from
> the place where they couched –

and, after the animal description that is ushered in by these lines, the eighteenth line brings a complete shift; after the initial sections of the poem we have reached the goal:

> How then dost thou sever the tie that binds thee in sincerity to a
> man of glorious fame, who desires not to withdraw from it?

The goal of ibn Qutaybah's description then seems to be the provision of some basic parameters for an analysis of structure that would match that of a substantial number of early Arabic poems in *qaṣīdah* form. A sizeable percentage of the earliest corpus of poetry shows considerable variation on his basic model. To provide just one of the more famous examples of poems that vary or elaborate on the pattern, the *muʿallaqah* of ʿAmr ibn Kulthūm, a piece of tribal boasting *par excellence*, makes mention of the beloved, but not until the poet has opened his performance (according to accounts, at the court of King ʿAmr of al-Ḥīrah) in a rather different fashion:

Ho there, maid, bring a morning draught in a goblet,
and do not stint on the best vintages of ʿAndarīn!

More recent analyses of this cherished repertoire of early Arabic poetry have examined the structure of the *qaṣīdah* in more mythopoetic terms, seeing the total poem as a dynamic process that shifts from moments of absence, deprivation, and nostalgia to those of presence, plenty, and celebration of life. Viewed within such a matrix (which appears to have much in common with the analysis of quest narratives and of rites of passage), the beginning of the poem finds the poet halting at an abandoned campsite, evoking images of both the absence of the present and companionship of the past; the atmosphere is one of loss, yearning, and nostalgia. These memories lead on to a process of separation, whereby the poet begins a journey into the dangerous world of the desert, a sphere of loneliness and 'liminality'. The constant danger associated with this journey and the complete reliance on animal traits leads to some elaborate depictions of the camel, one of the most famous of which is that of Ṭarafah in his *Muʿallaqah*. With this ritualistic sequence complete, the poet is then able to reintegrate himself into his society in a kind of homecoming ritual. The audience that has shared with the poet (and his bard) a full awareness of the perils that have been transcended now waits to hear the qualities of the group extolled in a boastful celebration of aggregation and solidarity. Here the closing section of the *Muʿallaqah* of Labīd, perhaps the greatest poetic expression of tribal mores, provides a splendid illustration. To the accompaniment of feasting, drinking, and gambling, the poem closes with a paean to the tribe that serves as man's primary source of security in his struggle against fate and the rigours of desert life.

The *qaṣīdah*, like other literary genres, was not to remain frozen in one static structural pattern based on the models provided by its earliest exemplars. In fact, the beginning in the history of the Muslim community provided occasions for elements of continuity within the poetic tradition. There is, for example, the poetry of Ḥassān ibn Thābit (*d. c.* 673), called 'the Prophet's poet', which celebrates the exploits of Muḥammad and pours scorn on his foes. The early years of the Muslim community itself were rife with doctrinal schisms and personal rivalries, all of which provided a continuingly fertile environment for the traditional mode of lampooning (*hijāʾ*). Most famous here were the famous 'flytings' (*naqāʾiḍ*), primarily between Jarīr (*d. c.* 732) and al-Farazdaq (*d. c.* 732) but also involving al-Akhṭal (*d. c.* 710) and al-Ṭirimmāḥ (*d. c.* 723).

However, while the poems composed during the initial stages of the post-Islamic era continued to display facets of the earlier tradition, the gradual process whereby allegiances shifted from those based on a system of tribal confederacies to that of the growing community of Muslims and their leaders inevitably had an effect on the generic purpose of the Arabic *qaṣīdah.* This type of poem, which had been an important element in the communal assertion of the tribe's self-identity and sense of chivalry, came to assume a more specifically panegyric function. The poem was now addressed to a specific figure, more often than not a patron who was to be recognised as protector of the Muslim community (or a subset of it); its primary function was to extol this leader's virtues as a representative of Islam and its community of believers. Furthermore, the emergence of an elaborate court system, with its accompanying panoply of bureaucrats and courtiers, also demanded of the poet that he be prepared to serve as an entertainer as well as morale-booster and propagandist. As a result of these changing expectations, the *qaṣīdah* now takes on a different structural logic for its new context and function. While the latter part of the poem focuses on eulogising the patron or other members of the court, earlier sections come to reflect the changed realities of performance context by moving away from the motifs of journeying through the desert and halting over encampments – concepts far removed from the courts of Baghdād or Cordoba and their mixture of Arab and non-Arab côteries. Thus, while Ghaylān ibn ʿUqbah (*d.* 735), a poet of the Umawī period best known by his nickname 'Dhū al-Rummah', is affectionately remembered as 'the last of the Bedouin poets' because of his continuing adherence to the conventions of the earlier poetry, Abū Nuwās (*d. c.* 803) reflects changing attitudes by using some of his openings to take pot-shots at the conventions of the traditional *qaṣīdah*:

> Some poor wretch turned aside to question a camp-ground;
> my purpose in turning aside was to ask for the local pub.

Within this new social context and purpose for the *qaṣīdah*, the evocation of the structural elements and imagery of early Arabic poetry now becomes the subject matter of allusion. Poets were, needless to say, eager to exploit the predilections of their audience to the full by using the intertextual possibilities that these motifs offered in order to exhibit the extent of their awareness of the tradition. Their ringing *qaṣāʾid* in praise of rulers remain a central element in the Arabic poetic tradition, seen most famously in the odes that al-Mutanabbī (*d.* 965) addressed to a sequence of rulers, but also in the works of many other poets among his contemporaries and successors, including, to cite just two examples, ibn Hāni' (*d.* 975), court poet of the Fāṭimī caliph al-Muʿizz in Tunis and ibn Darrāj (*d.* 1030) of al-Andalus. Eulogies (*madīḥ*) in *qaṣīdah* form, whether of rulers or religious figures, are the primary focus of the élite poetic tradition that has come down to us from the pre-modern period; among the more notable poets are al-Shābb al-Ẓarīf (*d.* 1289), ibn Nubātah al-Miṣrī (*d.* 1366), and Ibn Mālik al-Ḥamawī (*d.* 1511). The form continues well into the twentieth century where it is represented by the occasional poems of Aḥmad Shawqī (*d.* 1932), Khalīl Muṭrān (*d.* 1949), and other exponents of neo-classical poetry.

Rajaz

Commentaries on the Arabic poetic tradition link the *qitaʿah* and *qaṣīdah* into a single category known as *qarīḍ*. In that way the two structures that we have just analysed can be distinguished from another type of poem known as *rajaz* (also the name assigned to its metrical pattern). In this distinction we once again seem to be faced with the results of the process whereby the earliest phases in the development of the Arabic language and its cultural expressions were recorded. If we give credence to the idea that *sajʿ* does indeed represent an early manifestation of the poetic in Arabic, then *rajaz* emerges as a further step in the development of a mode of discourse characterised by its rhymes and rhythmic pulses. While one of the principal types of early *rajaz* poem is the camel-driver's song (*ḥidāʾ*), linguistic studies at the schools of al-Baṣrah and al-Kūfah (described in Chapter 2 above) seem to have inspired certain poets in the period of the Umawī caliphs to make use of the *rajaz* in order to compose virtuoso poems that have as a major purpose to explore the limits of Arabic lexicography. Al-ʿAjjāj (*d. c.* 717) and his son, Ruʿbah (*d.* 735), are particularly famous for their efforts in this domain. It needs to be added that the poem in *rajaz*, the *urjūzah* – with its more variable metrical and rhyming patterns than those of other metres subsumed within al-Khalīl's 'canonical' system – comes to be used by a number of Arab poets and for a variety of purposes: a hunt poem with ibn al-Muʿtazz (*d.* 908), for example, and a 445–line chronological account of the exploits of the Andalusian Umawī caliph, ʿAbd al-raḥmān III (*d.* 961), composed by the famous poet-anthologist, ibn ʿAbd Rabbihi (*d.* 940).

The prescriptive tendencies of the critical tradition may account for the fact that such variations on and adaptations of the hallowed *qaṣīdah* form are not plentifully represented in the collected works of the famous poets. However, it seems clear that, at least from the tenth century onwards, structures with different rhyming patterns – gathered together under the general heading *musammaṭ* (*ṣimt* meaning 'a string of thread') – became increasingly popular, adopting a variety of rhyming patterns in threes, fours, and fives (*muthallath*, *murabbaʿ*, and *mukhammas*).

The seven types

In quantitative terms the categories of poem that we have mentioned thus far would appear to constitute those that the recorders of the Arabic literary tradition thought most worthy of preservation for posterity. In addition to these categories there were others, most of which emerged at later stages in the history of the Muslim community and as a consequence of the interplay between the various cultural heritages involved. Commentators have often been inclined to dub these categories as 'popular', a designation that is not a little problematic in that it fuses and confuses aspects of language and performance occasion. The audience attending ceremonial occasions at which *qaṣāʾid* were recited would indeed be listening to a level of language that was not their normal mode of daily communication, but there would be many other types of less official occasion at which the recitation of poetry would be expected and welcomed, and for such events the type of language to be used would be adjustable in accordance with the nature of the audience and its linguistic predilections. Thus, any exclusive association of the literary language with the élite classes of society and the colloquial with the populace would be a false dichotomy; poetry which made use of levels of language other than the high literary was not 'popular', if by that is intended the notion that it was restricted to a plebeian audience.

With such linguistic postures in mind, we must consider ourselves fortunate in that a few poet-critics make a point of recording, alongside the categories of poem already mentioned, a seemingly lively tradition of what we will term 'less official' categories of poem. Later critics talk in terms of 'the seven types' of poem: *qarīḍ* (i.e. *qiṭʿah* and *qaṣīdah*), *kān wa-kān*, *dūbayt*, *muwashshaḥ*, *qūmā*, *mawwāl*, and *zajal*. The Iraqi-born poet, Ṣafī al-dīn al-Ḥillī (*d. c.* 1339), for example, composed an invaluable study of these genres entitled *al-ʿĀṭil al-ḥālī wa-al-murakhkhaṣ al-ghālī* (one of those more delightfully oxymoronic and therefore untranslatable of Arabic titles, roughly 'The unadorned now bedecked, the cheapened made costly') following the earlier example of the Egyptian poet, ibn Sanā' al-Mulk (*d.* 1211), who had written a study of the *muwashshaḥ* with the equally colourful title, *Dār al-ṭirāz* (The House of Brocade). Al-Ḥillī divides the categories of poem in two different ways: according to variations in metre and rhyme, and according to language. Three are said to be *muʿrabah*, meaning that they require the use of fully inflected literary Arabic (within which, as he colourfully notes, any lapse is unforgivable): *qarīḍ*, *muwashshaḥ*, and *dūbayt* (also known as *rubāʿī* (quatrain), the type of poem more famous within the Persian tradition and exemplified by the quatrains of the famous algebraist, ʿUmar al-Khayyām. Three other types are termed '*malḥūnah*', implying that a kind of language unacceptable to the grammarians is the norm: the *qūmā*, the *zajal*, and the *kān wa-kān* ('once upon a time').

The lion's share of al-Ḥillī's study is devoted to the *mawāliya* and the *zajal*. The former type of poem is alleged to have originated in Iraq and in its written forms consists of four rhyming lines. Under the alternative name of *mawwāl*, the *mawāliya* is also a popular category of folk poetry known in several countries within the Arab world. Regarding the *zajal* al-Ḥillī notes with disarming candour that 'the majority of people cannot distinguish between the *muwashshaḥ* and the *zajal*'.

As just noted, the very origins of both genres are not clear, nor indeed is the issue of which is anterior to the other (in spite of the common assumption that the *muwashshaḥ* is the earlier). The *zajal* (a word meaning literally 'shout') is a strophic poem composed in a language that permits the introduction of non-literary Arabic within the poem itself; such language might take the form of Arabic or romance dialectal forms. The structure consisted of alternating segments: those which had independent rhymes were called *aghṣān* (sing. *ghuṣn*), and those that had dependent rhymes *asmāṭ* (sing. *ṣimt*, a linkage to the *musammaṭ* categories mentioned above). The *zajal* was said to be 'complete' if it began with a prelude (*maṭlaʿ*), a section that shared its rhyme with the *asmāṭ*; if the poem had no prelude, it was given the somewhat pejorative designation 'bald'. A simple pattern might thus be: 'a bbb a ccc a' and so on; a more complex one: 'aba ccc aba ddd' and so on (where 'aba' represents the repeated pattern of the *simṭ* and 'ccc, ddd' the varying patterns of the *ghuṣn*).

The *muwashshaḥ* category (the word meaning 'girdled') shares some of the same structural characteristics: the majority of examples begins with a prelude and consists of a number of *asmāṭ* that share a rhyme with it and of *aghṣān* that do not. However, the content of the *muwashshaḥ* replicates many of the themes and images of the *qaṣīdah* tradition, and especially the conventions of courtly love poetry. What is most significant about the *muwashshaḥ*, however, is that its final rhyming segment (*simṭ*) is termed the *kharjah* (envoi) and is in the form of a quotation, or, some scholars would maintain, a deliberate attempt to imitate and surpass another poem or song. A *muwashshaḥah* by al-Saraqusṭī al-Jazzār (a poet of Saragossa, *fl.* eleventh century) begins with an anticipated expression of love-agony: 'Woe to the lovelorn wretch, my frame is in the grip of disease'. It finishes, however, with the female voice of the *kharjah* expressing sentiments in a rather different tone: 'Mamma, that boy's all mine, "legit" or otherwise'.

Neither the *zajal* nor the *muwashshaḥ* remained frozen in time, but underwent the normal processes of generic change. It is from the later compilations and analyses of the likes of ibn Sanā' al-Mulk and Ṣafī al-dīn al-Ḥillī that one attempts to extrapolate backwards to their beginnings. With regard to the *zajal*, its most famous exponent is clearly ibn Quzmān (*d.* 1160) who in addition to being a poet was also a Cordoban nobleman and minister. He provides an excellent example of the *zajal*'s use as a 'popular' medium in very genteel company; he is abundantly aware of the 'classical' tradition against which he is tilting (expressing in his poetry his desire to be distinguished from earlier poets like Jamīl Buthaynah (*d.* 701) and Abū Nuwās) and can write a *zajal* poem in which the final section, replete with the usual repertoire of panegyric (*madīḥ*) addressed to a patron, is preceded by a depiction of an encounter with a Bedouin prostitute that is astoundingly racy. The general acceptability of the *zajal*, with its variable characteristics, is seen through its different manifestations encountered in other regions of the Arab world: in the hymns of the Maronite liturgy, for example, and in a vigorous tradition of contemporary poetic jousting in Lebanon that boasts of its own celebrity poets. In a retrospective on the development of the *muwashahaḥ* we find that, as the *muwashshaḥ* made its way eastwards, it continued to serve as a medium for the poetic expression of a variety of themes: indeed ibn al-ʿArabī (*d.* 1240) and al-Shushtarī (*d.* 1269), both prominent Andalusian theologians who travelled to Syria, composed their own examples. It was still a particular favourite among poets in the nineteenth and early twentieth centuries, and most notably for those Lebanese Christians who make up the *émigré* (*mahjar*) school in the Americas.

THEMES

From the earliest stages of the critical tradition Arabic made use of the concept of the goal or purpose of the poem (*gharaḍ*, pl. *aghrāḍ*) as a means of discussing thematic content. Each purpose within what may be regarded as the most basic triad involved the element of praise. First and most significant was eulogy or panegyric (*madīḥ*) involving praise of the living. Here the primary task of the poet was to wax hyperbolic in extolling the virtues of the community and its leader(s); with the advent of the caliph's court and other seats of power, the language of these encomia of wealthy patrons would become flamboyant. Secondly, and stemming directly from the first, was the antithesis of praise: invective and lampoon (*hijā'*), whereby the virtues of the speaker's community would be enhanced by often scurrilous depictions of the faults of those inimical to it. Insult was the weapon in this case, and the target would be subject to withering ridicule. The third element of praise is that of the dead, namely elegy (*rithā'*), combining a sense of grief and consolation for loss with a rehearsal of the dead person's virtues that serve as an appropriate celebration of communal ideals.

Overriding the different occasions at which the poems would be performed and the atmospheres that they engendered were the universal values to which the society adhered: that of *muruwwah*, akin to a code of chivalry in its broadest sense, and of the above-mentioned *ḥamāsah*, a combination of heroism and élan. Early critics analysing the ways in which eulogy, lampoon, and elegy serve as celebrations of these communal values identify a series of further elements that contribute in different combinations to the poem's larger 'purpose': the love theme (*nasīb*), description (*wasf*), boasting (*fakhr*), and aphorism (*ḥikmah*).

It is these different modes of thematic organisation that will now be utilised as the basis for a survey of the Arabic poetic corpus. In order to accommodate within our purview the different categorisations that we have just discussed, we will begin by elaborating on the three major modes that reflect the preferred organising principles of the poetic collections themselves – eulogy, lampoon, and elegy – and append to them a discussion of 'description' (*wasf*). We will then discuss particular themes, many of which came to constitute separate categories within the collected works of poets – the wine poem, the love poem, and so on.

Eulogy, panegyric (madīḥ)

> You are a very sun and other monarchs are stars; when your
> light gleams bright, other stars disappear.

Thus the poet, al-Nābighah (*d. c.* 602), addresses al-Nuʿmān ibn al-Mundhir, the ruler of al-Ḥīrah. At a later date al-Mutanabbī appears to follow suit in a *qaṣīdah* addressed to Sayf al-dawlah, ruler of Aleppo, that celebrates the latter's recovery from illness:

> Light is now restored to the sun; it had gone out, as
> though the lack of it in its body were a disease.

Al-Mutanabbī's disease-image finds a still later echo in a eulogy composed by a poet who was a Circassian grandee of Damascus, Manjak Pāshā al-Yūsufī (*d.* 1669), when he lauds his patron with the following line:

> Intellects are cured of disease by his prudence; in his
> shadow the steadfast religion stands secure.

Conservative literalist critics in quest of a protocol for reading canonical texts were quick to point out that these poets (and others like them) are lying; poetry, they suggested, does not tell the truth. The poet-critic ibn Rashīq (*d.* 1064) is among those who point out that, while such verdicts may be correct on one, rather narrow, level, they are essentially missing the point. The *qaṣīdah* of the pre-Islamic poet was a celebration of the life and values of the tribe, and the generic expectations within which it functioned were clearly understood, indeed established, by its audience. During the Islamic period, the addressee of the *madīḥ* poem – be he caliph, *wazīr*, or sultan – now served as an authority-figure to a large and diverse community. Poetry composed in such a person's honour transcended the individual level to become an intrinsic part of the society's political and social fabric. The repertoire of communally accepted codes under which such poems were composed and performed were thus part of a system of publicity and propaganda that helped in the establishment of the society's sense of identity, the maintenance of its core values, and its relationship to the heritage of the past.

In the earlier discussion of the structure of the earliest examples of the tribal *qaṣīdah* it was noted that the third and last section was intended as a celebration of the virtues of aggregation and solidarity. The more direct form of poetic propaganda took the form of panegyrics addressed to tribal rulers, of boasts (*fakhr*) concerning the manly qualities of the tribesmen, and of aphorisms that would reflect the philosophy of life as envisaged by the tribal society. A superb illustration of this poetic environment is the *Muʿallaqah* of Zuhayr ibn Abī Sulmā (*d. c.* 607). Its historical context is the War of Dāḥis and Ghabrāʾ, a lengthy conflict between the tribes of ʿAbs and Dhubyān. Two chieftains made an enormously generous offer to bring the cycle of violence to an end, offering three thousand camels over a three-year period to settle the dispute. Zuhayr's poem shows considerable dispatch in reaching its point. At line 15 the intervention of the two chiefs is described:

> You have brought ʿAbs and Dhubyān together again after lethal
> conflict and the stench of death;
> We will achieve peace, you both said; should property and
> charitable words be needed, so it shall be.
> Thereby you placed yourselves in the best position, far removed
> from obstinacy or crime,
> Two great men of high rank in Maʿadd; may you be guided
> aright! Whoever condones a treasure-trove of glory will
> himself be glorified!

While Labīd's *muʿallaqah* celebrates the tribe through reference to the courage, generosity, and loyalty of its members, Zuhayr's poem concludes with a montage of moralistic utterances. His panegyric completed, he pronounces himself weary of the cares of an impermanent existence:

> I have grown weary of the cares of life; whoever lives eighty
> years will inevitably grow weary.

These panegyrical sections in celebration of the tribal values of bravery, fidelity, and generosity, coupled to an appreciation of the routines, comforts, and securities of communal living, find an exact obverse in the poems of the vagabond-poets. The *locus classicus* for this anti-tribal posture is the already mentioned 'L-poem' (*Lāmiyyah*) of al-Shanfarā. The mood is established from the very first line:

> Sons of my mother, stir up the breasts of your riding
> animals; for I am inclined to a tribe other than you . . .

The persona of the vagabond-poet is of one ostracised from society, relishing loneliness, danger, and the inevitable imminence of death. For such a person the advantages of integration into the tribe, as celebrated in the boasts and panegyrics of the tribal *qaṣīdah*, are not available, and indeed not desired.

This earliest tradition of Arabic panegyric poetry, with its established ideals and repertoire of images, was to see its context transformed in the seventh century with the advent of Islam. The many tensions that marked the initial phases in the development of the religious community are wonderfully captured in the famous '*burdah*' poem of Kaʿb, son of Zuhayr (so named because, when the poet completed the recitation of his poem, Muḥammad is alleged to have wrapped the poet in his own mantle (*burdah*) as a sign of his pleasure). The authentically pre-Islamic vision of the first half of the poem ends abruptly with the introduction of the poem's purpose: an account of the poet's dangerous position and the recitation of the poem itself as an act of contrition and conversion. At the close of the *qaṣīdah* the mood switches back to the past as Kaʿb makes use of his praise of the Prophet and his company as a point of transfer back to the mounted warriors of the pre-Islamic vision.

Muḥammad was quick to utilise poetry in the cause of Islam. Indeed Ḥassān ibn Thābit (*d. c.* 670) was dubbed 'the Prophet's poet'. Ḥassān's panegyric poems also mark the beginning of a particular strand of *madīḥ* poetry devoted to praise of the Prophet; during the centuries when the influence of popular mystical movements was at its height – extending from the thirteenth century well into the twentieth – this subgenre was to find particular favour as a mode of invoking the Prophet's intercession, a ritual that is seen most notably in the widespread popularity of another poem termed '*burdah*', that of al-Buṣīrī (*d.* 1295).

In view of the communal struggles and violence that beset the Muslim community after the unexpected death of Muḥammad, it is hardly surprising that the mood of defiance and the pride in hardship that had characterised the boasting segments of much pre-Islamic poetry were readily transferred to the several opposition groups engendered by such internal dissension – the Shīʿah and especially the Khawārij (both to be discussed in more detail below). Meanwhile the panegyrical aspect of the poem was co-opted by the Umawī caliphs. The poet who was known as 'the poet of the Umawī caliphs' was the Christian, al-Akhṭal (*d.* 710), whose verses invoke the qualities eulogised in the earlier tradition of panegyric but for the new purpose of glorifying the grandeur of a figure and indeed a dynasty that combined spiritual and temporal rule:

> Their ancestry is complete, and God Himself has selected them;
> the ancestry of any other clan is obscure and worthless.
> On the Day of Ṣiffīn, with eyes lowered, reinforcement came
> to them when they sought a favour from their Lord.
> You are from a house that has no peer when nobility and
> number are reckoned.

Al-Akhṭal was a member of the tribe of Taghlib, and his two famous contemporaries, Jarīr (*d.* 732) and al-Farazdaq (*d.* 729), both belonged to the Tamīm confederacy. Much of their poetry, and most especially the 'flytings' (*naqāʾiḍ*) that they aimed at each other (to be discussed in the section on lampoon below), provides an excellent reflection of the political tensions of the era.

While the early ʿAbbāsī caliphs may have been at some pains to contrast their conduct and priorities with the more secular proclivities attributed to the Umawī caliphs (mostly, it needs to be said, by historians who wrote during the ʿAbbāsī period), the demand for panegyric that would celebrate the achievements of Islam through the personage of its caliph remained constant. Indeed, opportunities for the panegyrist were to become more plentiful. In addition to the ʿAbbāsī caliph in Baghdād, other focuses of power made their influence felt: the Umawīs, now removed to their new centre in Cordoba, and the Fāṭimī dynasty in Tunisia and thereafter in Egypt.

As the performance venue for Arabic panegyric poetry shifted from a tribal gathering in the evening air of the desert or a gathering in the courts of pre-Islamic rulers to the pomp of the caliphal court in Damascus and later Baghdād, so did the generic purpose and organising logic of Arabic panegyric undergo a transformation. The career of the blind poet, Bashshār ibn Burd (*d.* 784), mostly spent in al-Baṣrah, was sufficiently long to permit him to compose panegyrics for members of both the Umawī and ʿAbbāsī caliphal families and their respective retinues. A panegyric addressed to Khālid al-Barmakī, minister of the caliph al-Mahdī (*d.* 785), provides a good illustration of the role that the theme of generosity now comes to play in the relationship between eulogiser and eulogised:

> While not every wealthy personage shows munificence, by my
> life ibn Barmak has shown generosity towards me.
> I have used my poems to milk his palms, and they have flowed
> copiously like rain-clouds in a thunderstorm.

Bashshār's panegyrics serve as excellent examples of the changing relationship between the opening of the *qaṣīdah* and the central section devoted to its principal purpose. The nostalgic references to the deserted encampment and the absent beloved will still occur as reminders of the inherited values of the past, but the quest for a more expeditious linkage of exordium to the recipient of the eulogy (more often than not mentioned by name) introduces a variety of other themes as possible preludes.

Bashshār is credited by the Arabic critical tradition as one of the pioneers in a movement that sought to exploit the new interest in the intrinsic lexical and syntactic riches of Arabic by rendering the language and imagery of poetry more complex, a trend which became known as *badīʿ*, an adjective implying newness and creativity. The ceremonial aspect of the panegyric and, one might say, the generic proclivity of the genre towards hyperbole made the Arabic panegyric poem a primary vehicle for *badīʿ* expression. Abū Tammām is the poet whose name is primarily associated with the critical controversies that raged around the function of *badīʿ*. As the later critic ʿAbd al-qāhir al-Jurjānī (*d.* 1078) pointed out, it was the impact of the unfamiliar juxtapositions in his imagery in particular that made him such an important catalyst for change within the Arabic poetic tradition:

> No veil can distance my expectations from you; for, when the
> heavens are veiled by cloud, much is hoped from them.

The Arab poet whose career and disposition personify the role of court poet, most especially as panegyrist, was Abū al-Ḥusayn, generally known by his nickname, al-Mutanabbī (*d.* 965); he is the Arab occasional poet par excellence. After a victory against the Byzantines at al-Ḥadath (954), the audience at the court of Sayf al-dawlah, Ḥamdānī ruler of Aleppo, heard the following ringing exordium:

> Resolutions come in accordance with the worth of the resolute;
> noble deeds come in accordance with the worth of the noble.
> In the eyes of the puny, puny deeds seem important; in the eyes
> of the important, important deeds seem puny.

Even in English translation (deliberately literal) the wordplay of these much-quoted verses conjure up an image of a fabulous occasion upon which al-Mutanabbī proclaimed this glorification of an Islamic ruler and his heroic deeds.

Perhaps nothing better illustrates al-Mutanabbī's mercurial personality and the close linkage between panegyric and its obverse, lampoon, than the succession of poems that he addressed to the Ikhshīdī regent of Egypt, a manumitted slave named Kāfūr. Upon his arrival, the poet greets his new patron:

> O father of musk, the face for which I have yearned, the time
> for which I have hoped . . .,
> You have not gained kingship merely by wishing, but through
> hair-whitening times,

but, when the anticipated munificence does not match the poet's expectations, he secretly departs, leaving behind some of the most scabrous invective in the entire literary tradition:

> Nothing can be more vile than a stallion with a penis, being
> led by a serving-girl with no womb;

> The nobility of every people come from among themselves;
> among Muslims however they are paltry slaves.

Adopting the terms used by Harold Bloom to describe the major influence that certain poets have on their successors, we can note that al-Mutanabbī is certainly the strongest of the strong Arab poets, the anxiety of whose influence was felt by all those who came after him.

The rulers of the Arabic-speaking world continued to employ poets to observe and celebrate the various occasions associated with their position: coronations, weddings, victories, birthdays, returns from the pilgrimage to Mecca, and so on. Aḥmad Shawqī (*d.* 1932), for example, is full of praise for the victories of Muṣṭafā Kamāl Pāshā, the Turkish army commander, urging him to replicate the exploits of one of the generals of early Islam:

> God is greatest! How joyous is victory! O Khālid of the Turks,
> repeat the exploits of the Arab Khālid . . .

but, when the government of that same commander, now known as Kamāl Ataturk, announces the abolition of the caliphate in 1924, Shawqī's joy at victory turns into sorrow and anger:

> Wedding songs now resound as wailing; in the midst of
> celebrations death is announced.

Political and social developments in the Arab world – the rise of nationalism as a response to European colonial incursions, the struggle for independence, and the quest for individual rights – have during the first half of the twentieth century led to the emergence of an entirely different set of imperatives and priorities for the poet. The rallying-cry of the Arab literary world in the 1950s was 'commitment' (*iltizām*), whereby the individual writer was supposed to devote his art to the cause of his nation – whether pan-Arab or local – and its people. Following the Suez débâcle in 1956, the Egyptian poet, Aḥmad ʿAbd al-muʿṭī Ḥijāzī (*b.* 1935), addresses a poem to the president of his country, Jamāl ʿAbd al-nāṣir (Nasser), that is certainly a panegyric but, equally certainly, a heartfelt expression of pride and support:

> Poets, I would have you write
> that here I behold the leader uniting the Arabs
> crying out: 'Freedom, justice, and peace'.

Hijāʾ: *lampoon, satire, invective*

The well-aimed barb, the personal smear, these now common and even accepted features of media-dominated political campaigns in our current era of Western politics have a very ancient history in the Arabic poetic tradition. Invective against one's foes (*hijā'*) – negative advertising, if you will – is found in poetry from the very earliest stages. A line attributed to ʿAmr ibn Qamīʾah makes the point unequivocally:

> Many's the tribal poet loaded with rancour I have tamed, so his
> folk have felt puny and ashamed.

Lampoon is the opposite of panegyric. Accounts of the occasion on which two of the *Muʿallaqāt* were alleged to have been first performed provide an excellent illustration. After a prolonged war, the tribes of Bakr and Taghlib sought mediation through the king of al-Ḥīrah. The poet, ʿAmr ibn Kulthūm, begins by expatiating about the Taghlib tribe and its prowess. This inappropriate use of the occasion goads al-Ḥārith ibn Ḥillizah, the poet of Bakr, into a retort that puts his braggart rival and the pretensions of his tribe firmly in their place:

> We turned our attention to the Banū Tamīm. As we observed
> the month of truce, their daughters were our servant-girls.
> On the open plain even their great men could not hold their
> ground; nor did it help the dishonoured to run away . . .
> The men of Taghlib who fell were unavenged, covered in death
> by the dust of oblivion.

As the above examples have shown, the most readily available targets of lampooning and invective were the chivalry of men (*muruwwah*, literally 'manliness') and the honour of women. Throughout the centuries both have provided ample scope for scurrilous attacks on adversaries. In particular, the good repute of the womenfolk of the family and tribe (the *ḥarīm*, a word with semantic connections to the notions of sanctuary and the need for protection) has always been and continues to be a primary means by which (masculine-based) honour is maintained and assessed.

In Arabic poetry's most famous episode of poetic jousting (a continuing contest in *hijā'* known as *naqā'iḍ* ('flytings')), the poet al-Farazdaq becomes a primary figure, with Jarīr as his most prominent opponent, but also involving other poets such as al-Akhṭal and al-Ṭirimmāḥ. In a sequence of poems, Jarīr, much feared for his pointed invective, chooses to turn an insult to al-Farazdaq's sister into a sexual orgy of major proportions:

> Do you recall how Jiʿthin screamed, while your goal was women's
> amulets and veils?
> When the disgrace of Jiʿthin's evil was known, weren't you afraid
> of it being brought to light?

Springing regularly to the defence of his sister's and therefrom his tribe's honour, al-Farazdaq responds in kind with a series of retorts. While replicating (and even expanding on) the prurience of Jarīr, he uses some of his poems to deliver a verbal savaging to Jarīr's tribe, unfortunately called Banū Kulayb ('sons of the puppy', thus affording al-Farazdaq an opportunity for all sorts of variations on the 'sons of bitches' theme).

Among those who witnessed this extended joust was Bashshār ibn Burd. While the examples of *hijā'* by Jarīr and al-Farazdaq that were cited above were from poems that open in a traditional way, Bashshār follows the trend found in many of their other poems by getting straight to the point. Talking sarcastically about a tribe of al-Baṣrah who have been boosting their numbers with new, non-Arab converts, he says:

> I have checked on the Banū Zayd: among their seniors there is no prudence; among their juniors none of unsullied repute . . .
> To their numbers they append sin-children, so that their throng surpasses everyone else's.

Abū Nuwās, secure perhaps in his status as renowned poet at the court of the caliph Hārūn al-Rashīd, manages to talk sarcastically about the latter's renowned minister, Jaʿfar al-Barmakī (Hārūn's faithful and long-suffering companion on many escapades in the *Thousand and One Nights*):

> This is the ape era. So just bow down and say: To hear is to obey.

The poet is even prepared to comment sarcastically on Jaʿfar's ill-starred marriage to Hārūn's sister, ʿAbbāsah, a union that is said to have led Hārūn to order his minister killed and his dismembered body displayed on the bridges of Baghdād:

> If you find pleasure in removing some rascal's head,
> Don't kill him with a sword; just marry him to ʿAbbāsah!

Arabic poetry's *locus classicus* for this type of sarcastic attack-poem lies – once again – with al-Mutanabbī, notably his series of *hijā'* poems (one of which was excerpted above) that he left behind when he departed Kāfūr's Egypt in a clearly disappointed rage. In another poem from the same series he insults the eunuch regent:

> Till I met this eunuch, I always assumed that the head was the seat of wisdom,
> but, when I looked into his intelligence, I discovered that all his wisdom resided in his testicles . . .
> Many's the panegyric I've recited to that rhinoceros, using verse and charms,

> but it was not a panegyric for him but rather a lampoon of
> mankind as a whole.

The changing political circumstances in the Arab world during the course of the twentieth century have radically transformed the social context of Arabic poetry and thus of *hijāʾ*. Burning issues, and especially cultural debates and rivalries, have continued to serve as stimuli for exchanges of insult and jousts. However, the post-revolutionary period in most Arab societies (roughly coinciding with the second half of the twentieth century) has been one in which the freedom of writers has been heavily circumscribed – to put it mildly, and, as a consequence, *hijāʾ* directed against authority figures of the kind we have just described has diminished considerably. One poet stands out as an exception to this general rule: Muẓaffar al-Nawwāb (*b.* 1934). His disgust with the entire authority structure of the Arab world spills out into poetry of a withering, venomous sarcasm:

> The son of Kaʿbah is having sex . . .
> The world's princes must wait!

Rithāʾ*: elegy*

In her autobiography, *Riḥlah jabaliyyah, riḥlah ṣaʿbah* (1985; *A Mountainous Journey*, 1990), the Palestinian poetess, Fadwā Ṭūqān (*b.* 1917), describes how her elder brother, the poet Ibrāhīm Ṭūqān, introduced her to the treasures of Arabic poetry. Opening Abū Tammām's famous anthology of early poetry, *al-Ḥamāsah*, he recited to her an ancient elegy (*rithāʾ*) by an unknown poetess (usually attributed to either Umm al-Sulayk or the mother of the infamous vagabond-poet, Taʾabbaṭa Sharran):

> He wandered the desert in quest of an escape from death, but he
> perished.
> If only I knew what it was – a terrible error – that killed you . . .
> Whatever track a young man follows, the Fates lie in wait.

Ibrāhīm Ṭūqān explains to his younger sister that he selected this particular poem to show what beautiful Arabic poetry was composed by women.

The elegy in Arabic (*marthiyah*, pl. *marāthī*) was intended to memorialise and eulogise someone who had recently died; in earliest times, that often implied death in tribal conflict or as a result of one of the many ways by which desert life could be an agent of imminent death. The large quantity of elegies composed by women that have been recorded suggests that this communal function was a particular province of women poets, the poems themselves being part of the funeral ritual. The two most celebrated names in the early history of this type of poem are Tumāḍir bint ʿAmr, renowned under the name of al-Khansāʾ (*d.* before 670), and Laylā al-Akhyaliyyah (*d.* 704).

Al-Khansāʾ mourns the deaths in tribal conflict of a brother, Muʿāwiyah, and a half-brother, Ṣakhr. The type of lament that is so associated with her name begins directly with a proclamation of the tragedy and the name of the dead hero:

> When night draws on, remembering keeps me wakeful
> And hinders my rest with grief upon grief returning
> For Ṣakhr . . .

The initial salute to the dead hero will often be followed by an account of the dire event itself and a recounting of his virtues, particularly as a warrior in battle:

> . . .What a man was he on the day of battle,
> When, snatching their chance, they swiftly exchange the
> spear-thrusts.

The elegy will often end with words of advice for the tribe, and, if the incident is part of a continuing feud, with calls for retribution against those who carried out the foul deed:

> O Ṣakhr! I will ne'er forget thee until in dying
> I part from my soul, and earth for my tomb is cloven.
> The rise of the sun recalls to me Ṣakhr my brother,
> And him I remember also at every sunset.
> (Nicholson, *Eastern Poetry & Prose*, 19)

In the case of Laylā al-Akhyaliyyah, the focus of her grief is a beloved named Tawbah; among the few recorded poems that make up her *dīwān* is this elegy:

> Splendid knight you were, O Tawbah, when high points came
> together and lowlands were raised.
> Splendid knight you were, O Tawbah, not to be surpassed on
> the day of your endeavour.
> Splendid knight you were, O Tawbah, when the timorous would
> seek your protection; splendid too were your fine deeds.

An early poet-warrior such as Durayd ibn al-Simmah (*d.* 630) manages to inject into one of his elegies for his slain brother, ʿAbdallāh, a vivid and particularised depiction of tribal conflict:

> My brother yelled out when we were separated by horsemen;
> when he called, he did not find me one to hold back.

I reached him to find spears piercing his body like the fall of
shuttles on an outstretched weave . . .
The horsemen have slain a warrior, they shouted; is it ʿAbdallāh
they have killed, I asked.
If indeed it is ʿAbdallāh who has left his space empty, he was
not one to shirk a fight, nor was his aim untrue . . .
As a youth he did youthful things, but then, when the grey hairs
appeared, he bade farewell to frivolity.

This heroic spirit – reflected in the themes of fighting for a worthy cause, confronting the inevitability of death, mourning lost comrades, and calling out for revenge – is carried over into the Islamic period most noticeably in the poetry of groups opposed to the policies of the central authorities; the anthologies record poems and extracts by poets of the Shīʿah and Khawārij. Shīʿī poets such as Kuthayyir ʿAzzah (*d.* 724 – also renowned as a love-poet) and al-Kumayt (*d.* 743), who was killed for satirising the Umawī governor of Iraq, certainly used their poems to express opposition to the interests of the Umawī dynasty, but the spirit of fierce defiance and struggle that is so much a part of the early desert poetry is best reflected in the work of Khārijī poets. ʿImrān ibn Ḥiṭṭān (*d.* 703) mourns the loss of one of the group's warriors thus:

Shed tears for Mirdas and his death, my eye; O Lord of Mirdās,
let me join him!
He has left me in despair, to mourn in a desolate dwelling that
was once abustle . . .
For a while I mourned for you, then my heart despaired; but that
could not dispel my tears.

The patronage afforded to poets within the elaborate structures of the caliphal court and other centres of authority provided a plethora of occasions for elegies of this official kind. Upon the death of the mother of Sayf al-dawlah, the Ḥamdānī ruler of Aleppo, for example, al-Mutanabbī composed an elaborate ceremonial elegy for the occasion. Beginning in that gnomic fashion for which his poems are so renowned, the poet notes that he is no stranger to adversity; this tragedy, however, is more than he can bear. The poem concludes with a stirring address to the poet's patron:

Sayf al-dawlah, seek help in forbearance; for what are mountains
when compared with yours?
You offer people counsel in consolation and in defying death in
the fickle chances of war.

Through the agency of the elegy composed by the patronised poet a family loss becomes a communal tragedy, and yet the presence of the enlightened Muslim ruler is a continuing source of consolation. The sense of disaster becomes more intense, needless to say, when the very fabric of Islamic society is attacked. In 871 for example, al-Baṣrah, the garrison city and port in Southern Iraq that had become a major intellectual centre, was devastated by the Zanj, an army of slave labourers. Ibn al-Rūmī (*d.* 896) composed an elegy bewailing the fall of the city and the massacre of its inhabitants; the repetitions which mark the beginnings of so many lines give the elegy a plangent quality:

> What sleep is there after the enormous catastrophes that have beset al-Baṣrah?
> What sleep is there now that the Zanj have flagrantly violated the sanctuaries of Islam itself? . . .
> My heart is seared with grief for you, poor al-Baṣrah, with flames of burning fire . . .
> My heart is seared with a grief for you, dome of Islam, a grief that prolongs my affliction;
> My heart is seared with a grief for you, port from lands afar, that will linger for many years . . .

In the ensuing centuries the elegy continues to fulfil this role as public record of the community's direst moments. Ibn al-Mujāwir (*d.* 1204) recounts the fall of the al-Aqṣā Mosque in Jerusalem to the Crusaders:

> The entire domain should weep over Jerusalem and proclaim its sorrow and grief;
> Mecca should do likewise, for it is Jerusalem's sister; and it should protest to ʿArafāt itself the treatment meted out.

Following the Mongol destruction of Baghdād in 1258 a poet from al-Kūfah, Shams al-dīn al-Kūfī, pays a return visit to the shattered city:

> What of the homes whose people are no longer my people, whose neighbours are not mine?
> By my life, what befell Baghdād after you was death, destruction, and torch . . .

In the twentieth century it is the Palestinian people that has often faced disaster; the corpus of its poetry contains, not surprisingly, many echoes of the elegaic tradition. In an elegy entitled 'My Sad City' (*Madinatī al-ḥazīnah*) Fadwā Ṭūqān, whose introduction to the genre by her brother opened this section, echoes the words of ibn al-Rūmī many centuries earlier:

> Children and songs vanished
> No shadow, no echo.

In my city sorrow crawled naked
With smattered tread.
In my city all is silence . . .
O my silent, sad city
At harvest time
Are grains and fruits on fire
Has everything thus come full-circle?

Along with these examples of the more 'public' type of elegy, the poets' *dīwān*s contain many expressions of grief in a more personal context. Al-Mutanabbī mourns his grandmother in a famous poem, and the Shīʿī poet, al-Sharīf al-Raḍī (*d.* 1016) writes a touching ode on the death of his sister. The lengthy elegy that Abū al-ʿAlāʾ al-Maʿarrī (*d.* 1958) composed on the death of a close relative was a heartfelt expression of the deepest sense of loss, providing a *locus classicus* for the '*ubi sunt*' (where are they now?) theme that is so prevalent in the tradition of Arabic ascetic poem (*zuhdiyyah*) – to be examined below – of which he was such a prominent exponent:

Lighten your tread; I think the surface of the earth is nothing but
the bodies of the dead,
so proceed slowly in the air and do not trample the remains of
God's servants underfoot.

However, few elegies can match the poignancy of those that recount the agonies of that most awful of family tragedies, the death of a child. Ibn al-Rūmī is one such father who mourns his middle son, Muḥammad:

Short indeed was his time between cradle and grave; he had not
even forgotten the cradle when he was enclosed in the grave . . .
My eyes! Be generous with your tears; for I have given the earth
the most precious gift I possess . . .
Though you [my son] may be alone in a desolate house, I am just
as desolate among the living . . .
God's peace be with you – a greeting from me and every
raincloud endowed with thunder and lightning.

A similar, albeit less intense, kind of personalised sentiment often emerges in the elegies that poets compose for their departed colleagues. A few months before his own death, Aḥmad Shawqī (*d.* 1932) found himself delivering an elegy on his long-time neo-classical companion in poetry, Ḥāfiẓ Ibrāhīm (*d.* 1932):

Preserver [Ḥāfiẓ] of literary Arabic, guardian of its glories,
leader of the eloquent,

You continued to proclaim the virtues of the past and protected
the authenticity of the ancient poets.
You renewed the style of al-Walīd [al-Buḥturī] and brought the
world the magic of al-Ṭāʾī [Abū Tammām].

Waṣf: *description*

The three modes that we have just discussed – eulogy, lampoon, and elegy – subsume within their purview a large percentage of ancient Arabic poetry. In addition to these three primary purposes (*aghrāḍ*), those who set about analysing the poetic corpus also identified a fourth feature, that of description (*wasf*).

In Chapter 2 it was observed that Arabian tribes eked out a living as animal herders and that this livelihood naturally led them to prize horses and camels in particular for their hardy qualities. This centrality of desert animals to the life and symbolic code of the community is graphically illustrated by the vast wealth of vocabulary used to depict them within the poetic corpus; some of the most colourful lexemes take the form of reserved epithets ('snub-nose', 'thick-hump', 'red-colour'). The poems create the most vivid images of an unfamiliar landscape. Here, for example, is part of the wonderful scene that ʿAbīd ibn al-Abraṣ (*d. c.* 554) narrates in comparing his horse with an eagle swooping down to pounce on a fox:

She spent the night, stock-still, on a hillock, like an old crone
whose children have died,
She was still there at dawn on a frigid morning, the frost dripping
off her feathers.
Then in a trice she spotted a fox, the barren desert between
them . . .
Swiftly she rose in the air towards him and then swooped
downwards.
Terrified at the sound of her wings, he raised his tail, the reaction
of one in a panic.
She grabbed him and dropped him from on high; beneath her the
prey is in torment.
She smashed him to the ground and crushed him, and the sharp
stones ripped his face apart.
He was screaming all the while, but her talons were embedded in
his side and his chest was ripped apart.

Passages such as this acquire a tremendous symbolic resonance and inevitably become a primary locus of the Arabic poetic tradition's classical ideals. The very size of the repertoires of poetry and anecdote dealing with desert flora and fauna that were gathered into anthologies beginning in the eighth century – al-Jāḥiẓ's *Kitāb al-ḥayawān* (Book of Animals) being merely the most renowned among many – serve to illustrate the enduring value that was attached to them.

The most elaborate and famous depictions of animal life are to be found in the central section of the early *qaṣīdah*, where the poet narrates a dangerous journey by camel into the desert wastes. The qualities of the trusted riding-beast are catalogued in great detail and compared with those of a variety of other denizens of the desert. When the poem turns to the process of reintegration and tribal solidarity, there is opportunity for a wide variety of other description. The latter part of Imru' al-Qays's *muʿallaqah* includes a much-cited picture of a horse, both as idealised riding animal and as proficient hunter, but the poem closes with a vivid picture of the desert after a thunderstorm, linking in a single scene the violence of sudden death and the promise of new growth:

> The storm pours its rain on Kutayfah, uprooting the lofty
> kanahbul trees,
> Then passes over Mount al-Qanān in a deluge, so that the goats
> have to leave their favoured spots,
> And on Mount Taymā' not a single palm-trunk or dwelling is left
> standing, unless bulwarked with stones . . .
> It unleashes its load on the desert of Ghabīṭ, like a Yemenī with
> loaded bales.
> At daybreak, the valley-birds sound as though they have drunk a
> draught of mulled wine,
> while at twilight the beasts who have drowned in its remote parts
> look like roots of wild-onion.

The changes that have already been noted above in connection with the performance context and generic purposes of the *qaṣīdah* and therefrom with its structural logic inevitably led to a transformation in the role of description. In the panegyric poem in particular, the journey section becomes less of an exploration of the risks of solitude and more of a process of directing oneself towards the person to be eulogised (*mamdūḥ*). While a poet like Dhū al-Rummah endeavoured to maintain the validity and authenticity of the pre-Islamic vision, the imagery that had been contained within the lengthy depictions of desert scenes and animal qualities becomes a classical repertoire of nostalgia for the glories of a lost past – in Jaroslav Stetkevych's terms, Arabia's Najd as a kind of Arcadia. Here, for example, is ibn Khafājah (*d. c.* 1039), the great Andalusian poet, so remote in both time and place:

Is Najd aware that in my eyes tears are welling which pour down,
while grief extends between them?
O tents of Najd, Tihāmah and Najd stand between us, a broad
pace for night-travel, and the camel's gentle tread.
O oryx of Najd, hardships are many through the dictates of
destiny, and few indeed are the loyal.

For al-Buḥturī, generally acknowledged as one of the finest exponents of descriptive poetry in Arabic, the resort in times of adversity is the ruins of the palace at Madā'in (Ctesiphon), the so-called *īwān* of Chosroes (Kisrā). He notices a striking wall-painting that depicts a battle at Antioch in 540 between Persian and Byzantine forces and visualises the fighting. Given a draught of wine by his companion, the poet imagines that the monarch Anūshirwān himself is offering him the drink; the building has been restored to its former glory and is filled with embassies and entertainers:

As though, when I have achieved the limit of my perception, I
can see ranks and people,
Delegations standing in the sun, ruing the delay as they wait in
line . . .

It is at the site of another palace that the Andalusian poet, ibn Zaydūn (*d.* 1070), recalls blissful times of old spent with his beloved, Wallādah:

Longingly I recalled you in al-Zahrā', when the horizon was
cloudless and the face of the earth gleamed,
When at eventide the breeze grew languid, as though it pitied my
plight and showed compassion;
The garden smiled to reveal its silvery fountains, as though you
had loosed necklaces from around the throats of maidens.

It has to be said that the lingering affection seems to have been entirely one-sided in that Wallādah's own poetry about ibn Zaydūn is excessively uncomplimentary:

For all his virtue ibn Zaydūn loves rods inside trousers.
If he spotted a penis up a palm-tree, he'd turn into a whole flock
of birds . . .

Ibn Zaydūn's image of the garden introduces another favourite topic of the Arabic poem. Bearing in mind the visual splendour of the gardens in Andalusian palaces such as al-Ḥamrā' (the Alhambra) in Granada, we should not be surprised to discover that they are a much favoured topic of poets. The basic Arabic word for garden (*jannah*) also carries connotations of Paradise, and the Qur'ān itself is not alone among sacred texts in linking the two. The delights of the hereafter and the path towards them were a subject of contemplation for some poets, but for the most part it was to the garden as terrestrial paradise that poets devoted the most attention. Al-Buḥturī describes one such in Iraq:

> Many are the gardens in the Jazīrah, the Tigris frolicking with
> their rivulets;
> They reveal emeralds to your gaze, all scattered; the light
> enhances their gleam,
> Strange delights that catch the eye when the sun reveals their
> hue . . .
> When a breeze rustles the branches, it is as though maidens were
> walking there . . .

With al-Ṣanawbarī (*d.* 945), the garden extravaganza reaches its acme:

> Many the narcissus, with its white and yellow, is doubled in beauty;
> Pearl and gold are blended in it, as are musk and ambergris.

In a final twist of the garden theme we can point to an interesting flight of the imagination by Ṣafī al-dīn al-Ḥillī. He composes a poem in which the garden serves as the venue for an argument, not between humans but among a group of flowers; the iris claims authority over the rose and lily, and the other flowers protest.

Groups of *wasf* poems, particularly those that continue this predilection for the portrayal of aspects of nature, remain a feature of *dīwān*s of Arab poets until the modern period. An eighteenth-century poet such as ʿAbd al-ghanī al-Nābulusī (*d.* 1731) composes a line devoted to the depiction of a flower:

> a carnation in the garden, resembling drops of blood on the
> water-surface,

while twentieth century poets such as Aḥmad Shawqī and Khalīl Muṭrān (*d.* 1949) devote several of their *wasf* poems to portrayals of nature. Some of Muṭrān's poems, and particularly 'Evening' ('*al-Masāʾ*'), give us an early glimpse of the romanticism that is to find a fuller bloom in the poetry of Khalīl Jubrān (*d.* 1931), notably in his 'Processions' ('*al-Mawākib*'), a lengthy contemplation of the human condition that advocates a return to the primitive realm of the forest (*al-ghāb*):

> In the forest is life to be lived, and, did I have gathered within my
> grasp the passing of days, it is there that I would scatter them.

The romantic poet situating himself in the midst of nature is personified by ʿAlī Maḥmūd Ṭāhā (*d.* 1949) in 'Rustic Song' ('*Ughniyyah rīfiyyah*'):

When the water strokes the shade of the tree and the clouds flirt
with the moonlight . . .
I have taken my place in its shade with distracted heart and
downcast eyes.

The most vivid contrast to these idyllic pictures of nature, the countryside, and gardens is provided by the city, that haven of political and administrative complications and of all that is cruel and corrupt. The Egyptian poet Aḥmad ʿAbd al-muʿṭī Ḥijāzī (*b.* 1935) uses a 'Basket of Lemons' ('*Sallat līmūn*') to symbolise the ways in which the metropolis exploits the surrounding countryside:

A basket of lemons left the village at dawn.
Green it was till that cursed moment and laden with dewdrops,
Floating on waves of shade . . .
Which hungry hand plucked it at today's dawn
And under cover of earliest twilight brought it
To congested, crowded streets,
Rushing feet, cars burning petrol
As they move by!

Poetic depictions of the modern city frequently portray its destructive features; one of the most richly complex and savage of these is that of Adūnīs in 'A Grave for New York' ('*Qabr min ajl Nyūyūrk*') – composed in the 1970s at the time of the Vietnam War:

New York:
A woman, statue of a woman
In one hand she holds up a scrap of paper we call freedom, so
called by another piece of paper we term history,
While with another hand she throttles a baby called the earth . . .

To return to our starting-point in this section devoted to the somewhat anomalous category of '*wasf*', a large percentage of Arabic poetry in all its variety can be reckoned as fitting its terms of reference. The topics that have been selected for illustration here are intended purely as examples, culled from a wealth of poetry and image which the contemporary poet has to confront, exploit, or reject.

Ghazal*: love poetry*

The precedents to the emergence of *ghazal* (love poetry) as a separate genre in Arabic can be seen most clearly in the opening section of the pre-Islamic *qaṣīdah*, known as the *nasīb*. The predominant mood in a large number of *nasīb* sections is one of nostalgia for times that are forever gone – of longing, absence, and wistful memories. ʿAlqamah's

Salmā, Labīd's Nawār, Ṭarafah's Khawlah, Zuhayr's Umm Awfā, al-Aʿshā's Suʿād, Laylā, and others, and, in the Umawī period, Dhū al-Rummah's Mayy, these are all female names used by the poets to invoke memories of the image of a now far-distant beloved, leaving the speaker of the poem, often in the company of companions, to question, to remember, to regret. Ṭarafah begins his *muʿallaqah*:

> Khawlah has left traces by the outcrops of Thahmad, that show
> like tattoo traces on the hand.

Labīd's *qaṣīdah* echoes the statement but without naming the beloved, and then goes on to note:

> Since the time when I knew the company of these ruins so well,
> many years have gone by, months sacred and otherwise . . .

These themes may perhaps be viewed as the natural expression of poetic sentiment in a society where gender roles were closely monitored, and occasions of aggregation (such as the annual 'gathering of the clans' during a month when all conflicts were suspended) might be followed by prolonged months of desert travel. Al-ʿArjī (*d.* 738) echoes the complaint of Labīd when he says:

> We spend a complete year without meeting, unless it is on the
> pilgrimage, if she undertakes it;
> And what of Minā and its folk, if she does not?

The most renowned of the *muʿallaqāt*, that of Imru' al-Qays, begins in a way that fits the pattern; indeed it is the *locus classicus* for the image:

> Tarry, my two companions, and let us weep for the memory of a
> beloved and a place, at the sand-dune's edge between al-
> Dakhūl and Ḥawmal.

However, Imru' al-Qays's poem then proceeds to break the above pattern. Indeed it is fondly remembered – and, as we will see in Chapter 7, roundly condemned by the conservative critic, al-Bāqillānī – for the series of episodes following this beginning in which the beloved, indeed a series of beloveds, is very much present:

> The day I entered 'Unayzah's howdah; 'Curses on you!' she
> protested, 'you'll make me dismount'.
> All the while the howdah kept swaying. 'You've hobbled my camel,
> Imru' al-Qays', she said, 'so get down'.

It is against this background that the *ghazal*, essentially a new development in Arabic poetry, emerged in the early days of the community of Muslims; the location was the Ḥijāz region of the Arabian Peninsula with its twin holy cities of Mecca and Medina. It was from this mercantile aristocracy of Mecca that one of Arabic's greatest love-poets, ʿUmar ibn Abī Rabīʿah (*d.* 712), emerged; indeed, so great is his repute that the adjective ʻʿUmarī' is regularly employed to refer to the unrestrained Ḥijāzī type of *ghazal*. The genuine innovation that he brought to love poetry was to relinquish the mood of nostalgia – love in the past tense – in favour of a view of love as a Don Juanesque sport very much in the present. For ʿUmar, amorous conquests are a continuing goal; love is a game, a process of overcoming obstacles. In a spirit of prankish irreverence, ʿUmar chooses some of his most exotic targets from among pilgrims to Mecca. He – or, perhaps more accurately, his poetic persona – is found 'standing on the corner, watching all the [pilgrim] girls go by':

> I spotted her at night walking with her women between the shrine and the [Kaʿbah] stone.
> 'Well then', she said to a companion, 'for ʿUmar's sake let us spoil this circumambulation.
> Go after him so that he may spot us, then, sweet sister, give him a coy wink'.
> 'But I already did', she said, 'and he turned away'.
> Whereupon she came rushing after me.

Besides providing an illustration of decidedly unholy behaviour in the sacred mosque in Mecca, these lines also illustrate some of the features that made ʿUmar's poetry so popular. He introduces realistic segments of flirtatious conversation in his poems, expressed in a level of language less complex than that of the ceremonial tribal *qaṣīdah*s of old. The essential narcissism of the persona is reflected in a particular delight in assuming the role of the female beloved and using the occasion to illustrate quite how devastating are his attractions to the opposite sex. The comments of Hind are a renowned example of this:

> One day, they claim, as she stripped to bathe herself, she asked our neighbour:
> 'Tell me, by God! The way he depicts me, is that how you see me, or does he show no restraint?'
> 'Ah', they replied with a chuckle, 'To every eye the one who is adored is beautiful!'

The popularity of these poems was considerably enhanced by the availability of a group of renowned singers (including ibn Surayj (*d.* 726) and al-Gharīḍ) who set the lilting, gentler rhythms of ʿUmar's poetic escapades to music.

Many poets followed the playful lead established by ʿUmar's poetry, including al-ʿArjī quoted above. However, if the accounts of trysts and escapades are to be believed, some of them carried their play in dangerous directions. Both ibn Qays al-Ruqayyāt (*d.* 704) and Waḍḍāḥ al-Yaman (*d.* 708) wrote poems depicting the attractions of Umm al-Banīn, the redoubtable wife of the Umawī caliph al-Walīd ibn ʿAbd al-Malik; while the charm of the former's tribute seems to have delighted the lady, the latter poet was allegedly put to death for taking his playfulness beyond the realm of poetry.

Another development in Arabic love poetry took the *ghazal* in a very different direction; since some of the poets who typify the trend, and especially the poet Jamīl (*d.* 701), came from the Banu ʿUdhrah tribe, this trend is usually termed 'ʿUdhrī'. The absence, longing, and distance characteristic of the *nasīb* of the earlier poetry are no longer matters of nostalgia, capable of being transcended by reference to other concerns and generic tribal benefits, but now become a lifelong situation, in fact an obsession. The story of Jamīl involves a breaking of the tribal code regarding contact between the sexes, in that he publicly revealed his feelings towards his beloved, Buthaynah. This attack on the honour of the tribe and especially of Buthaynah's family (maintained and enforced by her male relatives and particularly her father) led to a complete ban on any further contact between Jamīl and his beloved. Thus was established the classic situation of the ʿUdhrī love poem.

> Did you but realise how crazed I am with love, you would forgive me; if you did not, you would do wrong . . .
> As long as I live, my heart will adore you; should I die, my echo will trail yours among the graves.
> O to meet my fate suddenly, if the day of my reunion with you is not destined to happen!
> You and the promise you give are nothing but the lightning of a cloud that brings no rain.

The poet-lover places his beloved on a pedestal and worships her from afar. He is obsessed and tormented; he becomes debilitated, ill, and is doomed to a love-death. The beloved in turn becomes the personification of the ideal woman, a transcendental image of all that is beautiful and chaste. The cheek, the neck, the bosom, and, above all, the eyes – a mere glance – these are the cause of passion, longing, devastation, and exhaustion.

The tradition's greatest example of this compulsive and somewhat masochistic adulation is the poet Qays ibn al-Mulawwaḥ (*d.* 688), the beloved of Laylā, whose obsessions did indeed make him 'crazed' *majnūn*); he is thus known as Majnūn Laylā. Like Jamīl, he too will be faithful to the grave and beyond:

> Should our spirits meet after death, with high ground separating our graves,
> the echo of my voice will thrill to the echo of Laylā's, though I be dust in the ground.

As the *ghazal* genre develops, elements of the idealised love theme that are particularly associated with the ʿUdhrī tradition become integrated into the broader repertoire of love poetry. Indeed, as we will note in the section on religious poetry below, ʿUdhrī tropes and images are readily adopted by Ṣūfī poets at a later stage in order to provide a mode for the expression of another kind of devotional state, that of the mystic in quest of the transcendental experience.

Within the gradual process of generic change Bashshār ibn Burd is once again an important participant. His love poems addressed to his beloved, ʿAbdah, reflect the familiar sounds and images of the past:

> ʿAbdah has an abode; it speaks not to us, but looms like lines of writing.
> I question stones and a collapsed tent-trench, but how can such things give an answer?

So popular were these ʿAbdah poems (which contain much reference to the lover's suffering, to sleepless nights, and to the reproachful beloved) that, if we are to credit the contents of the poet's own verse, the caliph al-Mahdī forbade him to write any more. Bashshār, however, can also replicate the conversational tone of ʿUmar ibn Abī Rabīʿah:

> Many's the buxom maid who has told her companions: 'You people, this blind man is amazing!
> Can someone who cannot see be in love?' With tears streaming, I replied: 'Though my eyes may not see her face, in my heart it exists as an image'.

A poet who found particular favour with the caliph, Hārūn al-Rashīd, was ʿAbbās ibn al-Aḥnaf (*d.* after 808). His *ghazal* poetry is primarily concerned with the hopelessness of love, and the persona in his compositions seems resigned to a relationship of deprivation. The beloved's pedestal is now elevated to the sky:

> The very sun she is, residing in the heavens; so console the heart as best you may!
> Never will you ascend to her, nor will she descend to you . . .

However, it is al-Ḥasan ibn Hānī', renowned under his nickname Abū Nuwās (the man with the curl), whose name is most closely linked with the côterie of Hārūn al-Rashīd and of his son and successor, al-Amīn (*d.* 813). Many of his contributions to both love and wine poetry can be seen as the creations of an iconoclast eager to confront and contest the behavioural and cultural norms of his time. His love poems, divided between those addressed to women (*mu'annathāt*) and those to men (*mudhakkarāt*), cover a broad spectrum that ranges all the way from the deprivations associated with the ʿUdhrī love poem to depictions of sexual encounters that reflect his own bisexual predilections. Running through his collection of love (and especially wine) poetry there is an ongoing confrontation between his playful, ribald persona and a penitent alter ego:

> 'Hello!' said the Devil as he swooped down. 'Greetings to a
> penitent whose penitence is sheer illusion!
> What about a sensuous virgin-girl with a splendid bosom
> And a cascade of black hair down her back, its colour replicating
> the darkest grapes?
> 'No', I replied. 'Then what about a beardless youth whose plump
> buttocks are all aquiver,
> One who resembles a virgin in her boudoir, yet on his throat there
> is no necklace?'
> 'No', I said again. 'Then what about a notorious youth renowned
> for his singing and dancing?'
> 'No', I replied. 'Everything resembling what I've told you', the
> Devil continued, 'is sheer common sense.
> You'll change your tune, you fool! Of that I've no doubt!'

Within the broad domain that these poets established for the *ghazal* genre their successors were able to develop and elaborate on its repertoire of image and conceit. The *ghazal* now has a fixed place in the collected works of many poets; among the more famous who have already been mentioned are ibn al-Rūmī and ibn al-Muʿtazz, yet another caliph-poet:

> I passed by a flower-covered grave in the midst of a garden,
> covered in bay-leaves like anemones.
> 'Whose grave is this', I wondered. 'Be gentle with it', the soil
> responded, 'it's a lover's grave'.

The cultural environment of al-Andalus, initially at the caliphal court and later at the number of smaller centres of political patronage provided by the 'petty kingdoms', provided a rich environment for the elaboration of the *ghazal* tradition. Ibn ʿAbd Rabbihi (*d.* 940), the compiler of the famous literary anthology, *al-ʿIqd al-farīd* (The Unique Necklace), includes a section on love poetry that refers to most of the poets mentioned above and expresses a preference for the more courtly variety, something that also emerges from his own contributions to the genre. In addition to the renowned ibn Zaydūn whose storm-tossed affair with the princess, Wallādah, was described above, ibn Ḥazm (*d.* 1064) and ibn Khafājah (*d.* 1138) are renowned for their love poetry; the former is also the author of a manual on love, *Ṭawq al-ḥamāmah* (*The Dove's Neck-ring*), which is examined in more detail in the following chapter. Further insight into the inner dynamics of the tradition of Andalusian love poetry is provided by the recorded verses of the famous poetess, Ḥafṣah bint al-Ḥājj al-Rakūniyyah (*d.* 1190). Her beauty, it appears, aroused the passion of Abū Saʿīd, son of the ruler of Granada, but she responds caustically to his poetic advances:

> You who would lay claim to the head position in love and passion,
> Your poetry has arrived, but its composition failed to please me.

However, it is with Andalusian strophic poetry, the *muwashshaḥ* and *zajal* (the forms of which were discussed earlier in the chapter), that *ghazal* makes some of its most innovative contributions. Early examples of the *muwashshaḥ* poem are seen by some scholars as reflecting the cultural complexities of Andalusian society by juxtaposing a series of strophes and verses that bear an ʿUdhrī stamp with a final strophe – often a popular song – that is decidedly different. One of the fiercest of such contrasts occurs in an anonymous poem in ibn Sanāʾ al-Mulk's collection, *Dār al-ṭirāz* (House of Embroidery). It opens with the traditional repertoire of infatuation and suffering:

> He who has endowed eyelids with the qualities of Indian swords,
> And caused sweet basil to sprout on the side of his cheek,
> Has sentenced the infatuated lover to tears and sleeplessness;
> How can one keep silent?

With the final strophe (*kharjah*) of the poem we encounter an entirely different voice:

> Come on, my sweet, show some resolve! On your feet and give me a kiss! Embrace my breast and lift my anklets all the way up to my earrings. My husband's been called away.

Ibn Quzmān (*d.* 1160), the acknowledged master of the *zajal*, uses his poetry to boast about his prowess as lover and poet; he is quite explicit about his 'allegiance' to poetic forebears:

I am a man in love, by God!
My state shows I'm speaking the truth.
And in *zajal* I'm the tops.
Like a drawn sword poetry pierces my mind, and chainmail itself
will not stop my tongue.
Spare me, please, the religion of Jamīl and ʿUrwah!
Al-Ḥasan [Abū Nuwās] is a model for people!

Such is the enduring nature of the *ghazal* repertoire of landscape and image that we have just explored that in the eighteenth century we can still listen to the poet known as 'the prince of Ṣanʿāʾ ' (*'al-amīr al-ṣanʿānī'*, *d.* 1768) proudly proclaiming:

ʿUdhrī love is my art. Should I pine, do not blame me!
In love I am unique; neither mention nor extol any other . . .
Should you drink of the wine of love, then take it from my vat;
Should you be ignorant of some aspect, then ask your questions
of me.

The Majnūn Laylā legend becomes the source of Aḥmad Shawqī's (*d.* 1932) most famous poetic operetta, its verses remembered (like those of ʿUmar ibn Abī Rabīʿah many centuries earlier) through the popularity of song:

Laylā! Someone calls out that name – Laylā; and in my heart
a rapture takes wing, uncontrollable!
Laylā! the name is for ever implanted in my ear, in my very
soul, like the sound of birds in the forest.

The generation of romantic poets that came after Shawqī laid great stress on the centrality of the individual and the role of the soul in the imaginative process. As noted above, it was among the poets of the *émigré* communities in the Americas (*mahjar*) that the most accomplished examples of early romantic poetry are to be found. Iliyyā Abū Māḍī (*d.* 1957) finds his idealised beloved, Salmā, contemplating at sunset:

The clouds scurry across the spacious heavens as though scared,
while behind them the sun is yellow-hued with brow wrapped.
The sea a silent teak, humble as ascetics,
but your gaze is pallid as you stare at the distant horizon.
Salmā, what preoccupies your thoughts?
Salmā, of what are you dreaming?

For ʿUmar Abū Rīshah (*b.* 1910) the love poem was a vehicle for a newly liberated expression of the relationship between man and woman, whereas, for Ilyās Abū Shabakah (*d.* 1947), the passions of love become a source of nightmarish visions of personal agony and intolerant humanity. Sin, guilt, and lust are central themes of his collection, *Afāʿī firdaws* (Serpents of Paradise, 1938), and his preoccupation with them finds partial redemption through the prolonged process of composing '*Ghalwāʾ*', a poem addressed to Olga, the woman who was eventually to become his wife. A similarly tortured vision of love is later seen in the work of Tawfīq Ṣāyigh (*d.* 1971) whose collection, *Qaṣīdat K* (K's Poem, 1960), shows the emotional impact of his obsessive relationship with an English woman named Kay.

The gradual emergence of Arab women as a participating force in the public life of many Arab countries during the latter half of the twentieth century and the increased educational opportunities that have become available have served as the societal context within which the female voice has been able to offer fresh visions of love and gender relationships to the repertoire of Arabic poetry. Nāzik al-Malāʾikah (*b.* 1923), a pioneer in the process of change in the formal aspects of the poem, plays an important role here, as does the Palestinian poetess Fadwā Ṭūqān, some of whose poems, not unnaturally, link the theme of love to the fate of her homeland. As Fadwā Ṭūqān expresses it:

> In my homeland, O poet,
> in my precious homeland,
> there waits a lover,
> a fellow countryman;
> I shall not waste his heart . . .
> I am a female, so, whenever your whisper
> strokes my heart, please
> forgive its vanity.

The poetic voice of the modern Arab woman can be illustrated through numerous exemplars. From among them we choose an extract from a poem in the collection *Fī al-badʾ kānat al-unthā* (In the Beginning Was the Female, 1988) by the Kuwaitī poetess, Suʿād al-Ṣabāḥ (*b.* 1942); the feelings expressed by the speaker provide yet another linkage to the earlier tradition, one that echoes the sentiments expressed in ibn Quzmān's *zajal* cited above:

> I am tired of traditional words
> about love,
> I'm fed up with the *ghazal* of the dead,
> flowers of the dead;
> sitting down to dinner every night
> with Qays ibn Mulawwaḥ

and Jamīl Buthaynah,
and all the other permanent members
of the ʿUdhrī Love Club.
Please try to deviate a bit from the text,
try to invent me.

The name of one modern Arab poet is most closely linked to the theme of love: Nizār Qabbānī (*d.* 1998). Throughout his lengthy career he has garnered for himself enormous and widespread popularity by using his poems to express the younger generation's quest for liberation from the trammels of traditional morality. In his poems discretion is thrown to the winds:

Wake up from a night of burning passion
and put on your folded gown.
Wake up; the dewy morn will
expose your scandalous desires.
You with the roving breast, cover up
your bosom and voracious nipple.
Where are the clothes you scattered
in a moment of unrivalled pleasure?

The forthrightness with which Qabbānī has addressed love in its various aspects has also led him to compose a number of searing indictments of Arab society and its values, including '*Khubz wa-ḥashīsh wa-qamar*' (Bread, Hashish, and Moon) from the 1950s and '*Hawāmish ʿala daftar al-naksah*' (Commentary on the Notebook of the Disaster) in 1967 following the June War. In the following extract the vocabulary of love becomes immersed in a modern poem of political protest:

Ah, my darling!
What is this nation that treats love like a policeman?
A rose is considered a conspiracy against order;
A poem is a secret opposition pamphlet.
What is this nation, drawn like a yellow locust
crawling on its belly 'from the Ocean to the Gulf' . . .
talking like a saint by day,
and reeling around at night over a woman's navel.

Khamriyyah*: wine poetry*

In *Risālat al-ghufrān* (The Epistle of Forgiveness), a narrative by the poet-philosopher Abū al-ʿAlāʾ al-Maʿarrī (*d.* 1058) – to be discussed in the following chapter – a shaykh is taken on a tour of the next world in order to find answers to a burning question: How have some famous forebears, particularly those who lived during the pre-Islamic era, managed to obtain forgiveness for their conduct during their time on earth? Among those whom the shaykh meets are a number of poets whose fate is clearly in question because they have composed verses in celebration of wine (*khamr*), including ʿAmr ibn Kulthūm, ʿAlqamah ibn ʿAbadah, Labīd, and ʿAdī ibn Zayd. Among the first figures to be approached is the most famous of the pre-Islamic wine-poets, Maymūn ibn Qays, the much-travelled professional bard known as al-Aʿshā ('night-blind', *d. c.* 630?). In one of his most famous odes, he boasts:

I have gone to the tavern in the morning, with a bold, brazen,
  bawdy butcher in my tracks . . .
Reclining I have outdone my rivals for a sprig of sweet-basil and a
  dry wine from a moist jug.
As long as it is available, they only wake up to yell 'Give me more'
  after the first and second draft.

The poet narrates how, just as he was being hauled away to the nether regions, ʿAlī (the fourth caliph) appeared. Al-Aʿshā's reminded him of his poem in praise of Muḥammad, and that proved sufficient to persuade ʿAlī to ask the Prophet to intercede on the poet's behalf, the condition being that he drink no wine in Paradise. The shaykh later questions Ḥassān ibn Thābit, the 'poet of the Prophet', asking how the poet could introduce the theme of wine into a eulogy of the Prophet himself. The poet replies (and here we can appreciate the ironic tone of al-Maʿarrī's voice in this narrative) that he was only describing the phenomenon, not participating himself; and, in any case, the poet continues, the Prophet was not the puritanical figure that some subsequent scholars have made him out to be.

As is well known, proscriptions regarding wine-drinking are incorporated into official Islamic doctrine (although, as one might anticipate, there is considerable debate as to the precise definition of *khamr*). However, the application of any such rigid behavioural norms in a developing Muslim societal environment that remained culturally pluralistic and fractious provided – almost automatically – a ready device through which poets could exhibit a sense of defiance against received orthodoxy, whether in earnest or as a creative posture. It is within such a context that the *khamr* theme of the earliest period is developed into a separate genre in its own right, the *khamriyyah*.

That the court of the Umawī caliphs was hardly oblivious to the delights of wine (or, at the very least, to listening to poetry on that topic) can be illustrated not only in the celebrated poems of the Christian poet al-Akhṭal, but even more by the compositions of one of Arabic's most celebrated masters of the wine-poem, the Umawī caliph, al-Walīd ibn Yazīd (*d.* 744):

> Cast off hidden cares with frivolity; thwart fate by enjoying the
> daughter of the grape . . .
> How I long to drink from a maid of noble descent on her
> wedding-day,
> Resplendent in her jewels, wondrous to behold,
> As though her glass contained a firebrand gleaming into the
> watcher's eye.

Here the poet-caliph illustrates the developing imagery of the wine poem and its emerging cast of 'characters': the drinkers are challenging the fates (not to mention the tenets of the dominant faith), and the shape of the bottle and the promise that it offers is likened to that of a beautiful woman. These and other images are brought to their full flowering by the acknowledged master of the Arabic wine poem, Abū Nuwās.

Abū Nuwās's name has already occurred several times in this chapter on poetry, as is only fitting for a poet who was fully cognisant of the early heritage of Arabic poetry and of the primary Islamic canonical sources but whose creative persona was clearly unwilling to be trammelled by the perceived dictates of either. However, it is in the wine poem that his iconoclastic instincts are best combined with his poetic genius. It is the aim of Abū Nuwās's poetic world to create a replication of the heavenly realm on earth; it is a fools' paradise, of course, and, since it directly confronts and challenges the behavioural norms of the society, it is also fraught with risk. The primary resort with his rowdy group is the tavern which may have to be opened at a very late hour by the owner:

> Many's the lady publican I've roused from sleep, long after the
> Gemini has set and the Vulture Star is in the sky.
> 'Who's knocking?' she asks. 'A whole gang', we reply, 'short of
> goblet and in need of wine'.

The world into which the publican admits them is one where glasses gleam like stars ('like the sun, their gleam like the very Pleiades in exquisite glass') and bottles – slender-necked and unsealed, full of fine, old wine – are at the same time old crones and lithe virgin maids. Above all, the wine is served by the *sāqī*, a youth whose beauty is depicted in extravagant and sensual terms.

Abū Nuwās is not alone, of course, in choosing to explore (and exploit to the full) the many and various modes of challenge to orthopraxis, but his mischievous citation of phrases culled from the text of the Qur'ān itself clearly illustrates a conscious process of confrontational allusion. His corpus of wine poetry casts a giant shadow over the subsequent tradition of wine poetry in Arabic. The motifs and images that become an intrinsic feature of the false worldly paradise opened up by his poetry make their way into the works of Arab poets composing in a variety of forms and genres. Replicating not only Abū Nuwās but also one of his immediate successors, ibn al-Muʿtazz (*d.* 908), Ṣafī al-dīn al-Ḥillī (*d.* 1349) draws attention to the attractions that wine-making Christian monasteries (and their monks) provided:

> I roused a monk from sleep whose mellifluous voice accompanied
> us when he prayed or spoke.
> Opening the door he let us in . . .and brought us a superb vintage
> with a bouquet, well aged in its vat.
> He filled the cup till it overflowed on his hand, and gave me to
> drink after he had drunk himself . . .

In contrast with the public and declamatory nature of the panegyrical *qaṣīdah*, the *ghazal* and wine poem emerge as genres intended to express more private, personal types of sentiment, reserved perhaps for intimate, rather than ceremonial, occasions. This may at least help to account for the readiness with which the poetic repertoire of both genres came to be adopted by those poets who wished to find modes of expression suited to those more private, personal, and indeed ecstatic, forms of devotion associated with Sufism. When the most famous of the Ṣūfī poets who wrote in Arabic, the Egyptian ʿUmar ibn al-Fāriḍ (*d.* 1235), begins his Ṣūfī *khamriyyah*,

> In remembrance of the beloved we drank a wine through which
> we became drunk before ever the vine was created.
> For a cup it has a full moon; it is a sun circled by a new moon;
> when it is mixed, how many a star appears!

we are being introduced to a world where the imagery of love and wine constitutes a surface beneath which an elaborate code is at work. The 'beloved' here refers to God, while 'wine' serves as the medium through which a state of oblivion can be achieved; the gleaming of the stars represents sparks of inspiration that the mystic can receive once that state has been reached.

The *dīwān* of ibn al-Fāriḍ is generally regarded as marking the high point in Arabic mystical poetry, a genre in which, among the various literary cultures within the Islamic dominions, pride of place is generally accorded to Persian poets, notably ʿAṭṭār (*d. c.* 1230), Jalāl al-dīn Rūmī (*d.* 1273), and Ḥāfiẓ (*d.* 1390). The tradition upon which ibn al-Fāriḍ builds sees some of its earliest manifestation in the poetry of the renowned female mystic, Rābiʿah al-ʿAdawiyyah of al-Baṣrah (*d.* 801), whose life-span thus partially overlaps that of al-Ḥasan al-Baṣrī, an important figure in the early development of Ṣūfī thought and practice. In an often quoted poem attributed to her the linkage of the themes of devotion and love is direct, somewhat redolent of the poetry of famous European ecstatics of a later era such as Hildegard of Bingen (*d.* 1179) and Julian of Norwich (*d.* early fifteenth century):

> For You I have two loves: one of longing, the other because You are
> worthy of it.
> As for the one of longing, the mention of Your name diverts me
> from that of all others.
> As for the love of which you are worthy, that resides in Your lifting
> the veil for me so that I may behold You.
> There is no praise for me in one or the other, but in both the
> praise is Yours.

The love theme, and especially the notion of suffering in love that, as we have already noted, was an intrinsic feature of the ʿUdhrī tradition, was further developed in the poetry of the Egyptian mystic, Dhū al-nūn al-Miṣrī (*d.* 861). The idea of such longings leading to martyrdom in the cause of divine love is most famously represented by the renowned figure of Manṣūr al-Ḥallāj (*d.* 922), whose execution turned him literally into a martyr and a central symbol of the uneasy tensions between Sufism and Islamic orthodoxy. With him the vocabulary of love signifies at another level of meaning:

> The hearts of lovers have eyes which see what other beholders do
> not see,
> Tongues confiding secrets that remain hidden from distinguished
> clerks,
> And wings that fly featherless towards the realm of the Lord of
> the Worlds.

and, as the ecstatic vision takes over, the unification of aspirant with the transcendent becomes complete:

> I am You, without doubt. So Your praise is mine,
> Your Unity is mine; Your defiance is mine.

Those mystics who composed poetry during the four centuries that separate al-Ḥallāj and ibn al-Fāriḍ expressed their devotion and quest for the ascetic life in relatively stark and unadorned verse. Looking back from the poetic output of the two Ṣūfī masters of the thirteenth century, ibn al-Fāriḍ and ibn al-ʿArabī (*d.* 1240), Martin Lings suggests (*ʿAbbāsīd Belles-Lettres*, Ch. 14) that the changes evident in their poetry seem to result more from an awareness of developments in the more secular court tradition than to any line of continuity stretching back to al-Ḥallāj and his predecessors. In the case of ibn al-Fāriḍ we have already quoted the opening lines of his *khamriyyah*, but that poem's combination of the bacchic and erotic – the devotee is instructed to take his wine pure and not to shun the 'beloved's white teeth', i.e. the Prophet's word – is expanded into a much broader expression in the poet's '*al- Tā'iyyah al-kubrā*' (Great Poem rhyming on T, also known as '*Naẓm al-sulūk*' (Poem of the Path)), in which, following an opening verse,

> The palm of my eye gave me love's wine to drink, and my cup is
> the visage of the one who is beyond beauty,

the devotee explores over 760 lines the soul's journey in quest of God, filtered through the imagery of his relationship with his 'beloved': his suffering and self-denial, his instructions to his fellow devotees, and his desire for union.

Ibn al-Fāriḍ's contemporary, ibn al-ʿArabī, was also revered during his own lifetime and earned his own share of opprobrium from orthodox scholarship; as noted earlier, he was even accorded the curious distinction of having his books banned for a period by the Egyptian Ministry of the Interior during the 1980s. During a stay in Mecca, ibn al-ʿArabī was apparently inspired by an affection for his host's young daughter to write a collection of poetry, *Tarjumān al-ashwāq* (Interpreter of Desires). So convincingly authentic was this imagery and so complex its layering of symbolism that he found himself thereafter constrained to add a commentary on it in order to counteract more secular interpretations of its content. The following lines, often quoted, illustrate not only the links to the tradition of Arabic love poetry but also the resonances of ibn al-ʿArabī's language:

> O Marvel! A bower amidst the flames,
> My heart is now capable of every form,
> A meadow it is for gazelles, for monks a monastery;
> A shrine for idols, for pilgrims the very Kaʿbah;
> The tables of the Torah, the book of the Qur'ān.
> Love is my faith. Wherever its camels may roam,
> There is found my religion, my faith.

It is symptomatic of the tremendous devotional following attracted to popular Ṣūfī movements over large areas of the Islamic dominions that a single poem composed by an Egyptian poet named al-Būṣīrī (*d.* 1296), also known under the title of 'the mantle' (*al-Burdah*), was to become one of the most commented upon poems in the whole of Arabic. A 161–line record of the life of Muḥammad, its division into subsections detailing aspects of his prophetic mission, made it an ideal poetic vehicle for use in the *ḥaḍrah*, the gathering at which members of Ṣūfī brotherhoods would conduct their rituals of worship and listen to devotional texts. This poem also begins with a gesture to the early tradition:

> Is it from a memory of neighbours at Dhū Salam that you have
> mixed with blood tears that flowed from an eye?
> Has the wind blown from Kāẓimah's quarter, or a lightning flash
> gleamed in the dark by Iḍam?

After a lengthy exordium the poet moves on to praise Muḥammad and recount the details of his life and mission.

While the mellifluous complexities of ibn al-Fāriḍ and ibn al-ʿArabī may continue to delight adherents and disturb orthodoxy, it is the figure of the martyred al-Ḥallāj that provides many modern writers with a potent symbol. In addition to the play *Ma'sāt al-Ḥallāj* by ʿAbd al-Ṣabūr (discussed in Chapter 6), we may mention in closing Adūnīs's poem, '*Marthiyyat al-Ḥallāj*' (Elegy for al-Ḥallāj), in which the political defiance of the martyred Ṣūfī is transported into a modern Arab world much in need of such qualities:

> O star, arising from Baghdād
> laden with poems and birth,
> O poisoned green pen
> Nothing remains for those who come from afar
> bringing thirst, death, and ice.
> In this 'resurrectionist' land
> Nothing remains, save you and presence.

Ṭardiyyah*: hunt poetry*

That the *muʿallaqah* of Imru' al-Qays, that yardstick of the Arabic poetic tradition to which we have frequently had recourse, is just one among many earlier poems that contain a vivid description of a hunt is evidence enough of the antiquity of the Arabs' delight in this quest for food and sport. Besides weapons like the bow and spear (and, more recently, guns), specific types of animals and birds have traditionally been used to assist in the hunting of prey. Among the former, the category of hound known as Salūqī (English, Saluki) were particularly preferred; among birds, the falcon (*ṣaqr*), a sport that first came into vogue during the period of the Umawī caliphs.

In dealing with the hunt theme, we once again witness a process whereby such episodes within the larger framework of the pre-Islamic *qaṣīdah* become the topic of separate *qiṭʿah* structures during the Islamic period. As with the other genres we have discussed above, it appears to be in the *dīwān* of Abū Nuwās that the hunt poem is first categorised as a separate entity.

The majority of the poems of this type have a stock opening: the hunter ventures forth in the early morning, and his faithful hound is with him. The dog possesses heroic qualities:

> When a fox appears at the mountain foot, 'Ho!' I yell to my dog,
> and he is roused like a hero,
> A brave-hearted dog, a splendid worker, well trained, perfect in
> every quality . . .

and is a relentless pursuer:

> I have trained a dog for the chase, straight as an arrow, with collar
> and rope on his neck . . .
> He tears away from the squawk of the sand-grouse as he weighs in
> the balance the spotted hares.

Ibn al-Muʿtazz also contributes to the repertoire of poems on this theme:

> The dog-trainer brought out a slender saluki hound that he had
> often used,
> well trained, a wind-daughter – when you ask that she run, he
> sends her even faster;
> tongue sticking out of mouth the way daggers split through their
> sheathes.
> She grabs her prey without pause, just as suckling mothers hug
> their children.

The identification of the hunt poem as a separate category of topic-based poem during the Islamic period seems to reflect the particular tastes and predilections that characterised the court life and sporting activities of the Umawī and early ʿAbbāsī caliphs (including ibn al-Muʿtazz himself). While the hunt and chase, and indeed the animals involved as chaser and chased, continue to appear as images in court panegyric and indeed in poems that depict the continuing chase of love, the hunt poem itself appears to have fallen out of favour, at least with those who were entrusted with the task of committing the poetic record to written form.

Zuhdiyyah*: homiletic poetry*

Among the many tales in the expanded version of the *Thousand and One Nights* (a process examined in detail in Chapter 5), is '*Madīnat al-nuḥās*' (The City of Brass). During the reign of the Umawī caliph, ʿAbd al-Malik ibn Marwān, the Amīr Mūsā ibn Nuṣayr is sent on a journey to locate the bottles in which King Solomon has imprisoned the demon spirits known as *jinn*. Numerous sinister beacons point the travellers towards a mysterious 'city of brass'. The journey to the city is frequently interrupted by pauses in front of weird statues and pillars, on each of which are written poems that warn about the ephemerality of life on earth and the failure of humanity to reckon with what is to come. The journey serves as a splendid vehicle for the story-teller to include *ad libitum* copious examples of sermons in verse addressed directly to mortals:

> O man, consider what you see and take heed before you go on
> your final journey.
> Offer provision of charity for your benefit, for every house-dweller
> will depart.
> Consider too those who embellished their houses; under the earth
> they have become a pledge for their deeds.
> They built, but to no avail; they stored up goods, but their wealth
> was useless when their lifespan came to an end.

The word *zuhd* means literally 'asceticism', and the type of poetry that was to become the *zuhdiyyah* stresses the inevitability of death and thus an avoidance of life's excesses in favour of a path of self-denial and contemplation. The world created by such poetry is one of stark contrasts. Humans in their mortality are weak, at the beck and call of death whenever God so decrees; 'dust thou art, and to dust thou shalt return'. The coming of the Day of Judgement is inevitable; evil-doers will be punished, and the pious will earn their reward. Those who accrue wealth and power in this lifetime will discover its worth when the great leveller places their mortal remains in the grave.

Examples can be found in the pre-Islamic poetic corpus that acknowledge an awareness of the impermanence of life and imminence of death; the works of ʿAdī ibn Zayd (cited above for his hunt poetry) are often mentioned in this connection:

I have never seen the likes of young men, deluded by
passing time, who manage to overlook its consequences . . .
Their souls imagine that death's destruction will never
reach them, while random fates aim a straight arrow.

While such sentiments clearly form one kind of precedent to the later emergence of the homiletic poem, the Qur'ān's specific and frequent references to God's judgement and to rewards and punishments based on deeds and attitudes in life clearly provided a rich source of inspiration. The message is unambiguous:

Those who prefer this world and its embellishments, we will pay them full measure for their deeds there, and their rights will be observed.
They are the people who in the next world will have only Hellfire; whatever they have created will be as nought; their previous deeds will be futile.

(*Sūrat Hūd* (11, Hud), vv. 15 and 16)

Homilies and moral pronouncements were among the types of record that were committed to written form in collections, and the ideas and values that they contained were often couched in poetic form. The following lines, for example, are attributed to the famous grammarian, al-Khalīl ibn Aḥmad (*d.* 791):

Live as seems right to you. Death is your mansion, and there is no escape from it.
A house may be wealthy and glorious; the wealth will vanish, and the house will collapse.

The genre is regarded as reaching its acme with the work of two poets, both of whom were suspected of adhering to heterodox beliefs. The earlier of the two, Ṣāliḥ ibn ʿAbd al-Quddūs, sounds familiar themes:

Humans collect, and time divides; while fate tears things apart, they keep on patching.

but he also included in his poetry references to certain dualistic beliefs which, in the politically sensitive early decades of the ʿAbbāsī caliphate, were regarded as suspect; on the orders of the caliph al-Mahdī he was executed as a heretic (*zindīq*) in 784. The second and more famous poet, Abū al-ʿAtāhiyah (*d.* 826), managed to circumvent such accusations. Like most poets, accounts of his career come supplied with anecdote. One suggests that he devoted himself to homiletic poetry after failing in love, while another records that he demanded of his contemporary, Abū Nuwās, that he relinquish the field of homiletics and concentrate instead on his obvious forte, namely the poetic genres that focus on the celebration of life's pleasures. The relative balance of sections in each poet's *dīwān* lends some credence to the story, and yet Abū Nuwās's does include a section devoted to homiletic poetry and their cautionary message:

> Death is ever near us, never far removed.
> Every day brings death's call and the wailing of keening women . . .
> How long will you frolic and jest in delusion
> When every day death glows to the flint of your life?

Abū al-ʿAtāhiyah's concentration on this genre was sufficient to make him Arabic's homiletic poet *par excellence*. His poetry insists on the reality of humanity's mortality: death is inevitable and life a purely transitory phase that it is pointless to prolong. Wisdom therefore demands that humans in their impotence adhere to God's injunctions through piety and good works. They should be satisfied with what is enough (*kafāf*) and not embark on a useless quest for riches:

> Daily sustenance should meet your needs. How great is the sustenance of those who die!
> God is my sufficiency in every matter; in Him is my wealth and to Him do I express my need.
> If what suffices does not meet your needs, then the entire earth cannot do so.

The poetry of Abū al-ʿAlāʾ al-Maʿarrī (*d.* 1058) participates in the same homiletic tradition. Yet the poetic voice of this blind philosopher-poet, one of the most famous in the whole of Arabic literature, is less concerned with homiletics than with philosophical reflection tinged with pessimism. Such was his fame as a scholar that in 1008 he travelled from his native Syria to Baghdād in order to participate in the intellectual life of the great caliphal capital. However, he only stayed for some eighteen months, leaving in disillusion to return to his home town where he spent the rest of his life. Some of the themes of the homiletic poem are certainly present:

> The finest of time's gifts is to forsake what is given;
> God extends a predatory hand to what He has provided.
> Better than a life of wealth is one of poverty; a monk's
> garb is better than a king's fine clothes.

but al-Maʿarrī is constantly wondering about the meaning of a life that to him brings only misery. One of his most famous expressions of this gloomy vision is:

> If only a child died at its hour of birth and never suckled from its mother in confinement.
> Even before it can utter a word, it tells her: Grief and trouble is all you will get from me.

Such a life-view is a constant theme of al-Maʿarrī's great collection *Luzūm mā lā yalzam* (Adherence to What is Not Required (usually abbreviated to *al- Luzūmiyyāt*)), the title of which refers to his self-imposition of a more elaborate rhyming pattern than required by the poetic canon. For al-Maʿarrī every heartbeat is a further step towards the grave, and death itself is a relief from hardship:

> My clothing is my shroud, my grave is my home; my life is my fate, and for me death is resurrection.

Like the hunt poem described above, the homiletic poem does not appear to have retained its currency to any significant extent among al-Maʿarrī's successors. Those poets who did turn their attention to the genre hark back to the message and style of Abū al-ʿAtāhiyah. Sharaf al-dīn al-Anṣārī (*d.* 1264), for example, exhorts his listeners:

> Where are the quavering hearts, the copious tears
> For the sins committed, too countless to describe? . . .
> Weep many tears then till you imagine your eyelids to bleed,
> And seek God in order to gain the blessings of His goodness.

MODERN ARABIC POETRY

In the opening chapter of this book I suggested that one of the primary goals behind its mode of organisation was to emphasise continuities. In the preceding sections of this chapter on Arabic poetry I have attempted to illustrate the different ways in which themes and genres (*aghrāḍ*, to give them their Arabic term once again) developed during the pre-modern period and for modern poets became material for evocation or allusion (and, in the case of radical change, for rejection). However, the terms 'modern', 'modernity', and 'modernisation' imply a posture that acknowledges the continuing processes of change and in particular a way of confronting the heritage of the past. Thus, while the previous sections have sought to illustrate linkages between past and present, I will close this chapter with a section that investigates the differences that mark its modern manifestations.

Faced with the realities of a renewed encounter with the military and intellectual forces of Europe, poets found themselves constrained to confront both the Western other, simultaneously the symbol of their nation's occupation by foreign armies and the impetus for many of the social changes in which they found themselves involved; and the self, as they sought to come to terms with the 'anxiety of influence' implicit in their relationship with the poetic past. Changes within society itself – expanded educational opportunities, the emergence of a middle class, and, albeit at a more measured pace, the changing role of women in society – contributed to the emergence of new audiences for poetry and a very different system of patronage. All these features help to explain why in the early decades of the twentieth century a generation of Arab poets turned away from the directions that Arabic poetry had initially taken during the early stages of the revival (*al-nahḍah*) movement and found their inspiration in the poetry of European Romanticism. The neo-classical trend against which they were reacting had sought its models in the poetic heritage of the past. In the poetry of Maḥmūd Sāmī al-Bārūdī (*d.* 1904), Aḥmad Shawqī (*d.* 1932) and Ḥāfiẓ Ibrāhīm (*d.* 1932) in Egypt, form and occasion tended to echo the repertoire of the earlier tradition. That is a judgement on their collected poetry, but it should in fairness be added that each of them also composed some poems which made gestures to modernity, particularly in choice of themes. This trend is particularly noticeable in the poetry of Jamīl Ṣidqī al-Zahāwī (*d.* 1936) and Maʿrūf al-Ruṣāfī (*d.* 1945) in Iraq, both of whom seemed anxious to rid the classical *qaṣīdah* form of its lofty and detached associations. It should be added that, as modern Arabic poetry has witnessed the enormous processes of change that we are about to discuss, a number of poets, including Badawī al-Jabal (*b.* 1907), Bishārah al-Khūrī (renowned under the pen-name of 'Al-Akhṭal al-Ṣaghīr', *d.* 1968), and Muḥammad Mahdī al-Jawāhirī (*d.* 1998), continued to compose much admired poetry that maintains the neo-classical tradition while addressing itself with vigour and commitment to the concerns of the present.

Between these two approaches to poetry and modernity a key bridge role is often assigned to Khalīl Muṭrān (*d.* 1949), a Lebanese poet who spent most of his career in Egypt and is known as 'poet of the two regions'. While the bulk of his poetry is of the more occasional variety (panegyrics and elegies, for example), the language and mood of a few poems, '*al-Masāʾ*' ('Evening'), for example, which was cited earlier, affords an illustration of the kind of sensibility that seems to reflect Muṭrān's hopes for the future.

Romanticism, as a reaction against the definitional strictures of classicism, found its earliest creative impulse among Arab writers living within a set of communities that were themselves the consequence of a major change, the emigré (*mahjar*) communities of the Americas, North and South. In order to provide each other with support in both writing and publication, these writers established their own cultural societies: *al-Rābiṭah al-qalamiyyah* (The Bond of the Pen) founded in New York in 1920, and *al-ʿUṣbah al-Andalusiyyah* (The Andalusian Group) founded in Sao Paulo, Brazil in 1932. Of the northern group the undisputed leader is Jubrān; indeed he led from the front in his use of different forms – revivals of earlier strophic structures such as the *muwashshaḥ* and early experiments with prose poetry – and above all in his sensitivity to the creative potential of language. As has often happened within the Arabic poetic tradition, a refrain from his most famous poem, '*al-Mawākib*' ('Processions', already quoted above), is now known throughout the Middle East in the hauntingly beautiful musical version sung by Fayrūz:

> Give me the lyre and sing, for singing is the secret of existence,
> And, though it all vanish, the melody lingers on.

Jubrān's colleague in New York and the northern group's most significant critical writer was Mīkhā'īl Nuʿaymah (*d.* 1988). His most searing poetic statement reflects his experience as an American soldier of Arab descent who has fought in the First World War. The speaker in '*Akhī*' ('My Brother') localises the issue from the outset by noting the possibility that 'someone from the West' may brag about his accomplishments. However, as he notes in the final stanza, the Arab world has nothing to brag about:

> My brother! Who are we, with neither homeland, people, nor
> neighbour?
> Whether asleep or awake, our garb is shame and disgrace.

Of the poets in the northern group it is Īliyyā Abū Māḍī (*d.* 1957) whose works best illustrate the tensions involved in this process of change in poetic sensibility. His most famous collection, *al-Jadāwil* (Brooks, 1927, with an introduction by Nuʿaymah), is generally regarded as a major contribution to the development of Arabic romantic poetry. Song has once again made one of its poems, '*Ṭalāsim*' ('Charms'), widely known in the Arab world, and, in spite of its wayward length, the opening stanzas do establish a characteristically quizzical tone:

> I came, I know not where from, but I came.
> I had seen a way before me, so I took it
> And I will continue, whether I wish or not.

How did I come? How did I see my way?
I do not know.

Among the southern group of poets the most prominent names are Rashīd al-Khūrī (*d.* 1984) and Ilyās Farḥāt (*d.* 1980), both of whom are recalled for their advocacy, albeit from a substantial distance, of the cause of Arab nationalism, and the Maʿlūf brothers, Fawzī (*d.* 1930) – author of the famous long poem '*ʿAlā bisāṭ al-rīḥ*' ('On the Wind's Carpet', 1929) – and Shafīq (*b.* 1905).

The introduction to Nuʿaymah's collection of critical articles, *al-Ghurbāl* (The Sieve, 1923), was written by ʿAbbās Maḥmūd al-ʿAqqād, one of the most prominent early advocates of romantic ideals in Egypt. Al-ʿAqqād and his two colleagues, ʿAbd al-raḥmān Shukrī (*d.* 1958) and Ibrāhīm al-Māzinī (*d.* 1949), became avid devotees of the school of English romanticism as students, and, even though the group later split apart in acrimony, the causes that they espoused were still gathered around the title of the journal that they published in two parts in 1921, *al-Dīwān*. Part of the process involved debunking the pretensions of neo-classicism, and al-ʿAqqād undertook the mission with gusto in his attack on what he regarded as the outmoded artificiality of Shawqī's public poetry. As al-ʿAqqād's introduction to Nuʿaymah's collection also shows, the Egyptian poet-critic regarded it as part of his function to stand guardian at the gate of change and to monitor some of the more radical changes being advocated by the *mahjar* poets and others.

The creativity, whether in poetry, criticism, or both, of these pioneers laid the framework for the heyday of Arabic romantic poetry – the inter-war period stretching into the 1940s, a good deal of which has been cited above in the sections on description and love poetry. Following the lead of earlier romantic poets like Nuʿaymah and members of the South American *mahjar*, the renowned Tunisian poet, Abū al-qāsim al-Shābbī (*d.* 1934), was fired by the fervour of nationalist sentiment and sought to rouse his people in stirring tones:

If a people ever wills to live, then fate must respond.
Night must be revealed, and chains be severed.
Whoever is not embraced by a desire for life dissolves in the air
  and vanishes
So woe to the one who can find no solace in the life from the
  blows of an all-powerful nothingness.

Al-Shābbī, whose published lecture 'Poetic Imagination Among the Arabs' is a stirring statement of the ideals of romanticism, died at a tragically early age. Much of his poetry was published for the first time in Cairo, where another group of poets, *Jamāʿat Apollo* (The Apollo Society), was fostered by the supportive environment provided by a guiding figure, Aḥmad Zakī Abū Shādī (*d.* 1955). Unlike the other groups we have just mentioned, the Apollo Society was less polemical in its attitudes, endeavouring to stress continuity rather than confrontation; its first two presidents were Aḥmad Shawqī and Khalīl Muṭrān. For a period of just two years (1932–34), its journal, *Apollo*, was an important meeting-place for discussions about poetry, and it is not a little ironic that its closure came about as a result of a dispute involving al-ʿAqqād, an advocate of the modern, as we have seen, but only on his own terms. Abū Shādī himself was a prolific poet, the author of nineteen collections; *al-Shafaq al-bākī* (Weeping Twilight, 1926–27) alone contains some 1,380 pages. He was also an inspiration for the creativity of others: in addition to al-Shābbī, the most significant names are Ibrāhīm Nājī (*d.* 1953) and ʿAlī Maḥmūd Ṭāhā (*d.* 1949). These poets and their *mahjar* predecessors were an acknowledged influence on another writer who died tragically young, the Sudanese poet Yūsuf Bashīr al-Tījānī (*d.* 1937), whose poetry succeeds in fusing these modern sensibilities and a thorough acquaintance with classical poetry culled from a traditional Islamic education into verses that are marked by a unique mystical quality:

> True being, how vast its extent in the soul!
> Purest silence, how firm its links to the spirit!
> Everything in existence walks in the folds of God;
> This ant in miniature is the sound of His echo.

During these same decades, the Palestinian poet, Ibrāhīm Ṭūqān (*d.* 1941), cast an increasingly angry eye on the ever-worsening situation in his homeland and sought to rally people to the national cause:

> You people, your foes are not such as to be gentle and merciful.
> You people, before you is nothing but exile, so get ready.

For Ṭūqān, as for Ibrāhīm Nājī and ʿAlī Maḥmūd Ṭāhā, the game of love was one to be embarked on without guilt, but for their Lebanese contemporary, Ilyās Abū Shabakah (*d.* 1947), the animal desires provoked by love involve the horrors of sin and shame. While a later collection like *Ilā al-abad* (For Ever, 1945) may give expression to a more innocent and blissful love, the process of achieving that state sees the poet's persona laying bare his personal agonies; and no more so than in his appropriately named collection, *Afāʿī firdaws* (The Serpents of Paradise, 1938).

Alongside these developments in the 1930s and 1940s there emerged a group of symbolist poets. In view of the strong ties that have continued to link Lebanon with France and its culture, it is not surprising that most of the practitioners of this trend were of Lebanese origin or that they sought their models among the French symbolist poets. Indeed the most influential of the Arab symbolists, Saʿīd ʿAql (*b.* 1912), was throughout his career a fervent advocate of Lebanese nationalism ('Phoenicianism'), but his real significance lies in the groundwork that his poetry laid for future developments in Arabic poetry. ʿAql's etherial creations, couched in a symbolic language of great beauty, were criticised by his successors for their supreme detachment from 'reality', but the more perceptive poetic critics have come to realise the debt that those same successors owe to ʿAql in paving the way for the effective use of symbols during the decades following the Second World War.

As we have already noted, 1947 saw the appearance of two attempts to achieve a final break with the demands of *qaṣīdah* structure; Nāzik al-Malā'ikah, the author of one of them, proceeded to develop a new prosodic system that relied on the unit of the poetic foot rather than the line as a whole. However, the movements that we have just described were determined to sweep away *anciens régimes*, and that of poetry was no exception. In retrospect it is possible to see the changes in Arabic poetry since the 1950s as the major step in the direction of modernism. The achievements of the romantic movement were certainly considerable. The strong hold of the classical tradition (and its neo-classical manifestations) had been lessened; there had been a move from a patronised public voice to a more individual one, and poetic language had extended beyond the familiar repertoire of imagery to explore new associations of meaning. However, romantic poetry had veered in the direction of sentimentality, and symbolists like Saʿīd ʿAql were defining the aesthetics of their creations in terms of the sheer beauty of sound. The political corruption and social injustice that for them symbolised the desolation of the Arab world were to be stimuli for poetic creativity that focused on oppression, poverty, injustice, and exploitation and supported revolutionary change. If the title of T. S. Eliot's famous poem, 'The Wasteland', provided an emblematic text for so many Arab poets who read it in either the original or translation, then the rallying-cry of 'commitment' (*iltizām*) which came to prevail during the revolutionary decade of the 1950s afforded poetry (and other genres) a yardstick for social relevance.

Iraq, suffering under the joint burdens of British occupation and the corrupt regime of Nūrī al-Saʿīd, was a particularly fertile ground for the new, defiant voice of committed poetry, and also for the pattern of exile that has all too often been the automatic corollary of such expressions. ʿAbd al-wahhāb al-Bayātī (*d.* 1999), exiled from his homeland and later deprived of its citizenship, and Badr Shākir al-Sayyāb (*d.* 1964) graphically depict the conditions in which their fellow Iraqis live and work. Al-Bayātī's poem, '*Sifr al-faqr wa-al-thawrah*' ('The Book of Poverty and Revolution') proclaims:

'Let us burn,
So sparks will shoot from us
To light the revolutionaries' cries
And rouse the cock dead on the wall'.

The speaker of al-Sayyāb's poem, '*Unshūdat al-maṭar*' ('Song of the Rain'), generally acknowledged as one of the greatest poems in modern Arabic, is in exile and contemplates a future of untapped potential:

In every raindrop
A red or yellow flower-bud.
Each tear of hungry and naked people,
Each drop spilled from the blood of slaves,
Each is a smile awaiting new lips,
A teat rosy on a babe's mouth
In tomorrow's youthful world, giver of life.
Rain, rain, rain,
Iraq will blossom with rain.

While, for these poets, the city is the seat of tyrannical and corrupt political authority, it also represents the crushing power of the modern, technological metropolis to destroy the oppressed peasantry who flock to it in search of a livelihood. The Sudanese poet, Muḥammad al-Faytūrī (*b.* 1930), takes up this favourite theme of poets who responded to the call of commitment in '*Aḥzān al-madīnah al-sawdāʾ*' ('Sorrows of the Black City'):

When darkness erects
Over city streets
Barriers of black stone,
People extend their hands
To the morrow's balconies . . .
Their days are ancient memories
Of an ancient land,
Their faces, like their hands, gloomy . . .
You might think they are submissive,
But actually they are on fire!

For the poets of Palestine this general sense of oppression and alienation acquired a more particular and intense focus as their homeland became the arena of conflict in 1948 following the declaration of the State of Israel. Questions of land, home, and identity, confrontations with violence, injustice, and exile, these cogent factors prompted a number of poets to adopt the defiant voice of resistance. Most famous among them is Maḥmūd Darwīsh (*b.* 1942), whose poems range from the directly confrontational, as in '*Biṭāqat huwiyyah*' ('Identity Card'):

Write it down!
I'm Arab,
And my card number is fifty thousand;
I have eight children
And a ninth . . .is due late summer.
Does that annoy you?

to the more lyrical, although even in such poems (the renowned '*ʿĀshiq min Filasṭīn*' ('Lover from Palestine'), for example) the central message of exile, return, and confrontation is still present:

Wherever, however you are,
Take me and bring colour back
To my face and body
And light to my heart and eye . . .
Take me as a verse from the book of my tragedy,
As a toy, a stone from my house,
Then our next generation
Will remember the way back home!

For Palestinian poets like Darwīsh, Samīḥ al-Qāsim (*b.* 1939), and Rāshīd Ḥusayn (*d.* 1977), confrontation with the realities of the Israeli state was an almost daily event. For others, the dimensions of exile – within the Arab world and beyond – contributed to a somewhat different voice, still challenging, yet more nostalgic. One such was Tawfīq Ṣāyigh (*d.* 1971), whose collected works provide numerous examples of the sorrow, frustration, and anger that accompanied the continuing loss of identity. There is also a quest for a resolution of the internal conflicts resulting from his profound Christian faith. The conclusion of a poem of very direct reference, '*Al-mawʿiẓah ʿalā al-jabal*' ('The Sermon on the Mount'), would seem to be linking these latter two concerns:

I know he will return,
And I await his return.
(Our cemetery is now on yonder hill.)
He will return to it, abandoning the crowds,

Seeking a headrest . . .
Maybe he will open his mouth
And I may hear: 'Blessed are . . .'

Ṣāyigh's Palestinian colleague, Jabrā Ibrāhīm Jabrā (*d.* 1994) – poet, novelist, critic, and translator – served an invaluable function by making available through translation to the littérateurs of the Arab world some of the most significant works of English writing – including the tragedies of Shakespeare, and sections from Sir James Frazer's *The Golden Bough*. As poets in the 1950s and 1960s sought fresh sources of inspiration through which to express their reactions to new political and social realities within the larger Arab world and their particular nations – a process that inevitably required an exploration of the complex relationship with the Middle East of the past – the ancient figures of Tammūz, Ishtār, and Adonis, and symbols of regeneration such as the Phoenix (*al-ʿAnqāʾ*) and Christ, became newly powerful symbols of both indigenous cultural values and modernity in poetic expression.

As has been noted earlier in this chapter, a primary role in the process of 'modernising' Arabic poetry involved changes in form: the move to free verse forms and to the prose poem. Building on earlier experiments, the true pioneers here are Nāzik al-Malāʾikah and Badr Shākir al-Sayyāb. Following the latter's tragically early death in 1964, a generation of his poet-contemporaries followed his example; many of them were members of a circle of poets and critics that gathered around the Beirut journal, *Shiʿr* (Poetry), founded by Yūsuf al-Khāl (*d.* 1987) in 1957. Al-Khāl's famous poem '*al-Biʾr al-mahjūrah*' ('The Deserted Well'), for example, provides a good illustration of the way in which myth was invoked in new poetic form and language to form a powerful contemporary message of rebirth:

If I could spread my forehead
On the sail of light,
If it were granted to me to remain,
Would Ulysses return, I wonder,
The Prodigal Son, the Lamb,
The Sinner stricken with blindness,
So that he might see the Way?

Al-Khāl's Lebanese contemporary, Khalīl Ḥāwī (*d.* 1982), shares many of his poetic qualities, but his vision is a much darker one. Ḥāwī, uses '*al- Baḥḥār wa-al-Darwīsh*' ('The Sailor and the Dervish') to explore the clashing myths of East and West: the former with its vision of the great achievements of Western culture which to Ḥāwī's dervish had left behind nothing but 'ash from time's refuse', while to the latter the magical orient remains a haven of story-tellers, 'lazy tavern, myths, prayer, and the languid shade of palm-trees'. And, if his poem '*al-Jisr*' ('The Bridge') holds out some hope for a future generation that 'will deftly cross the bridge in the morning . . .to a new East, my own ribs laid out for them as a firm crossing', by the 1960s the always questioning mood of Ḥāwī's poetic voice has assumed a yet grimmer tone. '*La'āẓar 1962*' ('Lazarus 1962'), a work often seen as an uncanny prediction of the events of 1967, begins:

> Deepen the hole, gravedigger,
> Deepen it to a depth with no limits
> Ranging beyond the orbit of the sun . . .

Al-Khāl's closest colleague among the '*Shiʿr* group' was ʿAlī Aḥmad Saʿīd (*b.* 1928), universally known by his pen-name, Adūnīs. Through both his own poetry and his extended writings on modernity and its relationship to the cultural heritage Adūnīs has come to personify the vanguard of change in the cultural life of the Arab world. Quite how far the process of change in poetic creativity has gone can be gauged by comparing the form-based definition of poetry (still the prevalent norm in the 1940s) as 'discourse in metre and rhyme' with Adūnīs's notion that it is 'a vision [*ru'yā*]' and thus 'a leap outside of established notions'. The very function of poetry, he suggests, is to use language in innovative ways; if the transformation of meaning leads to difficulty and indeed obscurity, that should not inhibit the enjoyment of the poem's reception. However, even critics of Adūnīs's views on poetry and language acknowledge that he is the true modern successor of the great classical creators of the poetic image, such as al-Buḥturī. One often cited example from the short poem, '*Waṭan*' ('Homeland'), will illustrate:

> To a father who died green like a cloud
> On his face a sail,
> I bow . . .

The sail image, an aspiration to movement, provides a linkage to al-Khāl's poem cited above, but the striking conjunction of verdure – youth and fertility – and cloud – with its promise of rain and rebirth, a potent symbol for both the pre-Islamic poet and al-Sayyāb – creates a powerful sense of unfulfilled potential.

The influence of Adūnīs's poetry and theoretical writing on younger generations of poets has been considerable, but the emulations of those less gifted than he and less aware of the poetic heritage have not met with critical or popular success. Meanwhile, many poets of Adūnīs's own generation – for example, ʿAbd al-wahhāb al-Bayātī, Aḥmad ʿAbd al-muʿṭī Ḥijāzī, and Nizār Qabbānī (*d.* 1998) – continued to forge their own paths through the tumultuous decades that witnessed war and destruction in Palestine, Lebanon, Iraq, and the Gulf, and the concomitant vogues and conflicts within the cultural sector. If these poets constituted some of the major figures in modern Arabic poetry, then a somewhat younger generation has come to the fore at a more recent stage; among a host of possible names we would cite Saʿdī Yūsuf (*b.* 1943) in Iraq, Maḥmūd Darwīsh (*b.* 1942) in Palestine (and in exile), Muḥammad ʿAfīfī Maṭar (*b.* 1935) and Amal Dunqul (*d.* 1982) in Egypt, Muḥammad al-Māghūṭ (*b.* 1934) in Syria, and Muḥammad Bannīs (*b.* 1948) in Morocco.

Arabic poetry today finds itself in a confrontation with another aspect of modernity, one that is having a considerable impact on all literary genres: the media. For, while television and cinema (not to mention videotapes and the Internet) have enormous potential for the dissemination of culture of all kinds, it is poetry of all literary genres that seems to be taking a back-seat in this confrontation between one medium that is highly visual and another that provokes and relies on the power of the imagination. Even so, it remains the case that, when tragedy strikes – as it continues to do in the war-torn region that is the Middle East – the resort of the Arabic-speaking people is to poetry, the public literary mode that best reflects their sense of self-identity, history, and cultural values.

CHAPTER 5

Belletristic prose and narrative

INTRODUCTION

A regular perusal of book review periodicals such as those published in London and New York provides confirmation of the fact that biography has become a popular, perhaps the most popular, genre among what is often termed the general reading public. The arts of inclusion and omission have ensured that the existence of several biographies of the same prominent personage and the widely divergent pictures that they manage to create provide ready corroboration of our increasing awareness of the linkages between biography and fictional genres. Most particularly, recent research on the fascinating genre of autobiography, that ultimate act of self-arrogation, has served to identify unequivocally the intimate connections between that literary activity and fiction. Varieties of writing in such topics as history, biography, travel, as well as fiction, all come to be viewed as types of 'narrative', thereby sharing a number of structural and aesthetic features but differentiated by the contract that they establish with the reader, that contract itself being subject to varieties of manipulation by the author.

This immensely creative variety of modes whereby generic categories have been and are being blurred serves as an excellent preliminary to this chapter in which we will explore literary works in Arabic which fit within the terms of reference identified by Leder and Kilpatrick: 'works principally in prose, in which there is a pervasive concern with artistic expression as well as the communication of information' (*Journal of Arabic Literature* 23/1 (March, 1992): 2). In the contemporary Arab world, fiction, and especially the short story, is clearly the most popular mode of literary expression, having supplanted poetry in that role at some point in the mid-twentieth century. By contrast, in earlier centuries the prose genres existed in the shadow of a poetic tradition which, as we saw in the previous chapter, was the most prevalent force in the cultural life of society. Thus, any retrospective study of the development of belletristic genres and of the precedents to the emergence of modern narrative in Arabic finds itself confronted with an earlier tradition of writing in which not only was the balance between poetic and non-poetic expression tilted firmly in favour of the former but also the criteria and societal function of the latter were substantially different from their contemporary manifestations. One of the more surprising consequences of that difference can be illustrated by the contrasting attitudes of Western and Middle Eastern cultures to the Arab world's greatest collection of narratives, the *Thousand and One [Arabian] Nights* (originally translated into French by Antoine Galland and published in 1704). Whereas the Western world has for two centuries avidly devoured, adapted, and bowdlerised the contents of this great store of tales, it is only relatively recently that it has become the object of interest among the critical community in the Arab world. The 'different criteria' to which I have just drawn attention will thus be studied in detail below, not least because I intend to include in this chapter a discussion of not only those works that have been incorporated into the traditional canon but also the varieties of narrative (such as the *Thousand and One Nights*) that have not.

QUESTIONS OF DEFINITION: *ADAB* AND BELLES-LETTRES

The origins and development of a corpus of belles-lettres in Arabic are directly linked to the concept of *adab*, a term that has undergone a number of transformations in meaning over the centuries. In modern times *adab* serves as the equivalent of the English word 'literature' (in its narrower sense), but in earlier centuries the term was used to describe a field that was considerably broader in scope. The original meaning of the verbal root from which the noun *adab* is derived implied inviting someone to a meal, and from that developed the notion of enriching the mind, particularly by training in the social norms of politeness. The ideas of intellectual nourishment, manners, and education were thus present from the outset and remained important features of the concept as it developed and expanded within the general framework of the Islamic sciences. The person involved in those activities was the *adīb* (pl. *udabāʾ*), a term which in modern times is usually translated by the French term 'littérateur' but which in earlier centuries identified a scholar and mentor whose areas of interest included such fields as grammar, poetry, eloquence, oratory, epistolary art, history, and moral philosophy, and whose social status was a reflection of the love of learning and urbanity that were characteristics of the intellectual community within which the *adīb* fulfilled his function.

As the *udabāʾ* continued to practise their role as pedagogues and arbiters of literary taste, the concept itself underwent a process of change. Many *adab* works were, of course, a faithful record of the kinds of verbal debate and erudite exchanges that would characterise the variety of occasions – soirées (*musāmarāt*), sessions (*majālis*), and conferences (*muḥāḍarāt*) – at which intellectuals and wits were gathered together. However, with the development of the status of the *adīb* as practitioner and teacher, *adab*, elevated language, and text came to be closely associated with each other to the exclusion of other types of creativity that did not match those criteria.

As the tradition of *adab* expanded and diversified in its functions as both instruction and entertainment, the majority of works preserved for posterity that were subsumed within its definitional borders took the form of compendia of information and anecdote on an astonishing array of subjects. Their themes ranged from the morally uplifting to the socially marginalised, and the organising principles that governed the ordering of their subject matter ranged from the surface logic of chronology and geography to the apparently random collection of information that had in common only the fact that it was exotic and curious. There were also genres – types of fictional narrative, tales of history and travel, and autobiographies – that clearly bear the stamp of an individual author, but, as Abdelfattah Kilito has shown in a most interesting study (*L'auteur et ses doubles*, Paris, 1985), we need, in the context of *adab* works, to adjust our concept of authorship and originality in order to incorporate within it the contributions which the compilers of these many compendia, the *udabāʾ*, made to the library of Arabic belles-lettres.

THE EARLIEST TEXTS IN PROSE

As we noted in the previous chapter on the Qurʾān, the revelations of God to Muḥammad included a number of narratives of different kinds. Particularly during the Meccan period, these included many rhyming passages replete with colourful imagery which, from the reactions of Muḥammad's listeners recorded as questions and comments in the text of the Qurʾān, were frequently confused with the discourse used by soothsayers and other popular preachers. We also noted that the recording of the revelations in textual form marks the beginning of a lengthy and elaborate process whereby such a huge amount of information could be preserved, sifted, and studied; among categories of text recorded in this way were some of the earliest samples of Arabic prose.

The oldest and most basic mode by which information was transferred is known in Arabic as the *khabar* (meaning 'a report', pl. *akhbār*). It is a distinct characteristic of *akhbār* from the earliest times that they announce clearly their status as narratives by recording in detail the series of sources through whose mediation the information has become available, working back from the present into the past and finally to the alleged point of origin. This structure (known in Arabic as the *isnād* (chain of authorities)) takes a form similar to the following: 'X told me that he had heard Y telling a story which he had heard from Z, to the effect that he had been present when the following occurrence happened . . .' The actual account that follows the chain of authorities is termed the *matn* (the report itself). The placing of such information regarding the narrative act and its sources at the beginning of the report is characteristic of a large number of narrative genres in Arabic.

A series of accounts which are, no doubt, as much a mirror of the intertribal rivalries of the early stages in the development of the Muslim community as they are of the spirit of the pre-Islamic era itself are the *akhbār* known collectively as the *ayyām al-ʿarab*, the narratives of the wars and battles in pre-Islamic times through which the fighting men of the clan avenged wrongs and resolved their conflicts with other tribes. The War of Basūs, for example, set in an atmosphere fraught with tribal rivalries and family tensions, began with the slaying of a prized she-camel and degenerated into a prolonged period of intertribal strife.

Another characteristic mode of expression from the 'period of ignorance' is the rhyming utterances of the soothsayers, with their terse phraseology and prolific use of parallelism and colourful imagery. This very particular style of composition and delivery was echoed not only, as noted above, in the Meccan period *sūrah*s of the Qurʾān but also in a variety of examples of composition from the early period of Islamic history: testaments (*waṣāyā*), proverbs, sermons, and orations (*khuṭab*). Along with the extant examples of early legal texts, treaties, and the beginnings of official chancery documents, they form part of the recorded legacy of the early period in the development of the Muslim community in the seventh century.

When the third caliph, ʿUthmān ibn ʿAffān, declared a single version of the revelations to Muḥammad to be the only authorised Qurʾān, he may have resolved the issue of the canonicity of the central source of divine guidance for the community, but there remained numerous other areas of conduct and belief on which the Qurʾān is silent. Faced with these many situations the community resorted to reports on what the Prophet had said and done. By the end of the seventh century it was clear that, in order to disambiguate the sources for the code of belief and behaviour for the Muslim community in a number of areas, it was necessary to make a record of the statements and actions of Muḥammad during his lifetime. The movement thus set in motion provides Arabic literature with two important types of text that were to have a significant influence on the development of a tradition of prose discourse: the *ḥadīth* – a report of a statement by Muḥammad on a particular issue or occasion – and the *sīrah* – the record of the Prophet's life.

With the collection of accounts concerning the life and conduct of the Prophet, the *isnād* segment of each account (*khabar*) described above now assumes an increased significance, in that it provides religious scholars with the evidence needed to check the authenticity of a report. The *ḥadīth* accounts themselves vary widely in both length and degree of elaboration. Among the lengthier ones are those which elaborate on references found in the Qurʾān. The slander *ḥadīth* (*ḥadīth al-ifk*), for example, provides considerable detail on the incident in which the Prophet's wife, ʿĀʾishah, the daughter of Abū Bakr (later to become the first caliph), is slandered. The account dwells on her own emotions as the events unfold and on the tensions that inevitably arise between Muḥammad and his loyal companion until the entire issue is resolved.

The process of compiling the vast collection of reports that make up the *ḥadīth* collections – the second major source on matters of doctrine and behaviour after the Qurʾān itself – occurred in several stages, each involving different principles. The first stage (at the end of the seventh century) involved collections of materials preserved by companions and followers of the Prophet (named *ṣuḥuf*, sing. *ṣaḥīfah*). By the mid-eighth century, collections were being organised by category (*muṣannaf*); the best-known example is *al-Muwaṭṭaʾ* by Mālik ibn Anas (*d.* 770), the founder of one of the four major 'schools' of Islamic law. However, this mode of organising such a large corpus of materials did not address the increasing problem regarding *ḥadīth* of dubious authenticity. By the end of the eighth century, scholars were beginning to pay closer attention to the issues raised by the *isnād*; the kind of compilations that they produced, arranged according to the names of the Prophet's companions who served as the source of the account, was termed *Musnad* (from the same verbal root as *isnād*). One of the most famous examples of this kind of *ḥadīth* collection is that of yet another founder of a school of law, Aḥmad ibn Ḥanbal (*d.* 855), whose *al-Musnad* consists of some 30,000 *ḥadīth*. By the ninth century, the science of *ḥadīth* scholarship had refined a critical process that permitted the compilation of the two most famous collections, those of al-Bukhārī (*d.* 870) and Muslim ibn al-Ḥajjāj (*d.* 875) who are referred to together as *al-Shaykhān* (the two chiefs). Their works, called *al-Jāmiʿ al-ṣaḥīḥ*, are collections of *ḥadīth* that conform with the criteria for the most authenticated reports, termed *ṣaḥīḥ* (authentic).

Alongside and linked to trends in *ḥadīth* scholarship, an elaborate tradition developed to provide accounts of Muḥammad's life. Under the title *al-sīrah al-nabawiyyah* (the biography of the Prophet) numerous works were compiled throughout the pre-modern period. The earliest compilation appears to be that of Wahb ibn Munabbih (*d.* 732), but the most famous work to appear under this title is that of Muḥammad ibn Isḥāq (*d.* 767), as edited by ibn Hishām (*d. c.* 833). The primary focus of the biographical compilations was Muḥammad's life, with accounts of his contacts with family, companions, and adversaries, descriptions of battles and negotiations, and citations of correspondence. The collections (and segments of larger works) comprise a mixture of anecdotes, battle narratives, miraculous tales, and poetry; there are elaborations on incidents depicted in the Qur'ān, tales concerning the lives of prophets mentioned in the Qur'ān (such as Adam and Moses), and discussion of the genealogy of Arabian tribes.

From the many types of expression in the early Islamic period that are mostly in prose, we have focused in particular on the categories of *ḥadīth* and *sīrah* because the textual features that they display and the methods developed to compile and analyse them can serve as models for other types of individual work and compilation that are subsumed within the framework of this chapter. Some of those text-types have already been mentioned in the course of our discussion: commentaries of the Qur'ān (*tafsīr*) and historical writings are two such. To them we can add that of *ṭabaqāt* (classes), works which placed categories of people – jurisconsults, grammarians, and poets, for example – into groups according to particular characteristics or qualities.

THE DEVELOPMENT OF *ADAB*

Beginnings

By the end of the seventh century, the sheer dimensions of the area contained within the Islamic dominions, comprising an increasingly elaborate mixture of races, religions, and languages, demanded that the central administration of the caliphate in Damascus develop and maintain a sizeable and diverse chancery system. As the personnel in those departments, the secretaries (*kuttāb*, sing. *kātib*) – in effect a newly emerging class of bureaucrats – grew in number and as their tastes became more urbane and cosmopolitan, the growing complexity of the administrative apparatus and the requirement of the caliph ʿAbd al-Malik (*d.* 705) that Arabic become the language of chancery documents made it necessary not only to establish terms of reference within which the system of communication would function but also to develop texts and methods through which the desired norms of discourse and matters of taste could be inculcated into trainees.

The administration of the caliph's authority centred on a number of departments (Arabic *dīwān*); the chancery was termed *dīwān al-rasāʾil* (the correspondence department). The word *rasāʾil* (sing. *risālah*) shares with the English word 'epistles' the notion of a text of enduring significance and even of instructional intent, and it is in the realm of the *risālah*, the process of offering advice, and most especially, advice on good government, that the first monuments of Arabic belles-lettres are to found. Once again, there is a link to the multi-cultural environment of the early eighth century and, in this case, the desire of ʿAbd al-Malik's son, the caliph Hishām (*d.* 743), to see the Muslim community's perspective expanded through the translation of works from other cultural traditions. The head of Hishām's chancery was Sālim Abū al-ʿAlāʾ, who may well have been the translator of an advice manual on secretarial conduct towards the ruler perhaps based on Aristotle's correspondence with Alexander; whether or not he is the translator, his status as a pioneer in the development of *adab* needs to be acknowledged.

The name more usually associated with the earliest manifestations of a school of chancery writing is one of Sālim Abū al-ʿAlā's pupils, ʿAbd al-ḥamīd 'al-Kātib' (*d.* 750), who wrote several epistles; in his Epistle to the Secretaries, he goes into considerable detail about the training and duties of the office. His advice is proffered in the most direct of styles:

Then perfect your calligraphy, for it is the ornament of your writings. Recite poetry, and get to know its themes and less familiar aspects; the glorious battle-days of the Arabs and Persians as well, their tales and sagas. Such things are enjoined on you so as to conform with your high-reaching aspirations. Do not overlook computation either, for that is the basic skill of the tax official.

ʿAbd al-ḥamīd's epistles reflect a complete familiarity with the Qurʾān, its tropes and structures, and his style, with its predilection for balanced phrases and parallelisms, is a product of a keen awareness of the styles of not only the Qurʾān but also the other early Arabic sources that we have just analysed.

ʿAbd al-ḥamīd's name is often linked to, and more frequently overshadowed by, that of his contemporary, the Persian *kātib* originally named Rūzbīh who adopted the Arabic name, ʿAbdallāh Ibn al-Muqaffaʿ (*d.* 757). Like ʿAbd al-ḥamīd, ibn al-Muqaffaʿ contributed a manual on the politenesses of court officialdom, the *Kitāb al-adab al-kabīr* (Major Work on Courtly Etiquette). One feature of his career that is not in doubt is his major role in the realm of translation, in this context, as elsewhere, a major conduit of cultural cross-fertilisation and change. Ibn al-Muqaffaʿ applied his bilingual skills and stylistic sensitivity to the process of translating a number of works from the Persian tradition, the most famous of which is a collection of animal fables of Indian provenance concerning wise government, the *Panjatantra*, which he rendered into Arabic as *Kalīlah wa-Dimnah* (from the Pahlavi title of the work). Named for two jackals who appear in the frame-story of the collection, the work consists of a series of tales that are evoked by Bidpai, a wise philosopher, in response to questions posed by a king named Dabshalim. The way in which each section begins and the transition mechanism to the tale itself is illustrated by this example:

King Dabshalim ordered Bidpai to tell the tale of someone who, having been successful in the achievement of his goals, finds himself immediately losing what he has acquired. The Philosopher responded that the process of achieving a laudable goal is frequently less difficult than that of retaining it. The person who is unable to retain what he has acquired is like the tortoise in the following tale . . .

With the move of the caliph's capital from Damascus to the East in 756, the new capital city of Baghdād began to fulfil its function as a focus of the caliph's authority, thus initiating the process that would eventually turn it into a cultural centre of unrivalled influence. Meanwhile, the two traditional centres of learning in Iraq – al-Kūfah and al-Baṣrah – witnessed the heyday of their prestige. Al-Khalīl ibn Aḥmad (*d.* 786) pioneered the study of prosody, music, and lexicography, and his eminent pupil, Sibawayh (*d.* 792), compiled a work of grammar which is regarded as the *locus classicus* of the Arabic language system and is still known and revered as simply *al-Kitāb* (The Book). The work of compilation and analysis was continued by philologists who conducted what we would now term fieldwork by travelling to the desert (*bādiyah*) and recording from bards and story-tellers the memorised tribal lore of generations. As a result of these continuing efforts by scholars such as Abū ʿAmr ibn al-ʿAlāʾ (*d.* 770), and his successors, including Abū ʿUbaydah (*d.* 824) and al-Aṣmaʿī (*d.* 831), a large corpus of textual materials on language and poetry became available that was to serve as the basis for investigations by future generations. Since most of the names that we have just mentioned were connected with the 'Baṣran school' which maintained a healthy rivalry with al-Kūfah, we should also mention among members of the 'Kūfan school' the eminent grammarian, al-Kisāʾī (*d.* 804), who in the view of the scholarly community of Baghdād succeeded in besting Sibawayh himself, and the philologists, ibn al-Sikkīt (*d.* 857) and Thaʿlab (*d.* 903).

Al-Jāḥiẓ

Essayist, anthologiser, stylist, wit, polemicist, al-Jāḥiẓ is acknowledged as the master of classical Arabic prose. Of African origin and trained in the intellectual centre of al-Baṣrah, he quickly became renowned for his polymathic interests. The sheer variety of al-Jāḥiẓ's works that have been preserved is a reflection of not only his innate intellectual gifts but also his time – one of religious and cultural controversies, of translation from the Greek and Persian cultural traditions, and of assimilation of new ideas.

In his writings al-Jāḥiẓ involved himself directly in the religious and political controversies of his times. In a number of essays he explores the relative merits of the prominent families of pre-Islamic Arabia in order to provide evidence for the legitimacy of the ʿAbbāsī caliphs against the rival claims of those who, disapproving of the policies of the caliph al-Maʾmūn, expressed their opposition in terms of continuing adherence to the claims of the Umawī house. However, while these works provide a sample of the extent to which al-Jāḥiẓ involved himself in the intellectual debates of his day, he is better remembered (and recorded) for his thoroughly innovative contributions to the compilation genre. His *Kitāb al-ḥayawān* (Book of Animals), for example, is, on the surface, a vast collection of poems and stories about animals, but such is al-Jāḥiẓ's encyclopaedic knowledge that he is unable to resist indulging in asides on all manner of topics; thus alongside stories about snakes, foxes, camels, birds, rats, and a notable tale about a dog suckling a baby during a plague, we find other information on philosophy and society and even a description of his teacher, al-Naẓẓām. The *Kitāb al-bayān wa-al- tabyīn* (Book of Clarity and Clear Expression) is another huge reference work that provides a similarly discursive compilation of anecdotes and information on ideals of expression, whose general tone can be gauged from the following extract:

> Like people themselves, discourse falls into categories: it can be either serious or trivial, beautiful and fine or vile and nasty, entertaining or the reverse. It's all Arabic . . . For me, there is no speech on earth as enjoyable and useful, as elegant and sweet to the ear, as closely linked to sound intellect, liberating for the tongue, and beneficial for improving diction as a course of prolonged listening to the way the eloquent, intelligent and learned Bedouin talk. (al-Maqdisi, *Taṭawwur*, pp. 171–72)

Al-Jāḥiẓ also compiled anthologies that address themselves to questions of proper behaviour and morals. By far the most famous in this category is *Kitāb al-bukhalā'* (The Book of Misers), misers being a category which, in a culture that regards hospitality and generosity as behavioural norms, clearly offers a heaven-sent opportunity for an exploration of very peculiar people and situations. Such proves to be the case, and the work is the greatest outlet for al-Jāḥiẓ's wit and exploitation of irony.

Among the most characteristic aspects of al-Jāḥiẓ's works are their style and structure, both of which exploit to the full the morphological potential of the Arabic language. The richness of his vocabulary and the complex periods that he weaved within the boundaries of Arabic syntax combine with his pedagogical bent, predilection for debate, and ready wit, to create a style that his successors acknowledged as both masterly and inimitable. The cut and thrust of debate, the sheer delight in anecdote, and the desire to learn and to pass on that learning, these are all primary features of the career and personality of this genius of Arabic literature.

VARIETIES OF *ADAB*

Manuals and compilations

While some later writers aspired to imitate aspects of al-Jāḥiẓ's genius, it was ibn Qutaybah whose works provided the principal model for emulation by the bureaucrat class. Ibn Qutaybah was the author of a number of works including important studies on *ḥadīth* and problematic passages in the Qur'ān, but he made use of his status as the virtual tutor to the Baghdād administrative class to produce a variety of works that aimed at bringing about the reconciliation of a number of different groups and schools. By contrast with the somewhat wayward genius of al-Jāḥiẓ, ibn Qutaybah's view of the role of *adab* was more practical, prosaic perhaps. Following the lead of ʿAbd al-ḥamīd and ibn al-Muqaffaʿ he wrote a manual for bureaucrats, the very title of which, *Adab al-kātib* (The Bureaucrat's Manual of Etiquette), confirms the now firmly established linkage between the administrative class and *adab*. His *Kitāb al-shiʿr wa-al-shuʿarā'* is an anthology of Arabic poetry arranged chronologically from Imru' al-Qays and Zuhayr ibn Abī Sulmā to Abū Nuwās and ʿAbbas ibn al-Aḥnaf. With his *Kitāb al-maʿārif* he made an important and early contribution to the writing of history, gathering into a single work stories from the Bible, pre-Islamic narratives from Arabia and Iran, and accounts of the first two centuries of the Muslim community. However, in the context of the development of a compilation tradition, ibn Qutaybah's most significant contribution is *ʿUyūn al-akhbār* (Springs of Information), a work divided into ten separate sections, the general organising principles of which serve as a precedent for a huge number of similar contributions to *adab* that were to appear in ensuing centuries. Each section is devoted to a different topic: war, nobility, eloquence, asceticism, and friendship, for example, and a final section on women. For each subject ibn Qutaybah collects a number of anecdotes and extracts of poetry, the purpose being, as he instructs his readers in a tone of pedagogic fervour in the Introduction, 'that you should insert it into your conversation in meetings and make it part of your style whenever you put pen to paper'.

With the different approaches and styles of al-Jāḥiẓ and ibn Qutaybah as two key points in an expanding field, the tradition of *adab* proceeded to diversify, adopting a variety of forms and subjects that were united in their continuing goal to instruct, enlighten, and entertain. Such products found a ready market among the côterie that would attend formal and informal soirées at the caliph's court or at the residences of wealthier notables and courtiers. Among the primary participants in the repartee on such occasions was the boon-companion (*nadīm*) whose task it was to maintain the good humour of the ruler; compilations of anecdotes and fables provided him with an appropriate and ready repertoire with which to amuse his distinguished audience. Musical entertainment would be provided by distinguished male and female vocalists; the musical talents and alluring qualities of singing girls (*qiyān*), for example, are the particular focus of an epistle of al-Jāḥiẓ. Within the environment of such salons the maintenance of proper modes of etiquette was the province of arbiters of taste who were termed 'refined' (*ẓurafā'*, sing. *ẓarīf*). The above-mentioned *Kitāb al-aghānī* of al-Iṣfahānī is a primary source for accounts of the behaviour of rulers and their confidants on such occasions, while the *Kitāb al-muwashshā* (The Book of Brocade) of al-Washshā' (*d.* 936) provides a virtual manual of *ẓarīf* etiquette.

The contexts for the sharing and propagation of the principles and products of *adab* were *majālis* – literally 'sessions' but essentially 'salons' of the cultured élite, and *amālī* (the plural of *imlā'*, 'dictation'), a term that gives us an important insight into the way in which students of this field (and others) would be required to 'read' texts dictated to them by their masters. Both these words make their way into the titles of a number of compilations; one of the most famous of the former category is *al-Majālis* of Thaʿlab (*d.* 904), the famous grammarian of al-Kūfah, and of the latter, *al-Amālī* of al-Qālī (*d.* 967), a philologist who settled in Spain after receiving his education in Baghdād.

The model that had been established by ibn Qutaybah with *ʿUyūn al-akhbār* – a collection of information and anecdote organised by topic – was adapted by the great Cordoban poet and littérateur, ibn ʿAbd Rabbihi (*d.* 934), in his *al-ʿIqd al-farīd* (The Peerless Necklace). Divided into twenty-five sections entitled 'precious stones', it provides examples of various types of literary expression, poetry (including that of the compiler, for which this collection is a major source) and proverbs, as well as discussions of prosody and other literary topics. It still retains its status as one of Arabic's most favoured literary thesauri.

As literary salons (*majālis*) began to fashion their own modes of disputation and aesthetic vogues, so did the collections of texts that interested and diverted them become more elaborate and fanciful. Over the centuries this literary genre – for that is what these compilations really are – went through the normal processes of generic transformation that reflected the tastes and ideologies of the era in question. Compilations differ, for example, in the critical posture of the compiler towards the arrangement of his materials and in the categories of choice: among the latter are textual mode (prose and/or poetry), length of segment, and the question of the inclusion of the contemporary along with the old. A selection of famous examples of *adab* encyclopaedias might include: *Kitāb al-imtāʿ wa-al-muʾānasah* (Book of Enjoyment and Bonhomie) by Abū Ḥayyān al-Tawḥīdī (*d.* 1008), a collection of erudite and often witty conversations; *Tamthīl al-muḥāḍarah* (Exemplary Discussion) and *Laṭāʾif al-maʿārif* (Book of Wonderful Information) by al-Thaʿālibī (*d.* 1038); and *Rabīʿ al-abrār* (Springtime of the Innocent) of al-Zamakhsharī (*d.* 1143), a large and thematically organised collection of short quotations in both prose and poetry. As the tastes of the court audience for such modes of instruction and entertainment developed, this predilection for the curious and diverting extended in a number of directions. One such was still further into the realm of interesting and exotic stories. Al-Jahshiyārī (*d.* 942) is reported by ibn al-Nadīm (the compiler of the catalogue of works known as *al-Fihrist*) to have gathered a huge and carefully organised collection of tales from Arabic, Persian, Indian, and Greek sources, but regrettably the work has not come down to us. The titles of later collections that were preserved continue to reflect many of the same organising principles and intended audience as those we have already discussed: al-Ibshīhī's (*d. c.* 1446) manual for rulers, for example, *Al-Mustaṭraf fī kull fann mustaẓraf* (The Ultimate on Every Refined Art), is a diffuse collection of short, improving narratives, while his contemporary, ibn Arabshāh (*d.* 1450) – biographer of Tīmūr Lang (Tamerlaine) – produces a collection of fables, *Fākihat al-khulafāʾ wa-mufākahat al-ẓurafāʾ* (Fruit of Caliphs and Humour of the Refined), that incorporates a good deal of material drawn from Persian sources. A particularly favoured topic is that of amazing information (*ʿajāʾib*), 'tall tales' of the exotic and unbelievable that were presumably intended to amaze and even terrify, and, in so doing, to underscore for the audience the pleasing security of its own existence.

The changes in generic purposes and audience implicit in these titles and the works that they represent is also reflected in language and style. By the tenth century writers had access not only to a number of grammatical works that codified the elaborate system of morphology and syntax of Arabic but also to the lists of lexicographers who had begun the enormous process of recording its wonderfully diverse vocabulary. The application of this expanding branch of knowledge to the craft of *kātib*, illustrated by the manual genre of which ibn Qutaybah's *Adab al-kātib* is a fine example, was elaborated in a number of works, of which we would cite *Adab al-kuttāb* by Abū Bakr al-Ṣūlī (*d.* 948?) and *Kitāb ṣināʿat al-kitābah* (Book on the Craft of Writing) by Qudāmah ibn Jaʿfar (*d.* 938). However, as the ties that had linked many early pioneers of artistic prose writing (ʿAbd al-ḥamīd and ibn Qutaybah, for example) to the principles and practices of the religious sciences, and particularly *ḥadīth* scholarship, were gradually loosened, the epistolary school of writing was increasingly influenced by the tastes espoused by the *habitués* of literary salons. Stylistic priorities shifted away from a primary concern with the details of linguistic correctness and stylistic clarity towards a quest for the decorative and refined. The most famous literary salon of the era, that of ibn ʿAbbād (*d.* 995), a minister of the Buwayhī rulers who is renowned as 'al-Ṣāḥib' (the master), provides an excellent illustration of not only the process of change but also of the turbulent cultural background that lay behind it.

Ibn ʿAbbād's teacher and predecessor as minister in Rayy (near Tehran) was Abū al-Faḍl ibn al-ʿAmīd, whom renowned writers such as al-Thaʿālibī and the historian, Miskawayh (*d.* 1030) accord a primary role in leading the stylistic tastes of the school of bureaucratic prose-writing (dubbed *inshāʾ dīwānī* or 'chancery-composition') towards a greater emphasis on embellishment and elaboration, availing itself of the artifices of *sajʿ*, the tropes of *badīʿ*, and citations of poetry and proverbs. Such features are difficult, if not impossible, to illustrate in translation, but the following extract (from a letter of ibn al-ʿAmīd) does at least illustrate the parallelisms, repetitions, and contrasts:

> As I write to you, I waver between hope for you and despair of you, between reaching out to you and avoiding you. Your previous esteem is self-evident, your former service is clearly established. The least of the two would demand careful attention and require both protection and concern, but to them you now append a matter of malice and betrayal and attach dissension and revolt. The least part of it subverts your deeds and wipes out everything attributed to you.

At different periods al-Ṣāḥib ibn ʿAbbād managed to attract to his côterie in Rayy many illustrious figures: the grammarian ibn Fāris (*d.* 1005), the critic al-Qāḍī al-Jurjānī (*d.* 1001), and, among significant contributors to the development of artistic prose, Abū Bakr al-Khwārizmī (*d.* 993), Badīʿ al-zamān al-Hamadhānī (*d.* 1008) whose pioneering role in the development of the *maqāmah* genre we will explore below, and Abū Ḥayyān al-Tawḥīdī (*d.* 1023).

Al-Ṣāḥib ibn ʿAbbād was a major scholar and writer in his own right; in addition to works on theology, history, and philology, he published works of criticism (a review of the alleged plagiarisms of the poet al-Mutanabbī, for example) and a collection of poetry. However, it is his collected letters that best illustrate his explorations of a more elaborate mode of expression. The controversy provoked by his adoption of this style was intense, and we possess samples of nasty exchanges between him and both Miskawayh and Abū Bakr al-Khwārizmī, but the most vivid (if not the most accurate) picture of his personality comes to us from the pen of one of Arabic's most illustrious prose writers, Abū Ḥayyān al-Tawḥīdī.

Al-Tawḥīdī is regarded by many critics as the *adīb* whose works most closely approximate the virtuosity of al-Jāḥiẓ himself. To the tradition of *adab* compendia he contributed not only *Kitāb al-imtāʿ wa-al-muʾānasah*, but also *al- Baṣāʾir wa-al-dhakhāʾir* (Insights and Treasures), a collection of anecdotes and proverbs, and *al-Muqābasāt* (Book of Comments), which consists of 106 short discussions of a philosophical, grammatical, and literary nature of which the following is a selection: 'concerning the author's experience with certain doctors', 'useful anecdotes concerning higher philosophy', 'statements on asceticism and shunning the world', and 'on friends, true friendship, the philosophy of love and passion, and definitions of sound philosophy'.

Al-Tawḥīdī had been invited to Rayy by al-Ṣāḥib, but his high hopes of being welcomed at the salon and library as an *adīb* were disappointed; instead he found himself assigned the lowly task of copyist. By about 980, al-Tawḥīdī's pride had been battered enough, and he returned to Baghdād. The result of his rancour at the treatment he had received is *Kitāb mathālib al-wazīrayn*, also known as *Akhlāq al-wazīrayn* (Book on the Foibles of the Two Ministers), the people in question being Abū al-fatḥ ibn al-ʿAmīd and al-Ṣāḥib ibn ʿAbbād. The following extract gives an idea of both tone and content:

> Didn't ibn al-ʿAmīd hear what al-Ṣāḥib had to say about him?
>
> Oh yes, indeed! Abū al-fatḥ would retort that al-Ṣāḥib's rhyming prose showed signs of dissipation and loose living, while his script suggested someone who was paralysed or had the pox. Whenever he shouted, it sounded as though he was gambling in a pub. I've never laid eyes on him without thinking that some idiot's just given him some 'medicine'. He's stupid by nature, but there's some good in him too. Then there are days when his stupidity gets out of control. At that point all his goodness disappears, and decent, respectable and cultured people find themselves subjected to fits of jealousy, arrogance, and boorish behaviour.

With the rise of local dynasties and cultural centres such as that one at Rayy – each one requiring its own bureaucracy – those versed in the practicalities of the epistolographer's art and the various fields of *adab* were presented with a wealth of opportunities for patronage. Abū Bakr al-Khwārizmī, for example, who is credited with the further enhancement of the ornate style of prose, found service at the illustrious court of Sayf al-dawlah al-Ḥamdānī in Aleppo where his colleagues included the poets al-Mutanabbī and Abū Firās and the philosopher, al-Fārābī.

A century or so later, the court of Ṣalāḥ al-dīn provided another conducive environment for a number of eminent writers whose epistles are regarded as marking the acme of the *inshāʾ dīwānī* style. The most illustrious of these writers was al-Qāḍī al-Fāḍil (*d.* 1200), who served as minister and spokesman for Ṣalāḥ al-dīn. One of al-Qāḍī al-Fāḍil's subordinates was an equally famous writer, ʿImād al-dīn al-Iṣfahānī (*d.* 1201), whose account of Ṣalāḥ al-dīn's career, entitled *al-Barq al-Shāmī* (The Lightning of Syria), is regarded as the authoritative source and at the same time a model of *inshāʾ*.

Ensuing centuries witnessed the continued production of literary compendia that included instructions to writers along with varieties of other information and anecdote. Of these the most frequently cited are two compendia with quite different focuses: *Nihāyat al-arab fī funūn al-adab* (The Goal of Desire Concerning the Categories of *Adab*) by al-Nuwayrī (*d.* 1332), which resembles many of the earlier models cited above by including information on the heavens, mankind, animals, and plants, as well as a history of the Arabs up to his own time; and *Ṣubḥ al-aʿshā fī ṣināʿat al-inshāʾ* (Morning for the Night-blind Regarding the Craft of Secretarial Style) by al-Qalqashandī (*d.* 1418), a detailed survey of every aspect of the bureaucratic function, from filing techniques and types of ink, to matters of political acumen, grammar, geography, and history. The wide variety of anthologies that continued to appear is an apt reflection of the tastes and needs of a class whose interests were broad and open. One of the most colourful illustrations of such trends is provided by *Maṭāliʿ al-budūr fī manāzil al-surūr* (Rising of Full Moons in/regarding the Abodes of Delights) by al-Ghuzūlī (*d.* 1412), an anthology describing all kinds of worldly delight that is arranged in the form of a house; sections on site, neighbours, doors, gardens, food, and hygiene all evoke pertinent selections of poetry and anecdote.

Monographic works

The compilations of information and anecdote that we have just discussed were organised around topics and themes that were also the subject of monographic works; the earliest compilations were, one must assume, collected from already existing written or oral repertoires on individual topics. As we have already noted, al-Jāḥiẓ compiled a large collection of poetry and anecdote about animals in his *Kitāb al-ḥayawān*. He also wrote individual works on a variety of topics, from misers and singing slave-girls to envy and rhetoric. His successors in *adab* writing penned works on such categories as the blind and women. Al-Khaṭīb al-Baghdādī (*d.* 1071), an illustrious *adīb*, replicated al-Jāḥiẓ by composing a work on misers, and to him we owe a further addition to this list of fascinating social types, gate-crashers. This particular avocation links this work to a further subgenre that focuses on varieties of confidence tricks (*ḥiyal*). There is a substantial corpus of works on the organisations and activities of beggars – 'the mendicant's code' (*adab al-kudyah*). One such work is *al-Mukhtār fī kashf al-asrār wa-hatk al-astār* (Choicest Items Regarding the Uncovering of Secrets and Rending of Veils) composed by the widely travelled Damascene scholar, al-Jawbarī (thirteenth century); it takes the lid off, as it were, the repertoire of ruses practised on the public by rogues.

A theme that lent itself very well to the predilections of anecdote compilers for tales that would contain the maximum amount of incident and surprise was 'escape from hardship' (*al-faraj baʿd al-shiddah*). Among early works under this title are those of al-Madā'inī (*d.* 849) and ibn Abī al-Dunyā (*d.* 894), but the most famous collection is that of the judge, Abū al-Ḥusayn al-Tanūkhī (*d.* 994). The originality of the presentation of the anecdotes (and, some scholars maintain, of their contents as well) makes of this work a frequent point of reference in the development of imaginative narratives in Arabic. Here is a brief anecdote as an example:

> The judge Abū al-Ḥusayn mentioned in his book and said: ʿUmar ibn Hubayrah fell on really bad times. One day his condition made him feel so indolent, downcast, and aggravated that his family and retinue suggested that he ride over and see the caliph. If the caliph sees the way you are, they said, he might do something nice for you; or, if he asks you how you are, you can tell him. So ʿUmar rode over and went in to see [the Umawī caliph] Yazīd ibn ʿAbd al-Malik. After standing there for an hour, he addressed the caliph. Yazīd looked at him and noticed that ʿUmar seemed really different, and it disturbed him. 'Do you need to leave the room?' he asked. 'No', ʿUmar replied. 'Something's the matter', the caliph said. 'Something's hurting me between my shoulders', he said, 'but I don't know what it is'. 'Look and see!' the caliph ordered. They looked and found a scorpion between his shoulders that had bitten him several times. Before he left, he had been appointed governor of Iraq. Thereafter Yazīd would talk about his fortitude and high-mindedness. (Baghdād, 1955, p. 229).

There is, of course, no shortage of other themes that can be utilised to illustrate what is essentially an organisational spectrum: from compilations of anecdote and poetry arranged with the deliberate intent of providing variety, to others that are focused on a particular topic, and to monographic works that are the topic of this section. From among them we will focus on the theme of love, one that introduces a variety of its own in that we may subsume under the general heading works that range from explorations of divine love – most especially within the context of Ṣūfī writings – to a variety of compilations and studies on the delights and/or perils of profane love, to the most explicit of sex manuals.

In his '*Risālah fī al-ʿishq*' (Epistle on Passion), ibn Sīnā (*d.* 1037) discusses the intellect and passion as two qualities that are intrinsic to 'the necessary existent' (*wājib al-wujūd*). For Ṣūfīs, the concept of love, the agonies and delights that it engenders, and, above all, martyrdom in its worthy cause – all of them prominent themes in earlier love poetry – become symbols of a continuing struggle whereby the believer endeavours to mortify the demands of the flesh in a quest for transcendent experience. The title of one of the most prominent anthologies on the subject, in its mystical and more earthly manifestations, illustrates the same theme: *Maṣāriʿ al-ʿushshāq* (Demises of Lovers) by Jaʿfar al-Sarrāj (*d.* 1106), later expanded by al-Biqāʿī (*d.* 1480) as *Aswāq al-ashwāq fī maṣāriʿ al-ʿushshāq* (Markets of Desires Concerning Demises of Lovers).

Turning to the treatment of love in its more secular aspects, we still encounter in many works a concern with adherence to dictates elicited from the texts of the Qurʾān and *ḥadīth*; the concept of desire is regularly linked with the lower self (as opposed to the intellect) which, in the phrase from *Sūrat Yūsuf* (12:53) in the Qurʾān, 'encourages evil'. Such an attitude emerges clearly in the famous work, *Dhamm al-hawā* (Condemnation of Passion), an anthology compiled by ibn al-Jawzī (*d.* 1200), a Baghdādī preacher who resorts to *ḥadīth* and other sources in warning believers against the perils of passionate love. What might be termed the 'Summa' among such works is *Rawḍat al- muḥibbīn wa-nuzhat al-mushtāqīn* (Meadow of Lovers and Diversion of the Infatuated) by ibn Qayyim al-Jawziyyah (*d.* 1350). A major and original contribution to *adab* writing, this work explores the essence of desire and passion in the context of giving advice to a young man faced with the conflict between the joys of love and the ever-present perils of sin. He is scandalised by the approach adopted in what is the most individual and popular work on profane love in Arabic literature, *Ṭawq al-ḥamāmah* (The Dove's Neckring), by the renowned Andalusian jurisprudent and poet, ibn Ḥazm (*d.* 1064). The following extracts replicate to a degree the unusually intimate, indeed confidential, narrative tone that ibn Ḥazm adopts in this charming work:

> Love has characteristics which are easily recognised by intelligent people . . . Lovers will always rush to the spot where their beloved is to be found and make

a point of sitting as close as possible; they will drop all other work that might take them away and scoff at any weighty matter that might cause them to leave . . .

Weeping is another manifestation of love, although in this aspect people are quite different. Some, for example, weep copious tears, whereas others remain dry-eyed. I am among the latter, because I chew frankincense for my heart condition . . .

On a personal note, when I was young, I fell in love with a blonde, and ever since I haven't liked brunettes even though they may have been paragons of beauty.

It was qualities like these that made *Ṭawq al-ḥamāmah* so appealing to European tastes and ensured that it would be translated into a number of languages. Other sorts of appeal were, no doubt, at work when it came to the task of translating *al-Rawḍ al-ʿāṭir fī nuzhat al-khāṭir* (The Perfumed Garden for the Delight of the Heart), a sex manual written by Shaykh al-Nafzāwī (fifteenth century) at the behest of Muḥammad al-Zawāwī, the *wazīr* of Tunis (who is addressed at the beginning of many chapters). In the English-speaking world, the work became renowned through the abiding interest that Sir Richard Burton had in such materials. Burton seems to have overlooked an earlier survey of sexual practices by another Tunisian, al-Tifāshī (*d.* 1253), with the provocative title, *Nuzhat al-albāb fī-mā lā yūjad fī kitāb* (Delight of Hearts Concerning What Will Never Be Found in a Book), perhaps because it had not been translated at that time, but more likely because Victorian sensibilities would have fought shy – at least in the public domain – of a work that devotes so much attention to homosexual practices.

Adab *and the writing of history and geography*

As our discussion thus far has endeavoured to show, the term *adab* was used over a period of many centuries not only to identify the aesthetic norms of an intellectual élite, but also to designate the corpus of works that were the result of such activities. In turning to a consideration of some of those topics – history and geography in particular – within the context of *adab*, we confront an interestingly varied cluster of text-types. As the intellectual community's appetite for information and enlightenment increased, the fields of history and geography (and their subgenres) are often blended together, and their areas of focus can be seen as operating along a single, broad-scaled continuum.

Some of the types of early writing in prose that we examined above

– the battle accounts of pre-Islamic times (the *ayyām al-ʿarab*) and of Muḥammad's lifetime (the *maghāzī*) and the biography of Muḥammad himself – are, needless to say, historical data organised according to particular principles; they constitute some of the earliest examples of the generic requirements that characterise a good deal of historical writing in Arabic. That in turn led to the gathering of data on a variety of individuals, tribes, and categories. Such data were organised into 'classes' (*ṭabaqāt*) for easy reference, and the *ṭabaqāt* collections that resulted – on physicians, jurisconsults, poets, theologians, grammarians, and Ṣūfīs, to name just a few of the categories – provided a wealth of biographical information. Alongside this category of historical research there developed another that was concerned with the linkage of events to chronology. The current Arabic word for history, *tārīkh*, is a slight adaptation of the gerund form *taʾrīkh* which literally means 'the assignment of a date, the process of dating'.

In our brief assessment above of ibn Qutaybah's role as a compiler of manuals for bureaucrats, we have already drawn attention to his *Kitāb al-maʿārif* (Book of Knowledge), an early essay in historical writing that, with its readership clearly in mind, draws on a variety of sources. Among his contemporaries three names stand out for their contributions to the development of historical writing. The first is al-Balādhurī (*d.* 892), whose *Kitāb ansāb al-ashrāf* (Book on the Genealogies of the Noble) expands on previous biographical collections by organising information around the tribes and families of important figures within the Muslim community, with a particular concentration on the caliphs of the Umawī family. In his *Kitāb futūḥ al-buldān* (Book on the Conquests of Countries) he documents the processes of conquest and settlement within each province, thus answering an urgent need of the administrators of the widespread Muslim community. A second writer is al-Yaʿqūbī (*d. c.* 900), whose travels over a wide area permitted him to record a good deal of local and often original information. His *Tārīkh* (History) deals first with pre-Islamic cultures, such as those of Israel, India, Greece, and Africa, before turning to an account of the early centuries of Islam up to his own time. Most prominent of these three figures, however, is al-Ṭabarī (*d.* 923), whose *Kitāb taʾrīkh al-rusul wa-al-mulūk* (Book of History of Prophets and Kings) is the great monument of Arabic historical writing and, because of its very comprehensiveness, a transition point to new developments in historical writing. The great value of his work lies in the fact that, as the compiler of a major commentary (*tafsīr*) on the Qurʾān, he adopted the same standards of authentification of sources in his work of history. The information is laid out in annalistic form, the primary organising principle being the chronology created by the reigns of the caliphs. As several writers have observed, his work fails to represent the full breadth of the Islamic dominions either in his survey of the pre-Islamic period or in his coverage of his own times; concentration is on the Eastern part with which he is most familiar, while al-Andalus gets particularly short shrift. Even so, it provided the Muslim community with a comprehensive and chronologically organised account of its history, compiled in accordance with the strictest standards of authentification demanded by Qur'ān and *ḥadīth* scholarship.

A significant change in Arabic historical writing is brought about by al-Masʿūdī (*d.* 956), who combines historical and geographical information into a unified narrative framework (a feature which, as has been noted by several scholars, may reflect an awareness of the writings of Greek historians such as Herodotus). Even more widely travelled than his predecessor and fellow-Shīʿite, al-Yaʿqūbī, al-Masʿūdī's peregrinations took him from Persia to the borders of China, the Red Sea, Ceylon, and Palestine. The enormous work that he compiled under the title *Akhbār al-zamān* (Accounts of Time) has not come down to us, but a digest published under the colourful title *Murūj al-dhahab wa-maʿādin al-jawāhir* (Golden Meadows and Jewellery Mines) immediately became a major and popular source; the great historian of the fourteenth century, ibn Khaldūn, terms al-Masʿūdī *imām li-al-mu'arrikhīn* (a model for historians). Al-Masʿūdī begins his work with a survey of geographical phenomena – the creation of the world and a description of the earth – before surveying the ancient history of the peoples subsumed within the *dār al-Islām* and the history of Islam up to the year 947. What contributes to the originality of this work is not only the way in which it incorporates a personal knowledge of many regions and peoples into a continuous narrative but also the attractive and lively style in which the author couches his account.

In subsequent centuries the writing of universal histories tended to reflect the variety of organising principles adopted by these pioneers, although the majority of writers followed the model of al-Yaʿqūbī and, in particular, al-Masʿūdī by incorporating geographical information in their works. Prominent among such works were *Tajārib al-umam* (The Experiences of Peoples) by Miskawayh (*d.* 1030), *Al-Muntaẓam* (The Well-arranged) by ibn al-Jawzī (*d.* 1200), *al- Kāmil fī al-ta'rīkh* (The Complete Work on History) by ʿIzz al-dīn ibn al-Athīr (*d.* 1232 – the brother of the literary critic, Ḍiyā' al-dīn), and *Al-Bidāyah wa-al-nihāyah* (The Beginning and End) by ibn Kathīr (*d.* 1373), the organising principles of which, not to mention their aspirations to universal coverage, are evidenced by their very titles. The *Kitāb al-ʿibar wa-dīwān al-mubtadaʾ wa-al- khabar fī ayyām al-ʿArab wa-al-ʿAjam wa-al-Barbar* (Book of Lessons, the Record of Subject and Predicate on the Times of Arabs, Non-Arabs, and Berbers) by ibn Khaldūn (*d.* 1406) is similarly universal in its approach, but a number of features differentiate it from the other works that we have just listed. In the first place, ibn Khaldūn was born in Tunis and spent much of his life at courts in North Africa and al-Andalus; the knowledge that he acquired from those experiences is reflected in the comprehensive coverage of Western Islam that he provides. However, what has made him the most famous historian to have written in Arabic is that he prefaced his work with an introduction (*Muqaddimah*) in which he elaborated a theory of cyclic civilisational change involving the relationship between the peoples of the desert and the settled regions. He suggests that, through a process of softening that is the natural product of a sedentary and urban existence, the desert tribes lose their fierce, warrior-like qualities and are then prey to incursions from other tribes who still possess the qualities that they themselves have lost. The civilising process itself instigates dynastic decline, and so the cycle continues.

As the focus of political power moved from a model based on a single centre of caliphal authority in Baghdād to one with a number of widely scattered centres of authority – Cordoba, Cairo, Aleppo, Qayrawān, to name just a few – so did the writing of histories with a regional focus increase and diversify. The significance of Mecca and Medina – the two holiest sites in Islam – had ensured that they would be early topics of city-histories; one such is *Taʾrīkh Makkah* (History of Mecca) by ibn al-Azraq (*d.* 834). The prominence of Baghdād is reflected in the *Kitāb Baghdād* (Book on Baghdād) by ibn Abī Ṭāhir Ṭayfūr (*d.* 893), a strangely anonymous figure given the frequency with which his writings are cited (he is, for example, a major source for al-Ṭabarī).

Histories devoted to regions east and west abound: of Yemen by al-Ḥamdānī (*d.* 945) and al-Ḥakamī (*d.* 1175); of the Maghrib by ibn ʿAbd al-ḥakam (*d.* 870), ibn Raqīq al-Qayrawānī (fl. early eleventh century), and ibn Saʿīd (*d.* 1286). The case of al-Andalus is an interesting one, in that, while its intelligentsia showed an abiding interest in events and trends in 'al-Mashriq' (the East), writings literary and otherwise make clear that there was also a tremendous sense of local pride in the achievements of Andalusian culture. Many prominent scholars contributed to recording the history of the region: ibn Ḥabīb (*d.* 853), the theologian-poet ibn Ḥazm (*d.* 1063), and Lisān al-dīn ibn al-Khaṭīb (*d.* 1374). At a considerably later date, al-Maqqarī (*d.* 1631) of Tlemcen, looks back over the illustrious history of al-Andalus in a work written long after the fall of Granada in 1492 which carries the colourful and even nostalgic title, *Nafḥ al-ṭīb min ghuṣn al-Andalus al-raṭīb* (Waft of Fragrance from al-Andalus's Luscious Branch). The strategic importance of Egypt has always ensured that its history would be eventful, and two of its later historians were on hand to record momentous events: ibn ʿIyās (*d.* 1523) records in his *Badāʾiʿ al-zuhūr fī waqāʾiʿ al-duhūr* (The Choicest Blooms Concerning the Incidence of Dooms) the events surrounding the fall of Cairo to the Ottoman armies under Sultan Selim 'the Grim', and in 1798 ʿAbd al-raḥmān al-Jabartī (*d.* 1822) records in *ʿAjāʾib al-āthār fī al-tarājim wa-al-akhbār* (Remarkable Reports on Biography and History) his reactions to the arrival in Egypt of French forces under Napoleon. At any earlier date, al-Maqrīzī (*d.* 1441), who held the post of *muḥtasib* in Mamlūk Cairo and was thus responsible for public morality, introduces a good deal of economic insight into his works, based no doubt on his own practical experience. Most famous among them is *al-Mawāʿiẓ wa-al-iʿtibār fī dhikr al-khiṭaṭ wa-al-āthār* (Lessons to be Drawn from a Mention of Districts and Remains), which gives increased emphasis to the topographical aspect of city-history. This *khiṭaṭ* genre, which provides a detailed survey of streets, buildings and their histories, was expanded and updated in the nineteenth century by ʿAlī Mubārak (*d.* 1893) in his *Al-Khiṭaṭ al-Tawfīqiyyah al-jadīdah* (Modern Districts of Cairo [during the Reign of the Khedive Tawfīq]).

The continuing interest in genealogy ensured that the compilation of biographical records would remain a prominent part of historical scholarship. An important work in this category is *Taʾrīkh Baghdād* (The History of Baghdād) by al-Khaṭīb al-Baghdādī (1071), in that, in addition to supplying topographical detail on the city, he provided biographies of prominent citizens arranged in alphabetical order. Al-Khaṭīb's compilation provided a model for other city-based works, such as the enormous *Taʾrīkh madīnat Dimashq* (A History of the City of Damascus) of ibn ʿAsākir (*d.* 1175) and *al-Iḥāṭah fī akhbār Gharnaṭah* (Comprehensive Book on the History of Granada) by ibn al-Khaṭīb. The principles on which these more locally focused works were based were expanded in major collections of biographical data that were collected by Yāqūt (*d.* 1229) in his *Irshād al-arīb* (Guidance for the Intelligent) and, most notably, by ibn Khallikān (*d.* 1282), whose biographical dictionary, *Kitāb wafayāt al-aʿyān* (Book on the Deaths of Prominent People), was expanded by al-Ṣafadī (*d.* 1362) in a work entitled *al-Wāfī bi-al-Wafayāt* (The Complement to the 'Deaths'). While the bulk of the information provided in these works is biographical, the compilers occasionally include autobiographical accounts which tend to record incidents that reflect well on the subject involved rather than provide insights into aspects of personality. However, some individual works do stand out because of the glimpses they afford of the personae of their authors. In *Al-Munqidh min al-ḍalāl* (The Deliverer from the Stray Path) al-Ghazālī looks back in his latter years and surveys the circumstances of his life, and Usāmah ibn Munqidh (*d.* 1189) uses his *Kitāb al-iʿtibār* (Book of Example) to recount the adventures of a fighter against the Crusaders but is equally anxious to share with his readers the pleasures of hunting and literature along with a wealth of anecdote about himself and others.

While the Muslim community was clearly in need of geographical works that would describe the territories brought within the Islamic dominions by the Muslim conquests, there was also a need for other works of a more directly practical nature. Messengers and administrators had to travel on business from the centres of authority to the provinces and from one province to another, frequently traversing unknown terrain in the process. Among the first to respond to these needs was ibn Khurradādhbih (*d. c.* 885), apparently an official in the postal service, whose *Kitāb al-masālik wa-al-mamālik* (Book of Routes and Realms) is from one point of view a listing of itineraries, but the expectations of *adab* are also met through the inclusion of other types of information, including poetry. Among other works of what we might term descriptive geography were the *Kitāb al-buldān* of the widely travelled al-Yaʿqūbī (whose contribution to historical writing was mentioned above), the *Kitāb al-masālik wa-al-mamālik* of ibn Ḥawqal (*d. c.* 990) – itself a continuation of an earlier work of al-Iṣṭakhrī (*d.* 961) – and *Aḥsan al-taqāsīm fī maʿrifat al-aqālīm* (The Best Divisions for Knowing the Regions) by al-Muqaddasī (*d. c.* 1000), a work which is generally agreed to point to the future for both the rigour of its method and the elegance of its style. A century later, al-Idrīsī (*d.* 1165) composed a famous work for King Roger II, the Norman ruler of Sicily, under the title *Nuzhat al-mushtāq fī ikhtirāq al-āfāq* (The Dilectation of the One Who Desires to Traverse the Horizons) but also known as *Kitāb Rūjār* (Roger's Book), which provided not only a comprehensive geographical survey of the known world but also a series of maps to accompany the text. Yāqūt, whom we mentioned above in connection with biographies, compiled parts of the vast amount of information contained in these and other works in a geographical dictionary, a kind of gazetteer of place names arranged in alphabetical order, the *Muʿjam al-buldān* (Dictionary of Countries).

To the practicalities of communication were added the demands of commerce and diplomacy. 'The Voyages of Sindbād', originally a separate story tradition but later incorporated into the *Thousand and One Nights* collection, provides a clue as to the extent of the trade routes plied by Arab mariners. A repertoire of manuals on navigation parallel to the *masālik* genre described above for land travel was developed. On the diplomatic front we have the fascinating account of ibn Faḍlān who was dispatched by the caliph al-Muqtadir in 921 on an embassy to the Volga region and returned to record in his *al- Risālah* (The Treatise) the details of his encounters with the Slavic and Turkic peoples whom he met during his travels.

Quite apart from these motivations to travel and explore, Islam enjoined believers with the obligation to perform the pilgrimage to the holy city of Mecca. Two of the most renowned works of travel in Arabic begin by announcing that they are to be accounts of the pilgrimage, and both involve a journey from west – the Maghrib – to east. The pilgrimage of Ibn Jubayr (*d.* 1217) of Granada was, he tells us, an act of expiation for the sin of drinking. The *Riḥlah* (Journey) takes the form of a precisely organised chronological narrative of visits to the cities of Egypt, Syria, and Arabia, culminating in the description of Mecca itself. His descriptions are elaborate and often emphasise the more remarkable and unusual aspects of the places involved, an effect that is underlined by his hyperbolic mode of expression. In this he differs from his successor in this genre, Ibn Baṭṭūtah (*d.* 1377) of Tangier, whose *Tuḥfat al-nuẓẓar fī gharāʾib al-amṣār wa-ʿajāʾib al-asfār* (Delight of the Beholders Regarding Exotic Cities and Remarkable Journeys) continues the focus on the unusual (as his title clearly illustrates) but is written in a less complicated style. Between 1325 and 1349 he visited Africa, Constantinople, Russia, India, Ceylon, and China, following that with a shorter visit to Spain and Niger in 1353. He appears to have suffered the misfortune at one point in his travels of losing his notes, so that parts of the dictation of his account to ibn Juzayy had to be reconstructed from memory. Whether completely accurate or not, ibn Baṭṭūtah's narrative remains a remarkable and enjoyable record of a tradition that combined the adventure of travel with a quest for knowledge.

The contribution of mystical discourse

A variety of types of homiletic and contemplative discourse had already been part of the broad-scaled project of compilation that we have already described: sermons, for example, and testaments, two genres that offered the believer spiritual and ethical counsel. One of the acknowledged masters of the sermon genre was al-Ḥasan al-Baṣrī (*d.* 728), whose repute is based both on the personal example that he set in his scholarship and personal behaviour and on the attractive style in which his admonitions are couched. These foundations provided a base for the development of a more specifically mystical discourse, a process in which pioneer status is given to Dhū al-nūn al-Miṣrī (*d.* 861) whose innovative writings made use of allegory and parable as means of establishing interpretative layers through which to express the mystical path to spiritual ecstasy in terms of love and other more worldly sensations. Another renowned Ṣūfī teacher was al-Junayd (*d.* 910) who made use of the epistle genre to impart his wisdom to his Ṣufī brethren. One of al-Junayd's pupils, al-Daqqāq, served as master to al-Qushayrī (*d.* 1072) whose Epistle (usually known as *al- Risālah al-Qushayriyyah*; English translation, *Principles of Sufism*) served both to provide a systematic analysis of Ṣūfī tenets and, equally important, to exclude from consideration many of the more peculiar beliefs and practices that continued to attach themselves to the mystical path. The role of Sufism within Islam is also central to the thought of Shihāb al-dīn ʿUmar al-Suhrawardī (*d.* 1234), one of several contributors to mystical thought of that name, as expressed in his manual of Ṣūfī practice, *ʿAwārif al- maʿārif* (The Benefits of Knowledge). For that reason, he needs to be clearly distinguished from his fellow-townsman, Shihāb al-dīn Yaḥyā, whose contribution will be discussed below.

The imagery and discourse of Ṣūfī writing provides the tradition of Arabic prose with some of its most beautiful models. Following the example provided by Dhū al-nūn, Muḥammad al-Niffarī (*d.* 965) recorded his own experiences of the transcendent in two works, *Kitāb al-mawāqif* (Book of Stations) and *Kitāb al- mukhaṭabat* (Book of Intimations); the elements of imagery and repetition (here transcending its normal poetic role in the sonic realm to attain the more insistent function of entrancement) combine with an aphoristic and homiletic tone to remarkable effect:

STATION OF A SEA

He stationed me in a sea, but did not name it. He said to me: I do not name it because you belong to Me, not to it; when I let you know of other than Me, you are the most ignorant of the ignorant. The entire universe is other than Me. That which calls to Me and not to it, it is of Me. If you respond to it, I will punish you and will not accept what you bring. I cannot avoid having you; my entire need is in you. So seek bread and shirt from me. I bring delight. Sit with me, and I will make you happy; none other will do so. Look at Me, for I look at no one but you. When you bring me all of this and I tell you it is sound, you are not of Me, nor I of you. (Station 39)

The works of scholars such as al-Qushayrī and al-Ghazālī sought to place Ṣūfī thought and practice within the larger framework of Islam as a whole. However, such gestures of reconciliation did not prevent other Ṣūfī scholars from pursuing their own paths, challenging the norms of established dogma as they explored and expounded on the nature of the transcendental experience. Two of the most notable and controversial figures in this area were Shihāb al-dīn Yaḥyā al-Suhrawardī (*d.* 1191) and Muḥyi al-dīn ibn al-ʿArabī (*d.* 1240). The second Shihāb al-dīn from Suhraward, Yaḥyā, made use of his profound knowledge of philosophy to integrate the concepts of the Greek philosophy and particularly Neo-Platonism with concepts from Zoroastrianism, into a system that considered the place of the individual within God's universe. However, his speculative explorations on this topic ran afoul of the conservative religious establishment at a particularly sensitive moment during the ongoing conflict with the Crusaders. Executed on the order of Ṣalāḥ al-dīn, he thus shared the fate of his mystical forebear, al-Ḥallāj (*d.* 922).

No less controversial in his speculations was Muḥyī al-dīn ibn al-ʿArabī, known to his admirers as 'the supreme master' (*al-shaykh al-akbar*), whose contributions to the tradition of Ṣūfī poetry were briefly discussed in Chapter 4. He was born and educated in al-Andalus, and his travels throughout the Maghrib region had already earned him a wide reputation as a Ṣūfī divine when he decided – inspired by a dream, he tells us – to undertake the pilgrimage to Mecca in about 1202. Visiting Cairo, Baghdād, and Konya, as well as the holy cities of Arabia, he eventually settled in Damascus.

It was a period spent in Mecca that provided the inspiration for his monumental, thirty-seven-volume *al-Futuḥāt al-Makkiyyah.* They bring together within a single work speculative theology, philosophy, a personal spiritual diary, and information about other Ṣūfī masters, to become a virtual *summa* on esoteric wisdom in Islam. Later in his life, ibn al-ʿArabi was inspired – by a command from the Prophet Muḥammad in another dream, he tells his reader – to compose *Fuṣūṣ al-ḥikam* (The Gem-settings of Wisdom), a commentary on the Qurʾān based not on the numerical order of the *sūrahs* but rather on the prophetic narratives; in a series of meditations each prophet – Adam, Noah, Moses, Solomon, Jesus, and so on – becomes the locus for a discussion of one aspect of God's divine self-manifestation. The first chapter, for example, is on Adam, and takes as its topic the 'wisdom of divinity':

When the real willed
  from the perspective of its most beautiful names
  which are countless
to see their determination
or you could say
when it willed to see its own determination . . .
to reveal itself through itself
its mystery
  for the self-vision of a being through itself
  is not like its self-vision through something outside
  which acts like a mirror . . .
and when the real had brought into being
the universe
a vague, molded shape
without a spirit
it was like an unpolished mirror . . .

(Michael Sells, *Studia Islamica* (1986): 125)

For ibn al-ʿArabī the image of the mirror is a central one; the divinity of God is thereby reflected in the apportionment of part of His attributes to Prophets and 'saints' (*aqṭāb,* sing. *quṭb*). They are particular examples of the heights to which humanity can strive in its quest towards the ideal of the 'perfect man'. These concepts are all part of his overarching principle, 'the oneness of the universe' (*waḥdat al-wujūd*), whereby everything that is or might be is to be understood as a manifestation of the divine attributes of God illustrated by His 'beautiful names' and explored through the mystical path.

The five centuries following the death of ibn al-ʿArabī saw a vast increase in the influence of Ṣūfī brotherhoods. A natural consequence of this increase in the role and influence of Sufism at all levels of society was the composition of an enormous library of works intended for the inspiration of these communities: collections of miraculous tales concerning prominent Ṣūfīs and compendia of devotional texts. Alongside this ever-expanding store of hagiographic material the work of Ṣūfī scholars continued to enrich the Islamic sciences; two eminent examples are al-Shaʿrānī (*d.* 1566) and ʿAbd al-ghanī al-Nābulusī (*d.* 1731).

The contribution of Ṣūfī writings to the development of Arabic prose literature is immense and generally underestimated. In the eloquent words of Jamāl al-Ghīṭānī, the Egyptian novelist who has himself been much inspired by Ṣūfī writing (his novel *Kitāb al-tajalliyyāt* (Book of Illuminations) is modelled on the work of ibn al-ʿArabī), 'Ṣūfī expression presents a challenge to fixed, established patterns and an adventure into the unknown that aspires to limitless horizons'.

Journeys of the imagination

The debates over the place of philosophy and mysticism within the system of Islamic belief, which had preoccupied the minds of such great scholars as ibn Sīnā and al-Ghazālī, were reflected in several works in which writers used more indirect and allegorical modes to explore the dimensions of esoteric wisdom. One of the more famous allegorical treatments within the tradition is *Ḥayy ibn Yaqẓān, asrār al-ḥikmah al-mashriqiyyah* (Alive the Son of Awake, the Secrets of Eastern Wisdom). This allegory of the cosmic order served as inspiration for a number of writers, including the philosopher ibn Sīnā, but its most famous elaboration is that of the Andalusian philosopher, ibn Ṭufayl (*d.* 1185), who clearly acknowledges the influence of his great predecessor in philosophy.

At the beginning of the work, the narrator informs a friend who has asked him to reveal the secrets of philosophy as expounded by ibn Sīnā that he will make use of a story already used by 'the great master' (as ibn Sīnā is named) to illustrate the nature of the path ahead. The story he tells is that of Ḥayy ibn Yaqẓān, born in a process of spontaneous generation, who gradually learns to appreciate the rational nature of the cosmos and to develop a code of ethics. He then moves on from such earthly considerations to achieve a level of ecstatic contemplation, about which, as the narrator tells his friend, he can only provide hints since words are incapable of depicting it. It is at this point that Ḥayy – '*philosophus autodidactus*' in the words of Pococke – comes into contact with Asāl, the inhabitant of another island where social behaviour is governed by the teachings of a true religion. Ḥayy returns with Asāl to his island and endeavours to explain his acquired wisdom to them, but his teachings are given a cold reception. Realising the nature of the human condition and his hosts' inability to comprehend the essence of his insights, Ḥayy, accompanied by Asāl, returns to the other island.

The theme of a visit to the afterlife is adopted as the framework for two other famous works of the imagination. In *Risālat al-tawābiʿ wa-al-zawābiʿ* (Treatise of Familiar Spirits and Demons) the narrator of the

Andalusian poet, ibn Shuhayd (*d.* 1035), meets the spirits of a number of prominent littérateurs – poets such as Imru' al-Qays, Abū Nuwās, Abū Tammām and al-Mutanabbī, prose writers such as ʿAbd al-ḥamīd, al-Jāḥiẓ, and Badīʿ al-zamān al-Hamadhānī – and critics. However, it is the final section which may explain the rationale for this erudite and witty work: the narrator meets a number of animals, including a donkey and a goose, who duly provide their critical opinions on works of literature, suggesting that ibn Shuhayd was prompted to invoke the spirits of his forebears in order to counter some negative criticism among his local contemporaries. The other work is the *Risālat al-ghufrān* (Epistle of Forgiveness) by the renowned ascetic philosopher-poet, Abū al-ʿAlā' al-Maʿarrī (*d.* 1058). Having received from one ʿAlī ibn al-Qāriḥ a letter containing questions regarding aspects of heresy and belief, al-Maʿarrī decided to preface his response with an imaginary tour of the afterworld, during the course of which the Shaykh would be permitted to visit Paradise and Hell and interview various literary personages concerning their behaviour during their lifetime and its consequences. During the visit to Paradise he discovers that several pre-Islamic poets have been forgiven. The famous wine-poet, al-Aʿshā, has abandoned his former ways. When Ḥassān ibn Thābit, 'the poet of the Prophet', is challenged to justify a seemingly risky verse in his famous 'Mantle Poem' ('*Burdah*'), he observes that thc Prophet was not as puritanical as some people imagine. Visiting Hell, the Shaykh encounters Imru' al-Qays, Bashshār ibn Burd, and several other poets, including the famous vagabonds, Ta'abbaṭa Sharran and al-Shanfarā. In the second part of the work al-Maʿarrī finally broaches the task of responding to his correspondent's comments and questions on aspects of heresy, noting with a certain resignation that his statements on belief have been misinterpreted and that he is 'slandered just as the Arabs slander the ghoul'.

Maqāmāt

The genre of fictional narrative that became the most widespread and popular was the *maqāmah*; indeed it managed to retain that status until well into the twentieth century. The original meaning of *maqāmah* involves a place of standing. From there it came to mean a tribal assembly, to which was gradually attached the sense of an occasion for the delivery of an uplifting message. Al-Hamadhānī (*d.* 1008), dubbed 'the wonder of the age' (*badīʿ al-zamān*), chose to use, indeed to play on, these oratorical and homiletic dimensions by placing them into a societal context and by couching his narratives in a discourse that both exploited the potential of the Arabic language and evoked numerous intertextual linkages.

Each *maqāmah* of al-Hamadhānī begins with the phrase: 'ʿĪsā ibn Hishām reported to us and said'. This ʿĪsā, a fictional character who is nevertheless named after one of al-Hamadhānī's contemporaries, is one of two figures whose interaction forms the framework of the series of short narratives contained within the *maqāmāt*. The other character in the duo is named Abū al-fatḥ al-Iskandarī. His attitude to life is summed up in a number of short poems which conclude the *maqāmāt*:

> May God never put the likes of me at a distance; for where, O where, can you find the likes of me?
> God only knows how stupid people are; I have fleeced them with ease.
> I have asked of them charity in bulk, but in return I have merely given them a measure of deceit and lies. (*Maqāmah* of Mawṣil)

Abū al-fatḥ is a trickster, a master of disguise; he is never what he at first seems. In the majority of the *maqāmāt* ʿĪsā's role is as his companion and foil, his uncoverer; the recognition of the identity of Abū al-fath reveals the trickery that he has been working on his audience. In other *maqāmāt*, however, ʿĪsā fulfils a different function. In the Baghdād *maqāmah*, for example, it is ʿĪsā alone who dupes a country yokel into providing him with a lavish free meal before watching the wretched individual being pummelled into paying the bill. In the Maḍīriyyah *maqāmah*, ʿĪsā does not appear at all; instead the sight of a wonderful stew-like dish (*maḍīrah*) triggers in Abū al-fatḥ's memory an occasion when he encounters a *nouveau riche* merchant who insists on showing him every feature of his ultimate suburban residence, not least the toilet. However, while tales like these are indeed lively and entertaining, they are not representative of the bulk of al-Hamadhānī's *maqāmāt*. Other examples are far more static in nature and serve rather to provide replications, or perhaps pastiches, of different types of occasion and text: the *maqāmah* of al-Jāḥiẓ, for instance, takes the form of a literary circle where the works of al-Hamadhānī's great predecessor are discussed in learned (and critical) terms. The *maqāmah* of Saymarah recounts a lengthy and elaborate morality tale whose narrator is Abū al-ʿAnbas al-Ṣaymarī (*d. c.* 888), an actual poet, story-teller, and boon-companion of the caliph al-Mutawakkil.

Al-Hamadhānī's pioneer status is acknowledged by his great successor in the genre, Abū Muḥammad al-Qāsim al-Ḥarīrī (*d.* 1122), in the introduction to his set of *maqāmāt.* From the model presented by al-Ḥarīrī and his successors in the genre, it is clear that it was through stylistic virtuosity and its use for homiletic purposes that the *maqāmah* became for several centuries a popular mode of belletristic prose expression; to such an extent in fact that the role of al-Hamadhānī was largely eclipsed by the enormous amount of attention paid to the work of his famous successor.

With al-Ḥarīrī, the basic scenario of the *maqāmah* remains the same, but the names are different: the narrator is now called al-Ḥārith ibn Hammām, and the chameleon-like character whom it is his role to uncover is named Abū Zayd al-Sarūjī. The continuing ambivalence of the narrator towards his partner in narrative is well captured by al-Ḥārith himself when he notes in *al-Maqāmah al-wabariyyah*: 'As I weighed Abū Zayd's benefit and harm in the balance, I was at a loss as to whether to scold or thank him'. A few of al-Ḥarīrī's *maqāmāt* share the narrative qualities of some of al-Hamadhānī's examples that were mentioned above: that of Damascus, for example, depicts a desert journey, while others are concerned with Abū Zayd's feuds with his wife. However, al-Ḥarīrī's introduction specifies that he will be providing examples of other types of text, and this transtextual aspect, already present in al-Hamadhānī's *maqāmāt*, now becomes a more predominant feature. In several *maqāmāt* – those of Tannis and Rayy, for example – Abū Zayd is a hellfire preacher, advocating asceticism (*zuhd*) and reminding his listeners of the ephemerality of this world and all its goods. In the *maqāmah* of Sāsān, he delivers his last will and testament to his son, handing over to him the position of chief of the beggars' fraternity. Other *maqāmāt* take the form of a *majlis*: Abū Zayd's learning is shown through his discussions of metaphor and plagiarism in poetry (the *maqāmāt* of Hulwan and Poetry), of syntax (Qaṭīʿ), and of the comparative virtues of epistolary and financial expertise (Euphrates).

Whereas one can conceive of al-Hamadhānī improvising his brilliant vignettes in the public domain, al-Ḥarīrī's *maqāmāt* reflect the deliberate touch of a virtuoso creating his works within the more private world of the written text and crafting each example into a masterpiece of language. His *maqāmāt* are longer, and poetry assumes a much more prominent place within the structure of the text. Beyond that, however, al-Ḥarīrī provides examples of linguistic virtuosity that is unparalleled in Arabic literature: *al-Maqāmah al-marāghiyyah*, for example, contains a letter in which there is an alternation between words whose graphemes carry no dots and others in which every grapheme carries a dot.

After the death of al-Ḥarīrī, the *maqāmah* became a favoured mode of belletristic expression in Arabic, its continuing popularity as a genre serving as one of the more obvious manifestations of the literary élite's predilection for elaborate forms of prose discourse. Authors of works chose the *maqāmah* as the vehicle for their writing projects on a wide variety of topics, but the narrative structure established by al-Hamadhānī and followed to a certain extent by al-Ḥarīrī clearly did not provide a pattern that their successors felt called upon to replicate. The famous philologist, al-Zamakhsharī (*d.* 1143), who, in addition to the already mentioned *Rabīʿ al-abrār*, composed commentaries on the Qurʾān, a major source work in Arabic grammar, *al- Mufaṣṣal*, and a compendium volume entitled *Aṭwāq al-dhahab fī al-mawāʾiẓ wa-al-adab* (Golden Necklets on Homilies and *Adab*), informs his readers in an Introduction that he was prompted in a dream to complete fifty *maqāmāt*, which offer homiletic advice on various topics to the author himself and then proceed through question and command to issue warnings and counsel to the reader.

More similar to al-Ḥarīrī's work are *al-Maqāmāt al-luzūmiyyah* by al-Saraqusṭī (from Saragossa in Spain, d. 1143). Even though these *maqāmāt* do not carry particular titles, they reflect and discuss travel throughout the world of Islam, from the Arabian Peninsula to China. While al-Saraqusṭī does not set out to rival the verbal acrobatics of al-Ḥarīrī, the style of his writing and the variety of his themes (including two *maqāmāt* on literary topics) show clearly the inspiration that he drew from his illustrious forebear. In his *al-Maqāmāt al-zayniyyah* ibn Ṣayqal al-Jazarī (*d.* 1273), a teacher at the Mustanṣiriyyah College in Baghdād, debates issues of jurisprudence and grammar, while indulging in some Ḥarīrīan linguistic feats: the seventh *maqāmah*, entitled '*al-Sanjariyyah*', extols the work of al-Ḥarīrī and then proceeds to replicate his feat in producing a segment that can be read forwards or backwards. Since the Egyptian writer al-Suyūṭī (*d.* 1505) is renowned as one of Arabic culture's major polygraphs, it is hardly surprising that his collection of *maqāmāt* should be primarily a display of immense erudition. One of them is a stalwart defence of the beliefs of the famous Egyptian Ṣūfī poet, ibn al-Fāriḍ (*d.* 1245), citing all manner of textual authorities on the subject of Islamic orthodoxy, while another, '*al-Maqāmah al-miskiyyah*' (Of Musk), appears on the surface to be a survey of four perfumes but is almost certainly also a comparison of the political acumen of four Mamlūk rulers who were vying for power at a particular point in al-Suyūṭī's writing career.

The influence of al-Ḥarīrī's *maqāmāt*, already seen in many of the works we have just mentioned, is particularly evident in the records of literary activity in Egypt in the seventeenth and eigthteenth centuries. Shihāb al-dīn al-Khafājī (*d.* 1653) composed a commentary on al-Ḥarīrī's *maqāmāt* and produced some examples of his own, as did the poet, al-Idkāwī (*d.* 1770). The intellectual salon of al-Zabīdī (*d.* 1791), most renowned as the compiler of the dictionary, *Tāj al-ʿarūs* (The Bridal Crown), became a virtual centre for Ḥarīrī scholarship and imitation, including among its members Shaykh Ḥasan al-ʿAṭṭār (*d.* 1835) who not only wrote several *maqāmāt* (including one concerning his contacts with French scholars in 1799) but also served as mentor to Rifāʿah al-Ṭahṭāwī, who in 1826 was appointed the religious leader of the first Egyptian educational mission to France.

During the nineteenth century writers in Egypt, Iraq, and Syria turned to the *maqāmah* genre as an appropriate vehicle for participating in the changing cultural environment in which they were living. From among the many authors who contributed to this trend two writers stand out: Nāṣīf al-Yāzijī (*d.* 1871) and Aḥmad Fāris al-Shidyāq (*d.* 1887). Al-Yāzijī's *Majmaʿ al-baḥrayn* (The Meeting-point of the Two Seas, 1856) – the title itself being a quotation from the Qurʾān (*Sūrat al-Kahf* 18 (The Cave), v. 60) – is a genuine exercise in neo-classicism, in that it seeks to revive the glories of al-Ḥarīrī's classic work; in his Introduction, al-Yāzijī states his intention of using rare words and recherché usage, and the *maqāmah* of Sarūj consciously noted that it is in quest of the spirit of Abū Zayd al-Sarūjī, the renowned 'hero' of al-Ḥarīrī's *maqāmāt.* Al-Shidyāq's famous work, *Al-Sāq ʿalā al-sāq fī-mā huwa al-Fār-yāq* (The Pigeon on the Branch/One Leg Over Another/ Concerning Far-yaq, 1855), points in new directions. The deliberate ambiguity of the title illustrates an intrinsic part of its generic purpose, as he often resorts to the *sajʿ* style for rhetorical effect. The narrative is concerned with 'Fār-yāq's' travels to Europe – London, Paris, and Cambridge – and his encounters with cultural difference; a particular focus of that difference deals with the status of women, something that involves the pointed comments of 'Fāryāqah', his wife. The names 'Fār-yāq' and 'Fār-yāqah' are here cited in quotation marks because both consist of the first part of al-Shidyāq's first name, Fāris, and the last part of his family name; they suggest not only that this work provides al-Shidyāq with the opportunity to explore some of the interesting dimensions of autobiographical writing but also that al-Shidyāq is using the femininisation of his own name, 'Fār-yāq', to explore sexual difference within his own society and in its contacts with others.

When Muḥammad al-Muwayliḥī (*d.* 1930) began to publish his contribution to the genre as a series of newspaper articles under the title, '*Fatrah min al-zaman*' (A Period of Time), in 1898, he took the process back to its origins; his narrator is none other than ʿĪsā ibn Hishām, the narrator of al-Hamadhānī's *maqāmāt* of some nine centuries earlier; the linkage is made even clearer with the publication of the episodes in book form in 1907 as *Ḥadīth ʿĪsā ibn Hishām* (ʿĪsā ibn Hishām's Tale). ʿĪsā ibn Hishām is the narrative persona for the author, and, in the company of a Pāshā resurrected from the times of Muḥammad ʿAlī some eighty years earlier, he becomes an active participant in a lively and highly critical survey of life in the city of Cairo under British occupation at the turn of the century, and most notably its arcane legal system both secular and religious. In the latter part of the work, ʿĪsā and the Pāshā watch in amusement and disgust as a rustic village headman (*ʿumdah*) is introduced by a westernised fop to the ersatz attractions of 'modern' Cairo and in the process loses much of his wealth and reputation. *Ḥadīth ʿĪsā ibn Hishām* thus serves in an important bridging capacity, invoking styles, texts, and names from the past as a vehicle for a critical analysis of society that would be the primary generic purpose of modern fiction.

In spite of the increasing popularity of European fictional genres, fostered by a host of new magazines and journals that published translations in serial form, al-Muwayliḥī's model of the *maqāmah* as a modern vehicle was emulated by several other writers: Ḥāfiẓ Ibrāhīm (*d.* 1932), the famous Egyptian poet, for example, and the much travelled Bayram al-Tūnisī (*d.* 1961). Abandoning al-Muwayliḥī's concentration on the élite of society, Bayram takes the *maqāmah* back to its original focus on the poorer segments of society and their perpetual striving for the means of survival, often involving varieties of trickery.

The works of Bayram al-Tūnisī and other twentieth century authors (including ʿAbd al-salām al-ʿUjaylī (*b.* 1919), the illustrious Syrian writer of fiction) who have occasionally resorted to the *maqāmah* as a mode of expression show the continuing attraction to the educated readership of Arabic literature of this flamboyant genre that, while addressing itself to a wide variety of issues, exults in the sheer delight of exhibiting its own virtuosity.

POPULAR NARRATIVES

Introduction

In 1703 Antoine Galland, a French scholar who had made several visits to the Middle East, published the first two parts of *Mille et une nuit*, a translation of a manuscript collection of stories that he had acquired. Between 1704 and 1717 he was to publish other volumes in the series, completing the translation of the manuscript and adding to it some other tales from the oral repertoire of an obscure figure named Hanna from Aleppo, among them those of Aladdin and Ali Baba. The tales were organised into some 280 'nights', and were built around a frame story involving a King named Shahrayār who takes vengeance for the infidelity of his wife by marrying a virgin every night and killing her at dawn. Shahrazād, the daughter of the King's minister, takes it upon herself to put an end to the King's behaviour by means of story-telling, stopping her narration of a series of exciting tales at a crucial point that always coincides with the dawn – thus providing a *locus classicus* for the principles of serialised narratives.

The appearance of Galland's translation is one of the most remarkable success stories in the history of publication. The immense popularity with which these versions were greeted inevitably led to questions concerning the collection itself. This interest prompted the preparation of printed Arabic versions: the first began to appear in Calcutta in 1814, and a second was published in 1835 from the Būlāq Press that Muḥammad ʿAlī had founded in Cairo. Scholarly interest had also been aroused by this phenomenon. Influences and common bases in other cultural traditions were not hard to trace, but the search for manuscripts proved harder. As Edward Lane commented in the 1830s, 'when a complete copy of 'The *Thousand and One Nights*' is found, the price demanded for it is too great for a reciter to have it in his power to pay'. The key word in this extract is 'reciter'. For, while evidence on this topic is scanty in the extreme, one must assume that this huge collection is (or, at the very least, became) one among many examples of the huge repertoire of oral narratives that were performed on public and private occasions in the regions of Asia and North Africa. The principal reason why Lane found it so difficult to purchase any manuscript copies of the tales was that they had not been recorded in that medium; such copies as did exist were for the use of the *ḥakawātī* (story-teller), a figure who was till relatively recently one of the most prominent participants in the communal life of Middle Eastern societies.

In the Western world meanwhile the popularity of the *Thousand and One Nights* increased. There were many translations of the Arabic versions (as opposed to those that used Galland's French translation), and the variety of purposes reflected in the different approaches to translation provide us with interesting insights into the tastes of the European readership at the time. The language of the collection had been that of the *ḥakawātī* (whose gesturing cues form part of the recorded text of the second Calcutta edition of 1839–42), a register that, needless to say, contained a good deal of colloquial usage and was thus quite different from the elaborate style of *adab*. In rendering the texts into English, translators had to select an appropriate level of the target language; Edward Lane and Sir Richard Burton, for example, chose to exoticise their English versions by couching them in a style redolent of the King James Bible, thus creating a curious disjuncture between the impact of the original (in its authentic context) and the English translation. The images of the exotic Orient – with its swashbuckling adventurers, dusky maidens, magic lamps, fabulous riches, and wicked viziers – emerged from these and earlier versions, to become the contents of children's books, and to be performed in Christmas pantomimes (which, through an irony, were mostly based on Aladdin and Ali Baba, two of Galland's tales that were not part of the original collection). This exoticisation of the Middle East was, of course, also tailor-made for Hollywood extravaganzas, as a number of films, especially those devoted to the Sindbad voyages, make clear.

Here then is an interesting case of cultural contrasts. A work that had a major influence on any number of artistic genres in Western culture (one thinks for example of the lush Scheherazade scores of Rimsky-Korsakov and Ravel) and whose enormous popularity in the West has been responsible for the creation of so many stereotypes regarding the Middle East, has until recently been completely neglected as an object of study by the culture that fostered it.

Types of popular expression

The discussion of popular narratives in Arabic involves consideration of the various levels of the Arabic language and the cultural values attached to them. As I have already noted, the literary tradition has had no compunction about evaluating texts on such a basis, not only through its choice of terms (*al-fuṣḥā*, the more élite language, and *al-ʿāmmiyyah*, the language of the *plebs*) but also through the aesthetic criteria of the *adab* tradition. Secondly, the narratives within our purview are not all solely prose narratives; the *Thousand and One Nights* is just one among many collections of tales in which the *ḥakawātī* (story-teller) is at liberty to include within his narration large segments of poetry (as is the case with classical *adab*), a judgement that he will make according to the occasion of the performance and the desires and reactions of his audience. Lastly, research on Arabic prose genres of all types shows that tales with particular plots and themes would make their way into both 'élite' and 'popular' collections; tales concerning miraculous escapes, for example, are as much part of the material of the *Thousand and One Nights* as of the more explicitly titled *al-Faraj baʿd al-shiddah* of al-Tanūkhī (discussed above).

In our discussions above of historical, geographical, and religious works, we have noted that many writers – al-Ṭabarī and al-Masʿūdī for example – made use of the legends and fables that form part of the earliest lore of the Arabs. The stories of pre-Islamic lovers (like Laylā and Majnūn), of tribal wars (the *ayyām al-ʿArab*, such as the Basūs War between Bakr and Taghlib), of ancient Near Eastern heroes and prophets, these made their way into not only the works of those who contributed to the world of Islamic scholarship but also the repertoire of story-telling; indeed the Arabic word *sīrah* was used not only to describe biographies of the Prophet Muḥammad (as noted earlier) but also these collections of tales, the usage being specified by the addition of the adjective 'popular' (*al-sīrah al-shaʿbiyyah*). To these sources were added other types of narratives: animal fables and proverbs, such as those of the legendary figure of Luqmān (who gives his name to Sūrah 30 of the Qurʾān); storics of scmi-legendary poets such as Ḥātim al-Ṭāʾī, accounts of whose generosity have made his name proverbial; stories of conquest and *jihād*, tales of the expansion of Islam, of the Crusades, of the defeat of the Mongols; stories of migrations of peoples; and, of course, collections of humour, moralising anecdotes, accounts of pranksters, and tall tales of all kinds – the wily exploits of ʿAlī Zaybaq (the name means 'quicksilver') and Aḥmad al-Danaf (the 'mange'), and the numerous situations involving the Middle East's primary jokester, Juḥā, a character claimed by almost every nation in the region as its own (known within the Persian and Turkish traditions as Naṣr al-dīn (Nasreddin)):

One of Juḥā's neighbours came to ask him if he could borrow his donkey. Juḥā apologised and said that his donkey wasn't there. Just then the donkey let out a loud bray. The neighbour commented that he seemed to be in luck because the donkey was there after all. 'What's with you?' expostulated Juḥā. 'Do you believe my donkey rather than me?!'

The compilation of different types of narrative was, as we have noted above, part of the larger process of gathering all sorts of information during the initial centuries of Islam. Scholars have traced back references to collections of tales as far as the eighth century . However, given the oral nature of the processes of transmission and performance of the tales themselves, the dearth of textual sources is hardly surprising, thus making the precise chronology for the development of the large collections very unclear. Information concerning the different versions of the *Thousand and One Nights* collection is the most complete. It suggests that a core collection made up of an Indo-Persian frame-story and accretions from the Baghdād of Hārūn al-Rashīd (from the ninth century onwards) made its way to Syria and thence to Egypt; Muhsin Mahdi has published (in 1984) a reconstruction of the collection as it was in the fourteenth century, extrapolated back from manuscripts belonging to the Syrian stemma (including Galland's manuscript now in the Bibliothèque Nationale). Even in the 1830s Lane gives vivid descriptions of street performances by story-telling specialists of all kinds: some dealt with the epic tales of ʿAntar, the pre-Islamic poet, others with Abū Zayd, the hero of the migrating tribe of the Banī Hilāl. Here as elsewhere, however, such performers who thrived on the popular demand for their tales have not been able to rival the attractions of films, videos, and television. Public narration is a dying craft.

The major narrative collections

The popular tradition engendered many lengthy sagas, romances, and epics that were intended for public performance, each one constituting a narrative event that might extend over several evenings or be intended to celebrate a particular occasion (such as a wedding, for example, or a safe return from the pilgrimage or a long journey) or as entertainment during the nights of Ramaḍān.

The material for some of these narratives has the same provenance as many of the different kinds of *akhbār* collections that were listed above. The repertoire of *ayyām al-ʿArab* (tribal wars of pre-Islamic times), for example, is put into extended narrative form in the saga of *Al-Ẓīr Sālim* (Prince Sālim) which tells of the lengthy War of Basūs between the tribes of Bakr and Taghlib. Also of Arabian provenance is the huge *sīrah* of *Sayf ibn Dhī Yazan*, a work that seems to have been compiled in about the fourteenth century, in that one of its villains is named Sayf Arʿad, a ruler of Ethiopia at the time. However, while this *sīrah* may represent the anxiety of fourteenth-century Egyptians at the threat of attack from the south, the setting of its eponymous hero, Sayf ibn Dhī Yazan, is South Arabia during pre-Islamic times, the temporal disjuncture being vivid enough proof of the lack of concern that these narratives have with the niceties of chronology. Sayf undergoes a variety of adventures, not the least of which is a visit to the fabled land of Wāq al-wāq, an island paradise peopled by women where he becomes infatuated with a beautiful bird-woman named Munyat al-nufūs (Soul's desire). As many scholars have pointed out, this land of Wāq al-wāq is a prevalent theme in Arabic literature of all types. If *Sayf ibn Dhī Yazan* is frequently rescued from dire straits by the intervention of women, another *sīrah* takes the process one stage further: *Sīrah al-amīrah Dhāt al-Himmah* has a female warrior-princess as its heroine. Dhāt al-himmah (she who is possessed of resolve) is abandoned by her father who is disappointed that she is not a son, but she is a born warrior and, along with her son, ʿAbd al-wahhāb, she takes a valiant role in any number of battles. This further huge collection consisting of some seventy separate episodes is also known as *sīrat al-mujāhidīn* (of the strivers for Islam), suggesting a linkage to the textual tradition on *jihād* (the propagation of Islam). The *sīrah* of *al-Ẓāhir Baybars* recounts the glorious victory of the Mamlūk sultan over the invading Mongols in the thirteenth century and has thus become a favourite for those audiences desiring to listen to a narrative that reflects the traditional virtues of strategic resourcefulness and courage in battle.

During the nineteenth century *Sīrat ʿAntar*, a romance about the famous pre-Islamic poet-cavalier, ʿAntarah son of Shaddād, and his beloved and cousin, ʿAblah daughter of Mālik, was sufficiently well known in the Western world that it too was translated into several languages (including a partial translation into English) and Rimsky-Korsakov made an episode from the huge collection the subject of one of his earliest orchestral works. Born as a black child (an echo of the theme of Dhāt al-himmah's child) as a result of a union between the tribal chief and a black slave, Zabīdah, ʿAntar is initially ostracised; it is his tremendous courage and strength that come to earn him the grudging respect of the tribes. When he falls in love with the beautiful ʿAblah and her father refuses to contemplate a union, the stage is set for a whole series of impossible tasks that ʿAntar has to carry out in order to earn the right to marry his lady-love. In all this, ʿAntar's bravery, chivalry, and generosity to friend and foe alike are matched by the qualities of his beloved, ʿAblah, who is often subjected to the indignities of capture, confinement, and the lewd advances of rogues.

Among the most widespread of the *sīrah*s and certainly one of the most famous is that of the *Banī Hilāl*; researchers writing in English, for example, have recorded versions in Egypt, Nigeria, and Tunisia. This is a tale of migration, of the Banī Hilāl who left the Arabian Peninsula in the tenth and eleventh centuries and travelled via Sinai to Egypt. Initially sent south to Upper (southern) Egypt, they were dispatched westwards in the eleventh century as part of the struggle between the ʿAbbāsī caliphs in Baghdād and the rival Shīʿī Fāṭimī caliphs in Cairo. Like the other *sīrah*s we have discussed above, the *Sīrat Banī Hilāl* has its hero, Abū Zayd al-Hilālī, another personification of the courageous warrior, and a number of friends and foes who help or impede the progress of the tribes towards their goal.

In this short survey of some of the narrative collections that are a part of the popular heritage of Arab culture, I have emphasised context, themes and 'characters' (and especially heroes, villains, and beloveds). In discussing these works however, it is important to remember that each of the textual versions that we possess constitutes a written recording of one particular performance, and that the collections as a whole – in multiple volumes – represent a repertoire of tales built around a core theme and set of characters that would rarely, if ever, be performed complete. The narration of these segments would be occasions that were spread over a number of evenings, and the *ḥakawātī* would adjust his performance in accordance with the occasion and the duration of the segment in question. It is in such a context that we come to realise that the extreme variation in the recorded versions of individual tales – the amount of poetry included in some of the tales in the *Thousand and One Nights*, 'The City of Brass', for example – and in their English translation may represent the different circumstances in which the tale was performed as well as the editorial instincts of the translator.

The Thousand and One Nights

The most famous collections of Arabic popular narrative, the *Thousand and One Nights*, shares many features with those we have just discussed, although the reception of its translated versions in the West and the consequences of its world-wide popularity have served to complicate the investigation of its provenance and authenticity. It too contains tales of adventure, of war, of trickery, and of love; it also includes a number of animal fables like those of Luqmān. Furthermore, some of the tales are set in particular historical periods; notable in this category are those devoted to incidents involving the caliph Hārūn al-Rashīd, his famous minister, Jaʿfar al-Barmakī, and his boon-companion, the poet Abū Nuwās. However, whereas it is possible with the other *sīrah* collections to assign a general title containing the name of a hero or heroine to the often divergent collection of incidents and stories, the unique set of circumstances surrounding the compilation (and expansion) of the famous *Thousand and One Nights* collection, as outlined above, have furnished it with features that set it somewhat apart from the others. Shahrazād, the daughter of the king's minister, is a prominent participant in the frame-story of the collection, but thereafter she becomes a story-teller *par excellence*, using her frame-narrative – with its continuing threat of a violent conclusion if her narrative strategy should fail – as a context (and pretext) for the telling of other narrators' stories. The entire collection thus becomes a narrative about story-telling, its general goal being to offer, in the phrase repeated throughout the collection, 'a lesson for those who would learn'.

The frame-story of the collection performs a number of functions. It introduces the situation within which the primary characters will fulfil their roles. The way in which the brother kings, Shāhzamān and Shahrayār, dispense justice in response to their wives' infidelity is echoed in numerous tales involving rulers and their treatment of people; the caliph Hārūn al-Rashīd numbers prominently among such types. The behaviour of the wives themselves is taken as yet another illustration of the 'wiles of women' theme, which, as we saw in the chapter on the Qur'ān, finds a *locus classicus* in *Sūrat Yūsuf* (12, Joseph). But, beyond the thematic bases that are established, there is the narrative structure itself. Once the perfidy of their wives has been revealed, the two kings go on a journey, during which they encounter a brazen woman who has been locked up in a box by an evil genie and demands that the two kings make love to her. After the two kings have obliged, she demands their rings and adds them to the 572 others that she already possesses. The kings return home chastened; they too have learned a lesson of a sort, and the result is the killing of their wives, the need for Shahrazād's stratagem, and the start of the story-telling process. Shahrazād weaves her narrative thread for a thousand and one nights – at least, after the eighteenth century. At the conclusion of the final tale, that of 'Maʿrūf the Cobbler', Shahrazād asks the King whether he has abandoned his idea of killing her and brings in their sons to bolster her request. The King agrees, and the collection appears to end on a happy note.

The original collection of tales – as translated by Galland – gives every indication of being arranged in a way that will develop these themes. 'The Porter and the Three Ladies of Baghdād', for instance, is a wonderfully elaborate narrative structure, in which story-telling is a way of avoiding threatened violence and listening without question is a requirement for avoiding chastisement. 'The Story of the Murdered Girl' (also known as 'the Three Apples') is a thoroughly convincing crime narrative, again involving Hārūn al-Rashīd, whose demeanour towards his minister, Jaʿfar, shows striking parallels to that of King Shahrayār within the frame-story. A box is found in the River Tigris, containing the dissected body of a beautiful woman, and Jaʿfar is set the seemingly hopeless task of finding the murderer. An inner narrative reveals a tale of deceit and violence, involving one of the couple's children and Jaʿfar's black slave. The proven guilt of the slave is expiated when Jaʿfar, the guilty slave's master, volunteers to tell an even more unbelievable tale in exchange for the slave's pardon. Story-telling here not only prevents killing, but obtains pardon for it.

To this core collection of tales, containing, as we have just indicated, examples of great variety, were added others of different types. The lengthy and complex 'Tale of ʿUmar al-Nuʿmān' is, to all intents and purposes, a miniature *sīrah*, involving a number of sub-tales of battles and loves, all in the context of contacts between Christian and Muslim rulers and the eventual triumph of Islam. The collection also contains a large number of love stories. One of the most notable is 'Ghānim ibn Ayyāb with Hārūn al-Rashīd and Qūt al-Qulūb'. As the title implies, this is a multi-episodic tale in which the caliph, Hārūn al-Rashīd, moves beyond his function as facilitator or observer to become a full participant. A merchant named Ghānim witnesses a procession of eunuchs carrying a coffin, which to his horror contains a beautiful maiden, drugged but still alive. She is none other than Qūt al-Qulūb (Nourishment for the heart), the favourite concubine of Hārūn al-Rashīd; the caliph's wife, Zubaydah, has become jealous of her rival and has taken advantage of her husband's temporary absence to get rid of her. The scene now switches to the caliph's palace, which is in mourning for the 'death' of Qūt al-Qulūb. Inevitably, Hārūn learns that Qūt al-Qulūb is not dead, and Ghānim and his family are placed in mortal danger. However, when Qūt al-Qulūb explains to the caliph that Ghānim has been entirely honourable, he gives Qūt al-Qulūb to Ghānim, and, in one of those neat resolutions for which the Hārūn of the collection is renowned, he is married to Ghānim's sister, Fitnah.

The collection contains a number of travel-tales. 'The City of Brass' is a prolonged reflection on the ephemerality of life in this world. Beginning as the story of a quest (at the behest of the Umawī caliph, ʿAbd al-Malik) for the bottles in which Solomon had imprisoned the demons, it becomes a symbolic journey that reaches the 'City of Brass', a place with no visible entrance, a model of human delusion where nothing is the way it seems to be. A far different kind of audience was surely anticipated for the most famous travel tale of all, 'Sindbād the Sailor', a separate set of narratives that was added to the core collection. The structural patterns of Sindbād's seven separate voyages makes it clear that this discrete set of tales possesses a unity of its own, besides being a participant in the *Thousand and One Nights* collection. Sindbād's tales of adventure and commerce on the high seas are marked by a large degree of symmetry and, at the joins between the voyages, of formulaic repetition. Each tale begins with a voyage from al-Baṣrah in Iraq; some kind of disaster occurs; Sindbād finds himself washed up on some strange shore where humans, semi-humans, or animals do peculiar things. He has to resort to a variety of stratagems to avoid enslavement, capture, and even death, some of which involve acts of considerable violence: in the fourth tale, for example, he kills a succession of spouses who, like him, have been buried along with their deceased partner. The end of escape – and the continuation of the sequence of tales – apparently justifies the means. Thereafter, he finds himself in several of the tales living among the folk of the land, until a ship appears, whereupon he begins the return voyage, recording all the wondrous phenomena he sees on the way.

Of the tales in this huge collection, it is the most fantastic – of magic rings and lamps, of 'genies' and the instantaneous, yet varying changes they bring about – that have become the most popular in the West. 'Aladdin' (ʿAlāʾ al-dīn) is the most famous of these, of course, although, as we noted above, it is not part of the core collection but was added to the French translation by Galland. Another such tale is that of 'Maʿrūf the Cobbler', the final tale in the collection. In another lengthy and richly structured narrative, Maʿrūf, a poor and hen-pecked man of Cairo, is transported to a remote land where he meets a childhood friend named ʿAlī. They decide to try 'the caravan-on-the-way trick': that they have arrived ahead of a caravan loaded with the most precious items imaginable. The commercial sector of the city is duly impressed, and a line of considerable credit is opened. Maʿrūf falls into the part with gusto and liberally distributes money to the poor. The merchants become suspicious and take their concerns to the King and his Minister. The former, however, sees an opportunity for profit also; he puts the treasury at Maʿrūf's disposal and marries him to the Princess, his daughter. The Minister meanwhile, who was himself an aspirant for the Princess's hand, is deeply envious and suspicious. The Princess is told by her father to find out the truth about her husband, and he tells her his true situation. However, she has fallen in love with her husband and sends him away for his own safety. At this crucial point, Maʿrūf stumbles on a magic ring, creates his fabulous caravan, and returns to the city in triumph. Maʿrūf's fortunes seem to be secure, but the two inimical forces in the tale are not finished. The Minister steals the ring, but the Princess retrieves it; he is thereafter executed. Maʿrūf's improved circumstances are spoiled, however, when his beloved wife, the Princess, dies. In a return to the beginning of the tale, Maʿrūf's shrewish first wife reappears. When she too tries to steal the ring, she is cut down by Maʿrūf's son by the Princess. As the tale and the collection conclude, the many strands in this multi-textured narrative have been pulled together; all the forces inimical to the just King Maʿrūf have been eliminated and his line of succession is secure.

The *Thousand and One Nights* has been a popular resort for modern writers in all genres; motifs, images, and complete stories from the collection have been adopted in a continuing process that illustrates the central place of this and the other collections in the collective consciousness of the Arab world.

MODERN FICTION

Beginnings

When Najīb Maḥfūẓ, the Egyptian novelist and Nobel prize-winner, published a work in 1982 entitled *Layālī Alf Laylah* (Nights of a Thousand Nights), his invocation of the title of Arabic's most famous collection of narratives and the subtle change in its wording clearly invoked a renowned intertext. Indeed the work opens with a section that introduces a ruler named Shahrayār and contains other segments devoted to Maʿrūf, Sindbād, and Qūt al-Qulūb. However, this convenient linkage between a recent work by the Arab world's most illustrious novelist and the tradition of earlier narratives that we have just discussed is more a reflection of relatively recent developments in modern Arabic fiction than the culmination of a lengthy process of influence stemming from the beginnings of the modern literary revival. In those initial stages, evocations of the narratives of earlier centuries were rapidly superseded by the newly imported Western genres of fiction. During the course of the twentieth century these genres – the novel and short story – have become the most popular modes of literary expression.

The changes that occurred in the creation and reception of Arabic narratives during the nineteenth century were the consequence of a combination of factors. First there is translation activity, itself a natural outcome of renewed or intensified contacts with the West. The efforts of Rifāʿah al-Ṭahṭāwī and his students in Egypt and of numerous Christian families in Lebanon may initially have had other, more focused goals, but it was virtually inevitable that the interest of such a cadre of translators should turn to literary works, beginning with the processes of translation, adaptation, and imitation, but then leading to the appearance of the earliest examples of modern Arabic fiction. A second pair of factors can be grouped under the heading of 'press', implying on the one hand the establishment of printing presses and the increasing availability of books and journals (and libraries in which to make them accessible, such as the Egyptian Dār al-Kutub founded in 1870), and on the other hand the rapid expansion in the number of newspapers in the second half of the century. The foundation of general and specialised newspapers – dailies, weeklies, and monthlies – provided ample space not only for the political debates surrounding the presence of foreign occupying forces and the need for nationalist movements to resist them but also for cultural discussions about the need for a balance between the indigenous and the imported, the traditional and the modern, the teachings of Islam and those of Western culture.

It was in this socio-political environment and for a broader readership founded on entirely new modes of access that initial attempts at fiction were written; research suggests that, as in other cultural contexts, women constituted a sizeable portion of the readership involved. Clearly there was no shortage of current topics to address, and yet the very earliest examples looked elsewhere for subject matter. An early favourite for translation (in almost every Middle Eastern country) was Dumas's *The Count of Monte Cristo*, and the historical romance novel immediately acquired a wide audience. It was part of the literary (and commercial) genius of the Lebanese *émigré* journalist, Zurjī Zaydān (*d.* 1914), to appreciate that this trend could be adopted for educational and even nationalist purposes. In a whole series of historical novels, he portrayed in fictional form significant events from the history of the Arabs and Islam. Following Zaydān's example, a number of writers published historical novels, including Nīqūlā Ḥaddād (*d.* 1954), Yaʿqāb Ṣarrūf (*d.* 1927), and Faraḥ Anṭūn (*d.* 1922).

While this library of romantic fiction played an invaluable role in developing both a readership and a sense of national and local identity, it did not focus on the societal issues of the times – the great topic of the Western novel in the nineteenth century. The columns of the press were also the publication venue for the first attempts at creating fictional narratives that would be new in content, form, and style. ʿAbdallāh Nadīm (*d.* 1896) and Yaʿqūb Ṣannūʿ (*d.* 1912) wrote witty vignettes that exploited mimicry of specific dialectal speech patterns to portray particular character types, and especially those operating in those social contexts where Western and indigenous cultures came into contact. Muṣṭafā Luṭfī al-Manfalūṭī (*d.* 1924) published a series of moralistic and sentimental 'essays' in which he made use of fictional contexts as a means of discussing pressing social and moral issues. Jubrān Khalīl Jubrān (*d.* 1931) addressed himself to conflicts of gender and generations in a series of early stories in Arabic. And in 1913 a young Egyptian named Muḥammad Ḥusayn Haykal (*d.* 1956), recently returned from France, published a novel, *Zaynab*. Filled with nostalgic depictions of the Egyptian countryside and of discussions of social philosophy, it criticises Egyptian society and its attitudes to marriage through a portrayal of the agonies of love among Egyptian peasants.

While what we term the novel may provide the earliest examples of modern Arabic fiction, it was the short story that was the first to achieve maturity within the Arabic tradition. Its generic features were adopted with relish by Arab writers during the early decades of the twentieth century; it has now developed into the most favoured mode of literary expression in the Arab world.

The short story

Any number of writers on the short story (many of whom are themselves short-story writers) have noted that the genre demands of its writer a good deal of artifice, since our experiences of life do not come in the form of stories that are short. The encapsulation of scene, character, and mood demands a craft that combines very particular powers of observation and use of language akin to that of a poet. While the narratives that pioneer writers such as Nadīm and al-Manfalūṭī published in Egyptian newspapers in the late nineteenth century may not contain all the features of the short story noted by Western critics, there can surely be no denying the concision of their expression – the stock-in-trade of any journalist – while their short narratives certainly reflect 'the nervousness and restlessness of modern life' (V. S. Pritchett) as it impacted upon Egyptian society at the time. In Lebanon, both Jubrān

Khalīl Jubrān and Mīkhā'īl Nuʿaymah (*d.* 1988) addressed themselves in their earliest stories composed in the first two decades of this century to one of the most hotly debated topics of the period: the position of women in society. The trials of 'Mārtā from Bān', snatched from the rural simplicity of her home and placed into the dens of iniquity in the evil city and of '*Wardah al-Hāniyyah*' who deserts a comfortable home with a husband she hates in order to live with her real love, these stories are told by Jubrān with both passion and sentimentality. Mīkhā'īl Nuʿaymah's early stories show a greater sense of both subtlety and detachment, something that stems in no small part from his extensive readings in the Russian masters of the short story such as Chekhov and Gogol; their influence is clearly visible in the themes and techniques of stories such as '*Sanatuhā al-jadīdah*' ('Her New Year') and '*Maṣraʿ Sattūt*' ('Sattūt's Death').

These early writers who addressed themselves to current social issues and participated in the crafting of new forms and styles provided a base on which a new generation could develop the genre. In Egypt the acknowledged pioneer in that process was Muḥammad Taymūr (*d.* 1921), who, in spite of his early death, made a major contribution to the development of the short story. He was followed by a group of writers known as 'The New School' (*Al-Madrasah al-ḥadīthah*) – including such major figures as Maḥmūd Taymūr (younger brother of Muḥammad, *d.* 1973), by far the most prolific writer in the group, Yaḥyā Ḥaqqī (*d.* 1993?), and Maḥmūd Ṭāhir Lāshīn (*d.* 1954). Within different time-frames other regions had their analogues: in Iraq, for example, Maḥmūd al-Sayyid (*d.* 1937) and Dhū al-nūn Ayyūb (*d.* 1988); in Palestine, Khalīl Baydas (*d.* 1949); in Tunisia, ʿAlī al-Duʿājī (*d.* 1949); and in Lebanon, Tawfīq Yūsuf ʿAwwād (*d.* 1989).

One of the most favoured types of story among this group of writers was the vignette: the first part of the story consists of a character sketch of an individual whose name or description often provides the title; once this unusual person has been portrayed, the narrative proceeds to describe one particular incident. Maḥmūd Taymūr's '*ʿAmm Mitwallī*' tells the story of a poor man from the Sudan who has come to Cairo; from his behaviour people conclude that he is the expected Mahdī (the title of a later revised version of the story) and follow his pronouncements avidly until it becomes clear that he has become absolutely mad. Ibrāhīm al-Māzinī (*d.* 1949) adds an additional element to this type of story by lacing many of his examples with his particular brand of farcical humour, as, for example in '*Ḥallāq al-qaryah*' ('The Village Barber') where the character in question uses the same set of implements on his human and animal customers.

The ability of the short story to provide encapsulated portraits of broader social institutions made it a powerful tool in the analysis of a topic that just a few decades earlier had been essentially off-limits: the family and in particular the role of women within its structure. Short stories from across the Arab world address themselves to every aspect of family life: the frustrations of teenagers living in a fishbowl society that watches their every move, the stages of marriage and divorce, the treatment of children, and the functioning of the larger Middle Eastern family with its many generations living in close proximity. As changing societal attitudes and improving educational opportunity bring more women writers out of the confines of the family home and into the public domain, these same topics are addressed from an entirely different perspective. Suhayr al-Qalamāwī (*b.* 1911) and Ulfat Idlibī (*b.* 1912) are among the first generation of women writers who use their stories to illustrate the female view of the life of women within the Arab family and society at large.

During the 1930s the romantic spirit that characterised much of this fiction led some writers in the direction of sentimentality, culminating in the immensely popular oeuvre of Iḥsān ʿAbd al-Quddūs (*d.* 1990). While this trend may have gained the short story a considerable readership, it was left to other writers to develop the more artistic aspects of the craft. Prime amongst them was Yaḥyā Ḥaqqī, a member of the 'New School' mentioned above, who wrote a relatively small output of stories. Ḥaqqī produces exquisite narratives that explore motivations while providing the reader with a vivid picture of Egypt in all its variety of people and place. '*Qiṣṣah min al-sijn*' ('A Story from Prison'), for example, is set in the countryside of Upper Egypt and tells the story of a law-abiding peasant whose life falls apart when he is bewitched by a beautiful gypsy girl. These qualities in Ḥaqqī's writing are brought to superb heights in his famous novella, *Qindīl Umm Hāshim* (1944; *The Saint's Lamp*, 1973). Among other writers who contributed to the development of the craft of short-story writing, we would mention Tawfīq Yūsuf ʿAwwād, whose stories are notable for their depiction of rural life and the hypocrisies of authority, Maḥmūd al-Badawī (*d.* 1985), ʿAbd al-salām al-ʿUjaylī (*b.* 1919), and Samīrah ʿAzzām (*d.* 1967).

To these aspects of theme, language, and form, Yūsuf Idrīs (*d.* 1991) adds an instinctive genius for the genre, producing volume after volume of stories that seem to be an apt reflection of both the dysfunctional nature of his rural upbringing and his own wayward and colourful personality. Beginning with an outburst of productivity in the 1950s, Idrīs captures as never before the life of the Egyptian provinces and the abject poverty of the older quarters of Cairo. Incidents and character types of extraordinary variety are portrayed with an intimacy and vividness that reflects not only a profound familiarity with the environments involved but a remarkable ability to depict the sensory aspects of the scene in a new blend of language that Idrīs made entirely his own. '*Arkhaṣ layālī*' ('The Cheapest of Nights') finds a man in a village wading through hordes of children and cursing the hole in the sky from which they fell to earth; unable to find anything else to do, he heads to his house and, climbing over the sleeping bodies of his own children, warms himself with the body of his wife.

While the realistic short story clearly matched the era of revolutionary political and social change of the 1950s, it soon found itself confronting the unpleasant realities of a new set of regimes for whom the littérateur's depiction of social conditions was expected to conform with certain implicit or explicit expectations. Many short stories now become allegories of complete alienation and the quest for meaning. Najīb Maḥfūẓ's masterpiece, '*Zaʿbalāwī*', is such a quest through the older quarters of Cairo; the narrator has 'an illness for which there is no cure', and he visits a number of 'stations' on his way to a devoutly desired encounter with a 'saint' named Zaʿbalāwī. He fails to find him, and yet the search is not a complete failure in that, as the narrative returns to its starting-point, the narrator has learned that an entity with the supernatural powers needed to cure him exists. Yūsuf Idrīs also contributes stories in the form of parables: '*Al-Āurṭā*' ('The Aorta'), for example, paints a horrifying picture of the human herd instinct, impervious to any concern for the fate of the individual.

A peer of Idrīs in short-story writing is the Syrian writer, Zakariyyā Tāmir (*b.* 1931), who is renowned for his symbolic narratives of alienation and oppression, stories that take the reader into an illogical world, a universe of sheer cruelty and callousness. The very relationship between title and beginning is often intentionally disconcerting: '*Jūʿ*' ('Hunger') opens with the sentence, 'Aḥmad was not a king', using the lack of any logical connection as a means of drawing the perplexed reader into the core of the narrative. Each story is couched in a style whose terseness and clarity suggests a naïve detachment from what is being narrated that is as disturbing as it is misleading; a style that, in its subtlety and imagery, turns many of his stories into virtual prose poems.

Among other figures of primary importance in developing the craft of the short story, we should mention the Iraqi writer, Fu'ād al-Tikirlī (*b.* 1927), whose small output nevertheless manages to reveal his mastery of the structuring of the genre; '*Al-Tannūr*' ('The Oven') is a masterpiece of ironic play between the reader and an utterly unreliable narrator. The Moroccan novelist and critic Muḥammad Barrādah has also made some notable contributions to the experimental short story; his collection, *Salkh al-jild* (Hide Flaying, 1979) reveals the subtle worlds of an author much concerned with the expression of different levels of consciousness. In Egypt, Yūsuf al-Shārūnī (*b.* 1924) and Edwar al-Kharrāṭ (*b.* 1926), both influential writers and critics, present an interesting contrast: al-Shārūnī's stories are immaculately constructed narratives that show an awareness of many of the narrative strategies of the contemporary short story and yet are couched in a style that is stark and unadorned; al-Kharrāṭ, on the other hand, relishes his ability to compose his symbolic and ambiguous stories in a style that is highly elaborate and image-laden.

The writers mentioned thus far have been mostly male. Women writers of the short story, taking their lead from pioneers such as Suhayr al-Qalamāwī, Ulfat Idlibī, and Samīrah ʿAzzām, have been making major contributions to every aspect of the genre. During the 1950s and 1960s, Laylā Baʿalbakkī (*b.* 1936) and Colette Khūrī (*b.* 1937) published works of fiction that showed a new frankness in their discussion of relationships between the sexes; Baʿalbakkī's story, '*Safīnat ḥanān ilā al-qamar*' ('Spaceship of Tenderness to the Moon') was considered sufficiently subversive to have her charged in court with an offence against public decency; she was acquitted. The successors of these courageous pioneers, writers such as Ḥanān al-Shaykh (*b.* 1945), Salwā Bakr (*b. c.* 1950), and Laylā al-ʿUthmān (*b.* 1945), have been able to contribute to the Arabic short-story tradition works of considerable artistry and social insight.

The short story has now become the most popular mode of Arabic literary expression. Large numbers of collections are published annually throughout the Arab world; for many decades Egypt and Lebanon were generally regarded as the primary centres of publication, but more recently the output in the countries of the Gulf states, the Arabian Peninsula, and the Maghrib has been an addition in both quantity and variety.

The novel

In our survey of the early history of modern Arabic fiction above, we noted that the early popularity of the novel genre was engendered in large part by the serialised publication of historical romance novels. This tendency was one of several factors that made the development of an Arabic genre which would replicate the structures, styles, and generic purposes of the nineteenth-century novel in the West a complex and even disjointed process in comparison with that of the short story. The ability to project aspects of 'life on a large scale', to place realistically drawn characters into authentic environments, and to do so in a style that was palatable to the newly emerging readership, these were skills that needed a prolonged and concentrated period of application and technical development, something that was and, in many cases, remains, a luxury that many would-be novelists cannot afford.

As was the case in other literary genres, a number of geographical and cultural factors – not the least being the emigration of many Syrian families to Egypt in the 1860s and 1870s – made the Egyptian tradition an early focal point of both creativity and emulation. Elsewhere in the Arab world, the timetable involved was different, often considerably so. In the countries of the Maghrib, for example, the deep penetration of French culture into the educational system has meant that the balance between French and Arabic expression remains a hotly debated issue, with programmes of 'Arabicisation' (*taʿrib*) endeavouring to promote the use of Arabic within cultural milieux. The first Algerian novel in Arabic, for example, is Aḥmad Riḍā Hūhū's *Ghādat umm al-qurā* (Maid of the City) published in 1947, and the first by an Algerian woman writer is Aḥlām Mustaghānimī's *Dhākirat al-jasad* (Body's Memory, 1993). Under Ottoman suzerainty (and censorship) Iraqi literature was kept under tight control and tended to adhere to traditional modes; a few historical romances were published, but it was not till the 1920s, when the British mandate was in effect, that the Iraqi novel began to address pressing contemporary issues.

In any historical survey of the development of the novel, Haykal's *Ẓaynab* clearly occupies an important position; the Egyptian countryside is lovingly depicted with the overwhelming sentiment of a writer recalling it from abroad in its most idealistic and romanticised garb (although it needs to be added that, even when compared with the descriptive detail of al-Muwayliḥī's work of a decade earlier, *Ẓaynab* comes up short on authenticity). Another milestone in the development of the multifaceted aspects of novel writing came in 1926 when Ṭāhā Ḥusayn published in serial form a fictionalised account of his early childhood, entitled *Al-Ayyām* (The Days, 1925; *An Egyptian Childhood*, 1932), the narrative features of which – especially the ironic play between the narrator and the protagonist (his childhood self) – have rightly earned it a significant place in the history of the development of modern Arabic fiction.

It was during the 1930s that a group of writers in different parts of the Arab world accepted the challenge of establishing the novel in Arabic as a ready and powerful literary mode whereby to explore topics of current concern and to experiment with aspects of technique. The dual role of the West as the seat of colonial hegemony and of cultural influence was a favourite topic: Tawfīq Yūsuf ʿAwwād's novel *al-Raghīf* (The Loaf, 1939), explores the tensions created by the conflict during the First World War; Shakīb al-Jābirī's *Naham* (Greed, 1936) and Dhū al-Nūn Ayyūb's *al-Duktūr Ibrāhīm* (Doctor Ibrāhīm, 1939) both discuss the impact of a period of study in Europe on Arab students – a favourite theme of Arab writers from the outset and one which finds its most distinguished expression in Yaḥyā Ḥaqqī's novella, *Qindīl Umm Hāshim* (1944; *The Saint's Lamp*, 1973), and al-Ṭayyib Ṣāliḥ's *Mawsim al-hijrah ilā al-shamāl* (1966; *Season of Migration to the North*, 1969). In *Ibrāhīm al-kātib* (1931; *Ibrāhīm the Writer*, 1976) Ibrāhīm al-Māzinī brings his well-known humour and insight to the portrayal of a number of characters and situations in a story of the narrator's love for three women. Tawfīq al-Ḥakīm contributes several notable works: *ʿAwdat al-rūḥ* (1933; *Return of the Spirit*, 1990) provides a lively colloquial dialogue as a means of introducing his reader to the tensions of a large Egyptian family living through the tensions of life in Egypt in 1919; *Yawmiyyāt nāʾib fī al-aryāf* (1937; *The Maze of Justice*, 1947) is a beautifully constructed picture of the Egyptian countryside in which a young urbanised Egyptian makes a mostly vain attempt to explain the machinations of Egyptian law to the bemused peasantry. One of the most accomplished Egyptian novels of this period, notable by contrast for its apparent lack of autobiographical content, is also one of the most neglected: Maḥmūd Ṭāhir Lāshīn's *Ḥawwāʾ bi-lā Ādam* (1934; *Eve Without Adam*, 1986), which explores the tortured feelings of a woman who falls in love with the brother of the girl she is tutoring and whose despair leads her to suicide.

It was also during the 1930s that another Egyptian writer, Najīb Maḥfūẓ (*b.* 1911), set himself the task of tying together all these various strands of the novelist's craft by undertaking a systematic survey of the themes and techniques of Western fiction. Over a period of five decades

Maḥfūẓ has taken as his major theme the novel's primary topic: the city – in his case, Cairo and, to a lesser extent, Alexandria – and the aspirations and sufferings of its middle class of artisans, traders, and bureaucrats. The Nobel Laureate in Literature for 1988, he is widely recognised as the founding father of the Arabic novel.

By the time the Egyptian Revolution of 1952 had swept away the *ancien régime*, Maḥfūẓ had penned a series of novels that showed in graphic detail the political corruption and social disparities that had bred such discontent. In each case a particular district of old Cairo, depicted with the loving attention of one who is intimately familiar with the area, became the focus for a story that explored the aspirations of Egyptians and the many ways in which they were crushed by forces over which they had no control. The three-volume trilogy, *Bayn al-qaṣrayn* (1956; *Palace Walk*, 1990), *Qaṣr al-shawq* (1957; *Palace of Desire*, 1991), and *al-Sukkariyyah* (1957; *Sugar Street*, 1992), uses the ʿAbd al-Jawwād family as the focus for a huge canvas of Egyptian political and cultural life from 1917 till 1944, placing the loves, dreams, ideas, and foibles of successive generations within the inexorable forward march of time and the often painful processes of change. The readership of the Arab world as a whole, searching for new directions in the post-independence era, found in Maḥfūẓ's masterpiece a graphic illustration of the circumstances that had brought about the profound political and social transformations that occurred in Egypt and elsewhere during the 1950s. However, while the need for change had united disparate groups and classes in a common goal (as *al-Sukkariyyah* clearly shows), the direction of the newly independent nations and their political agenda were very unclear. For novelists who penned works that showed a commitment to governmental policies, the rewards often came in the form of positions in the new cultural hierarchy. For those, on the other hand, who chose to challenge those policies, the result was imprisonment, exile or worse; the long list of novelists who have been imprisoned and the repertoire of novels that discuss the prison experience – including notable contributions from Ṣunʿallāh Ibrāhīm (*Tilka al-rāʾiḥah*, 1966; *The Smell of It*, 1961) and ʿAbd al-raḥmān Munīf (*Sharq al-Mutawassiṭ* (East of the Mediterranean), 1975) – is a sobering commentary on the lack of a genuine freedom of expression that has been the lot of most Arab writers in the second half of the twentieth century. Maḥfūẓ's response to this situation was a fictional silence that was broken in 1959 by a very different kind of work, an allegorical novel that treated one of his favourite topics, the role of religion in the history of mankind and the dilemma of its relationship to modern scientific knowledge. *Awlād ḥāratinā* (1959, 1967; *Children of Gebelawi*, 1981; *Children of the Alley*, 1996) follows the course of mankind's history of faith through a series of leaders who attempt to provide a moral and spiritual base that will bring the unruly conduct of the gangs in the community under some sort of control. It is this religious aspect, and especially the overarching figure of Jabalāwī who is eventually killed by ʿArafah (scientia), that has made this work Maḥfūẓ's most controversial piece of fiction.

When Maḥfūẓ did turn his attention to the course of the Egyptian revolution in the 1960s, it was in a series of highly allusive works that move away from the depiction of the community as a whole to explore the alienated world of the individual. Using a newly economical language to provide details of place and time, these novels – beginning with *al-Liṣṣ wa-al-kilāb* (1961; *The Thief and the Dogs*, 1984), and culminating with *Thartharah fawq al-Nīl* (1966; *Adrift on the Nile*, 1993) and *Mīrāmār* (1967; *Miramar*, 1978) – constitute a rising crescendo of disillusion and anger towards the rulers of Egypt and the grim atmosphere that their societal machinations had created. The June War of 1967 came as a brutal confirmation of the scenario that Maḥfūẓ and others had painted, and once again Maḥfūẓ wrote no novels for a time, concentrating instead on a series of lengthy and cryptic short stories. When he did return to the novel, it was in changed circumstances: he himself had retired, and Anwar al-Sādāt had become president on the death of ʿAbd al-nāṣir (Nasser). To Maḥfūẓ's personal disillusion over the way that the revolution's promise had been thwarted, obvious enough in works like *al-Marāyā* (1972; *Mirrors*, 1977) and *al-Karnak* (1974; *Al-Karnak*, 1988), was now added a deep antipathy to the president's personality and style and to the open-markets policy (*infitāḥ*) which served to exacerbate the class divisions within Egyptian society. Novels such as *Malḥamat al-ḥarāfish* (1977; *The Harafish*, 1994), *Al-Bāqī min al- zaman sāʿah* (Just One Hour Left, 1982), and *Yawm qutila al-zaʿīm* (The Day the Leader Was Killed, 1985) show a society of glaring contrasts, one in which basic amenities such as housing remain a dream and there is little mobility. As Maḥfūẓ has aged, his work has also become more retrospective. In some works he has repeated earlier experiments in structure and language; in others – such as *Riḥlat ibn Faṭṭūmah* (1983; *The Journey of Ibn Fattouma*, 1992) and *Layālī alf laylah* (1982; *Arabian Nights and Days*, 1995) – he has looked for inspiration in the narrative genres of the classical tradition. And with age has come also a certain wistful and nostalgic tone; both *Qushtumur* (the name of a cafe, 1989) and *Aṣdā al-sīrah al-dhatiyyah* ('Echoes of

Autobiography', 1994) – the latter a remarkable evocation of classical Ṣūfī writings – take the reader back to earlier days in the narrator's life, days of hopes and loves, and of struggles both physical and intellectual.

As the novel has attained a position of prestige that allows, indeed requires, it to fulfil its primary generic purpose as a reflector and advocate of social change, so male and female writers have begun to experiment with a variety of techniques in the process of exploring the significant issues of the time. A few authors have now successfully undertaken the challenge of replicating the mammoth scale of Maḥfūẓ's *Trilogy*. ʿAbd al-raḥmān Munīf's quintet of novels, published under the general title *Mudun al-milḥ* (1984–88; in English thus far, *Cities of Salt*, 1984; *The Trench*, 1991; and *Variations on Night and Day*, 1993) is a carefully crafted and highly critical fictional study of the impact of the discovery of oil on the traditional life of Saudi Arabia and the morals of its rulers. The Libyan novelist, Ibrāhīm al-Kūnī (*b.* 1948), introduces the readers of his novels to an unfamiliar landscape and environment, the nomadic tribes of the deserts of North Africa. Lengthy works such as *al-Majūs* (The Magi, 1991) and *al-Saḥarah* (The Sorcerers, 1993) take their readers far from the modern cities of the Middle East and place them into a transient society that invokes many of the images and values of the earliest stages in the Arabic literary tradition.

Oil and desert are, of course, closely linked as themes, in reality as in fiction. The discovery of oil in the early twentieth century has guaranteed that the Middle East will remain for the nations of the West a focus of strategic and economic concern. As the Gulf War of 1991 has already proved convincingly, it needs to be added to the large number of points of potential and actual conflict in the region, many of which have, not unnaturally, been the topics of works of fiction. Principal among them is the fate of the Palestinian people; while the focus of some works has been on the conflicts themselves – 1948, 1956, 1967, 1973, and 1982 – the most accomplished pieces of fiction have dealt with the life of the fragmented community during the interstices. The works of Ghassān Kanafānī (assassinated in 1972) are emblematic of a period when, for all the empty rhetoric from Arab leaders and with the indifference of the rest of the world, little was done to ameliorate the situation of the exiled Palestinians; *Rijāl fī al-shams* (1963; *Men in the Sun*, 1978) captures the situation with superb artistry, as three Palestinians from different generations suffocate to death as they try to escape to Kuwait inside a water-tanker. Completely different but equally powerful is Emil Ḥabībī's (*d.* 1996), *Al-Waqāʾiʿ al- gharībah fī ikhtifāʾ Saʿīd Abī al-naḥs al-mutashāʾil*

(1972, 1974, 1977; *The Secret Life of Saeed, the Ill-Fated Pessoptimist*, 1982). One of the finest exercises in irony in all of Arabic fiction, it depicts the wise fool, Saʿīd, coping in his unique way with the crushing realities of the life of a Palestinian living in the State of Israel. Different again are the novels of Jabrā Ibrāhīm Jabrā (*d.* 1994) which portray the alienation and nostalgia of the Palestinian intellectual community condemned to a life of exile. Novels like *al- Safīnah* (1970; *The Ship*, 1985) and *al-Baḥth ʿan Walīd Masʿūd* (The Search for Walīd Masʿūd, 1978), make excellent use of the multi-narrator technique to portray the agonies of the exiled Arab intellectual and specifically the plight of the Palestinians as emblematic of the region as a whole. Saḥar Khalīfah (*b.* 1941) has taken as a major theme in her novels the often tortuous relationship between the peoples of Israel and the West Bank; in *al-Ṣubbār* (1976; *Wild Thorns*, 1985) we see the reverse of Kanafānī's *Men in the Sun*, in that a Palestinian man returns from the Gulf in order to disrupt the daily transfer of workers from the West Bank to jobs in Israel.

Other conflicts have also provided inspiration for novels. The prolonged War of Liberation in Algeria (1954–62) is still a potent memory, and no more so than in the vivid narratives of the Algerian novelist, al-Ṭāhir Waṭṭār (*b.* 1936); in two works, he creates the character of *al-Lāz* (1974, 1982), a fighter for the nationalist cause who spies on the French. Social complexity of an even greater kind has been a feature of Lebanese communal life, and the civil war during the 1970s and 1980s, with its linkages to the Palestine question and other regional issues of hegemony and control, was a fertile breeding ground for societal chaos, reflected in vivid detail in several distinguished contributions to fiction. The early pioneer Tawfīq Yūsuf ʿAwwād may actually be seen as foretelling the conflict in his novel, *Ṭawāḥīn Bayrūt* (1972; *Death in Beirut*, 1976), in which a Shīʿī girl from South Lebanon encounters the fault-lines in the social structure during her time in Beirut. However, it is Ḥanān al-Shaykh's (*b.* 1945) *Ḥikāyat Ẓahrah* (1980; *The Story of Ẓahrah*, 1986) that, again using a Shīʿī girl as its focus, reveals in most graphic and accomplished detail the full scale of the insane destruction that the armies of the various political and religious subgroups rained upon each other. The same atmosphere of normalised violence and despair characterises the several novels of Ilyās Khūrī; the narrator of *Riḥlat Ghāndī al-ṣaghīr* (1989; *The Journey of Little Ghandi*, 1994) continually questions 'the author' as he finds himself placed into a nightmare world in which personal relationships and narrative linkages of any kind are tenuous and death is an ever-present reality.

The Arabic novel has also addressed itself to a whole series of other confrontations and problems within the society itself. For example, a number of Egyptian novelists have addressed the nature of the relationship between the city and the rural life of the provinces, including ʿAbd al-raḥmān al-Sharqāwī (*d.* 1987), Yūsuf Idrīs (*d.* 1991), Fatḥī Ghānim (*b.* 1927), and Yaḥyā al-Ṭāhir ʿAbdallāh (*d.* 1981); the works of Yūsuf al-Qaʿīd (*b.* 1944) such as *Akhbār ʿizbat al-Minaysī* (1971; *New from the Meneisi Farm*, 1987), ʿAbd al-ḥakīm Qāsim in *Ayyām al-insān al-sabʿah* (1969; *The Seven Days of Man*, 1989), and of Bahāʾ Ṭāhir in *Sharq al-nakhīl* (East of the Palm-trees, 1985) are notable examples of this subgenre. In a country such as Algeria and Syria where the relationship between the urbanised littoral and the countryside has always been tense, works of fiction devoted to the topic have a particularly fervent quality; thus, ʿAbd al-ḥamīd ibn Hadūqah's *Rīḥ al-janūb* (South Wind, 1971) and al-Ṭāhir Waṭṭār's *al-Zilzāl* (The Earthquake, 1974) from the former, and ʿAbd al-nabī Ḥijāzī's *al-Sindyānah* (The Oak-Tree, 1971) from the latter.

A number of authors have created works that explore crisis situations in family life, often brought about by the death of the father: Maḥfūẓ's *Bidāyah wa-nihāyah* (1951; *The Beginning and the End*, 1985) and Fāḍil al-Sibāʿī's (*b.* 1929) *Thumma azhar al-ḥuzn* (Then Sorrow Bloomed, 1963) are two examples of this theme. A number of Maghribī novelists paint a gruesome picture of family life and, in particular, of the tyrannical role of the father within it: Muḥammad Barrādah, for example, in *Luʿbat al-nisyān* (1987; *Game of Forgetting*, 1996) and Muḥammad Shukrī in his 'fictional autobiography', *Al- Khubz al-ḥāfī* (1982; *For Bread Alone*, 1973), but the most shocking picture is painted by the Algerian novelist, Rashīd Abū Jadrah [Boujedra] (*b.* 1941), most notably in *La Répudiation* (1969; *al-Taṭlīq* (Repudiation), 1982), and *al-Marth* (The Soaking, 1984). A number of women novelists have expressed themselves on this topic in increasingly forthright terms. Particularly noteworthy are Laylā Baʿalbakkī with *Anā aḥyā* (I Am Alive, 1958) – a pioneer in the forthright fictional expression of women's liberation – Laṭīfah al-Zayyāt (*b.* 1925) with *al-Bāb al-maftūḥ* (The Open Door, 1960), and Ghādah al-Sammān (*b.* 1942) with *Bayrūt '75* (Beirut '75, 1975) and *Kawābīs Bayrūt* (Beirut Nightmares, 1976). Loudest of all in expressing her opposition to traditional, male-dominated family values is the Egyptian writer, Nawāl al-Saʿdāwī (*b.* 1930) who, in addition to serving as a courageous publicist of women's issues in Egypt, has also written several works of fiction, the most famous of which is *Imraʾah ʿinda nuqṭat ṣifr* (1975; *Woman at Point Zero*, 1983), the story of a prostitute who is killed for the murder of her pimp. The courageous way in which Baʿalbakkī, al-Sammān, al-Shaykh, and al-Saʿdāwī have expressed their feminine vision of current Arab social realities in such a frank fashion – often at the risk of personal attacks from the more conservative segments of society – has served to open up fictional creativity to a richer and variegated exploration of gender relationships with the family and society as a whole.

We have already drawn attention to the repertoire of novels about prisons and the loneliness and alienation that they of necessity engender, but the theme of exile, be it physical and external or psychological and internal, has also been a feature of much writing, as in Ḥannā Mīnah's (*b.* 1924) *al-Thalj ya'tī min al-nāfidhah* (1969), ʿAbd al-ḥakīm Qāsim's (*d.* 1990) *Qadar al-ghuraf al-muqbiḍah* (Fate of the Oppressive Rooms, 1982), Jūrj Sālim's (*d.* 1976) *Fī al-manfā* (In Exile, 1962), and Ḥabībī's *Ikhṭiyyeh* ('Oh dear', 1985), set in a transformed city of Haifa that is now divorced from its Arab past and site of a static internal exile.

The intangible essence of the novel genre lies in its role as an agent of change and thus the necessity of its susceptibility to the very phenomenon that it depicts. Arab writers have made use of its changing nature to the fullest extent. Like many of their Western colleagues they have chosen to represent the complex and fragmented conditions that confront them through what Frank Kermode has described as 'a recognisable estrangement from what used to be known as reality'. Narrative coherence is no longer a given; it is often eschewed. Chronological time is fractured through flashbacks (as, for example, in Jabrā's works) or through the cinematic sweep of Ḥalīm Barakāt's novel of the June 1967 War, *ʿAwdat al-ṭā'ir ilā al-baḥr* (1969; *Days of Dust*, 1974); the reliability of a single, omniscient narrator is replaced by the different versions of several narrators and then by a challenge to the entire concept as the narrators of the fiction of Muḥammad Barrādah and Ilyās Khūrī argue with their 'authors' about the course of the narrative in which they are involved. This is, of course, one aspect of the process of 'metafiction', what Frank Kermode describes as 'the use of fiction as an instrument of research into the nature of fiction'. One of the most remarkable examples of this narrative strategy is *ʿĀlam bi-lā kharā'iṭ* (A World Without Maps, 1983), a joint work of ʿAbd al-raḥmān Munīf and Jabrā Ibrāhīm Jabrā, that is interesting not only because of its actual authorship but also because one of the characters is in the process of writing a novel and discusses the process at length. At the hands of many contemporary Arab novelists the process of composition involves an elaborate process of textual play. Ḥabībī evokes all manner of styles and references, Arab and Western, as he covers the bitter realities of daily life in Israel with a layer of improbable erudition. In *Maʿrakat al-zuqāq* (Struggle in the Alley, 1986) Rashīd Abū Jadrah's school-boy protagonist has to make vocabulary lists for his classroom courses in Latin and Arabic. Jamāl al-Ghīṭānī (*b.* 1945) and ʿAbd al-raḥmān Munīf incorporate into their works of fiction segments from, and pastiches of, the works of the classical littérateurs we have mentioned earlier in this chapter (including al-Jāḥiẓ and ibn ʿArabī).

CONCLUSION

The cumbersome title of this chapter is an appropriate indication of the definitional difficulties associated with the material included in it and, it needs to be added, with any attempt to find a context within which to analyse the literary production of a cultural system (particularly a non-Western one) different from our own. The changing nature of the phenomenon of *adab* during the earlier period and the way that it now represents the equally problematic concept of 'literature' provides one cluster of problems, while the exclusion of popular genres and particularly narratives from the pale is another. Different parameters are clearly involved here, and we have not tried to hide them.

That said, however, much contemporary literary criticism has been at pains to break down the barriers between different types of text. For a work such as this, whose organisational principle implies continuities rather than ruptures, perhaps the most convenient aspect of current narrative writing in Arabic is that the use and imitation of the themes, structures, and language of classical Arabic prose genres – popular as well as élite – is now regarded by many authors as a modernist gesture.

CHAPTER 6

Drama

INTRODUCTION

In 1963 the prominent Egyptian short-story writer and playwright Yūsuf Idrīs chose to publish a series of articles in the Cairene literary monthly, *Al-Kātib*, under the title, 'Towards an Egyptian Theatre'. Whatever yardstick one may wish to use in deciding what the terms 'theatre' and 'drama' may imply in the Arab world context – a point we will discuss in detail below – there can be little argument about the fact that by 1963 an Egyptian tradition of modern Arabic drama was well over a century old. Surveying the development of the drama genre up to that point, Idrīs suggests that, while the processes of translation, 'Arabicisation', and adaptation may have been able to transfer certain elements of drama into the Egyptian context, and indeed while certain Egyptian playwrights may have produced accomplished works that made use of local themes, the end result of all this creative activity was still culturally derivative. There remained a disjuncture between Arabic drama in Egypt and the indigenous cultural tradition. Were there, Idrīs wondered, no examples of drama to be found within the heritage of the Egyptian people? Idrīs's response to these questions took the form of a remarkable and innovative play, *Farāfīr*, that was performed in 1964. However, in the context of the series of articles he continued by exploring the nature of the dramatic in the Middle East and the West and the kinds of drama performance that had been popular in the pre-modern period of Middle Eastern history. The questions that he raised at that time and the answers he provided constitute a conveniently modern point of reference through which to consider the nature of drama in its Arab world context and the types of dramatic event that were the precedents to the modern tradition.

DRAMA AND ARABIC DRAMA

The theoretical beginnings of the European dramatic tradition which Idrīs is confronting in his comments are generally agreed to be found in the *Poetics* of Aristotle where he tells his readers that drama is based in the principle of 'representation' (*mimesis*), a process that involves impersonation. An expansion, indeed a corollary, of this classic definition is represented by the notion that, in order to fulfil its dramatic function to the full, a play needs to be acted, performed; such a process requires a place where the drama may be presented – a theatre of one kind or another – and an audience who will engage themselves in the performance with both their eyes and ears. For the most part, the 'action' will involve actors performing on stage by using gestures and dialogue as means of representing the deeds and emotions of characters in order to 'show' the import of the play being presented. While in the Greek tradition the relationship between the performance on stage and the audience was viewed as one that involved the stimulus of the audience's empathy followed by a sense of catharsis, more recent trends, particularly those associated with the plays and productions of Piscator and Brecht, have endeavoured to prevent such empathy; in fact, to distance the audience from the action so that the performance can fulfil a more educational purpose.

Within the context of that broad concept known as society the history of drama shows that the genre has managed to fulfil a number of functions, including those of liturgy, entertainment, and education. In origin the genre was connected to religious or communal festivals, as in the case of much Greek and Roman drama. In a more popular vein, the drama was co-opted by medieval Christianity through the often lengthy cycles of plays recorded in the archives of such English cities as Chester, Wakefield, and York, or in the Oberammergau Passion play. Above all, the very fact that drama is the most public of all literary genres, a performance, an act of impersonation and showing in front of an audience, has also made it in many, if not most, cultures and historical periods the focus of political oversight – in a word, censorship.

Within the Western tradition of drama the performance element gravitates towards the formalities and conventions of the theatre as structure, something that led Brecht to frame part of his own dramatic theory in terms of the effect of the theatre's 'walls' on audience response to the performance. In the same way the script of the play has assumed the status of a text. The works of Sophocles, Racine, Shakespeare, Goethe, Pirandello, and Chekhov are regarded as major contributions to the literary heritage and have joined the list of canonical works of Western culture, a status confirmed in numerous ways, not least by their presence on the reading lists of national school curricula.

It is as part of the nineteenth-century cultural renaissance in the Arab world that the literary community encounters and adopts the generic tradition that we have just outlined. The pre-modern Arabic literary heritage does not provide us with examples of types of drama that can be conveniently linked to the Western tradition, but, as Yūsuf Idrīs's remarks cited above imply, there are a number of indigenous genres which exhibit dramatic qualities. Mirroring the combination of religious memorial and public performance that marks the medieval mystery plays mentioned above, a first example can be provided by a performance tradition that survives from great antiquity till the present day. Within the Shīʿī communities of the Middle East (and thus especially in Iran), there is a tradition of the *taʿziyah* (a term implying both mourning and consolation), a passion play which serves as a commemoration of the death of the Prophet Muḥammad's grandson, al-Ḥusayn, at the battle of Karbalāʾ in AD 680. Performances of this particular form of drama take place during the Islamic month of Muḥarram and consist of a highly ritualised public performance.

The period preceding the nineteenth-century renaissance in the Arab world – an era that, as we noted in Chapter 1 above, spans no less than five centuries – witnessed an efflorescence of a variety of popular genres, many of which can be considered as dramatic. Prime amongst these was the shadow play in which coloured figures were manipulated by wires from behind a transparent screen. We are fortunate to possess the manuscript of three 'plays' composed by the Egyptian Shams al-dīn Muḥammad ibn Dāniyāl (*d.* 1311), for this particular form. It is clear from the introduction to his plays that the genre was not a new one in his day; one of the purposes that ibn Dāniyāl has in recording these examples is to provide fresh materials for a medium where much of the material has become hackneyed. The plays themselves clearly fall into the realm of comedy, intending to show up the very worst foibles of mankind, most particularly where matters sexual are concerned. The contents are bawdy to the point of obscenity. In one play, *Ṭayf al-khayāl*, the chief character is named Prince Wiṣāl, a name that implies sexual congress. Farcical and scatological effects are provided by having the characters stumble, babble, and fart on stage. In another play, *ʿAjīb wa-gharīb*, every form of profession, particularly those of the less desirable elements of the populace, is explored.

A particularly popular and widespread form of this type of presentation was the genre known as *karagöz*. This genre bears a very close resemblance to the traditional Punch and Judy show, perhaps not so common at the end of the twentieth century as it was in this writer's childhood. In imitation of what would appear to be a Chinese tradition, a single performer would wrap himself in a tent-like structure and proceed to manipulate hand-held puppets on a stage above his head. A number of sketches involving different characters might be involved, but the basic hero would always be Karagöz – Everyman – the bumbling and boisterous simpleton, who would endeavour to outsmart any pretentious hypocrite who chose to stand in his way, usually resorting to beatings as the preferred mode of resolving disputes.

One final aspect of the 'dramatic' during the pre-modern period concerns a particular function that has been much exploited by modern dramatists: the *ḥakawātī* or story-teller. As Edward Lane records in *Manners and Customs of the Modern Egyptians*, his unique account of Cairene life in the 1860s, story-tellers would accompany themselves on musical instruments and would gesticulate at appropriate points in the narrative. That several contemporary playwrights should invoke the figure of the *ḥakawātī* in order to provide a Brechtian distancing mechanism to their dramas and that a prominent group of Palestinian actors should call themselves the Ḥakawātī Troupe is clearly no accident.

BEGINNINGS IN SYRIA AND EGYPT

European travellers have provided us with accounts of these types of public performance from all parts of the Middle East; in certain areas, the genre of shadow play has lasted well into the twentieth century. Alongside these accounts we encounter – particularly during the period of Western colonial expansion into the region – descriptions of performances by Western troupes for residents from European countries and the local cultural élite who could, at least partially, understand performances in one or other European language. Thus, the Egyptian historian, ʿAbd al-raḥmān al-Jabartī, apparently a somewhat bemused member of the audience, gives us his own account of a performance in 1800 by a French troupe during the French occupation that followed Napoleon's invasion of Egypt in 1798.

Mārūn al-Naqqāsh (*d.* 1855), a member of a prosperous family of Lebanese businessmen, returned from a visit to Italy in 1847 and put on a performance of his play, *Al-Bakhīl* (The Miser), in his own home in the following year. As the title suggests, the theme of the play shares much in common with Molière's play of the same name, but the script was no mere slavish copy. The majority, perhaps all, of the play was sung, in that, to cite al-Naqqāsh, the presence of singing would make the new genre more palatable to its audience. This linkage between dramatic performances and music has remained a predominant feature of much modern Arabic drama. Spurred on by the success of his initial experiment al-Naqqāsh adapted a tale from the *Thousand and One Nights* for his second and most successful play, *Abū al-Ḥasan al-mughaffal aw Hārūn al-Rashīd* (Abū al-Ḥasan the Simpleton or Hārūn al-Rashīd, 1849–50). This tale concerning the Abbāsī caliph, Hārūn al-Rashīd, and his *wazīr*, Jaʿfar, and the way in which they have some fun at the expense of Abū al-Ḥasan, who in an unguarded moment wishes that he could have real power, provides much opportunity for comedy and for some none too subtle insights into the realities of authority.

Al-Naqqāsh had to obtain a decree from the Ottoman authorities before he could perform plays in his home. Just how sensitive the situation was can be illustrated by the career of another pioneer, the Syrian dramatist, actor, and troupe manager, Abū Khalīl al-Qabbānī (*d.* 1902). In the early 1870s he was encouraged by the Ottoman governor, Ṣubḥī Pāshā, and later by Midḥat Pāshā (*d.* 1883), the famous reformer, to put on some plays – in particular yet another piece inspired by the tales of Hārūn al-Rashīd to be found in the *Thousand and One Nights*. The conservative religious establishment in Damascus, already deeply suspicious of the permissibility and probity of this new medium, was aroused to a fury by the appearance on stage of Hārūn al-Rashīd the caliph in disguise and obtained a decree from Istanbul ordering the theatre to close. In 1884 al-Qabbānī emulated the al-Naqqāsh family by moving his troupe to Egypt. There he enjoyed a very fruitful two decades of work, directing numerous plays by himself and others until his theatre was burned down in an act of arson in 1900.

The Egypt to which the troupes of al-Naqqāsh and al-Qabbānī travelled provided a much more conducive atmosphere for these and other pioneers in Arabic drama. The Khedive Ismāʿīl, who had ruled the country since 1863, had set himself to replicate within Egyptian society as many aspects of Western culture as possible. The city of Cairo had been extended to the banks of the Nile, and where this new city adjoined the old, a large square had been opened up to accommodate the new Cairo Opera House. Just half a mile from the site of the opera house, foreign acting troupes regularly performed plays on an open-air stage in the newly refurbished Ezbekiyya Gardens. It was among these troupes that another pioneer of modern Arabic drama, Yaʿqūb Ṣannūʿ (*d.* 1912), obtained his early practical experience in the theatre.

Like al-Naqqāsh, Ṣannūʿ had previously encountered the genre at first hand in Europe. Born into an Egyptian Jewish family, he had been sent to further his education in Livorno, Italy. In the early 1870s he determined to gather together a troupe of actors to perform in Arabic on stage. Details of the particular plays have not come down to us, but they appear to have combined dialogues with episodes of music and singing in much the same way as al-Naqqāsh had done, although in Ṣannūʿ's case the dialogue was composed in the colloquial dialect of Cairo – something that marks an important shift in the communication between stage and audience. News of these performances attracted the Khedives's attention, and Ṣannūʿ was invited to perform a set of plays before a large and prestigious audience in the Khedive's private theatre in Qaṣr al-Nīl. The plays presented on this occasion were all relatively brief comedies, and initially amused the ruler, until, that is, he realised that he himself appeared to be the butt of some of the humour. In spite of warnings, Ṣannūʿ seems to have been unwilling to tone down his satirical attacks, and his theatre was closed down in 1872; the Khedive exiled him in 1878.

Within the Egyptian context, mention must also be made of another important figure, Muḥammad ʿUthmān Jalāl (*d.* 1894), who managed to produce a remarkably accomplished transformation of Molière's *Tartuffe* into an Egyptian version, *Al-Shaykh Matlūf*, published in 1873 but not performed on stage till 1912. What is so important about this and other translation efforts by Jalāl (including three other plays by Molière published in 1889) was not merely the authenticity of the resulting texts couched in the Arabic poetic genre of *zajal* and the colloquial level of language into which the original text was transposed, but also the highly successful process whereby the characters and scenario were 'Egyptianised'.

As the brief account above makes clear, Egyptian audiences in the latter half of the nineteenth century found themselves presented with an extremely varied fare within the larger context of the theatre. On the stage there were plays based on traditional tales of romances which were performed in the literary language by a constantly expanding collection of troupes. Elsewhere, there were other performances of a more popular kind in terms of both themes (with emphasis on domestic farce and socio-political satire) and language. The reaction of audiences to this wealth of opportunity ranged from the obvious appreciation of the educated élite to sheer bemusement among large segments of the populace. What, for example, was one supposed to make of women who not only appeared unveiled in public, but also portrayed their emotions on stage with such apparent facility? One commentator, Muḥammad al-Muwayliḥī (*d.* 1930), was appalled by what he witnessed:

> The curtain went up to reveal a group of actors and actresses on stage. They started performing something best described as halfway between chanting and singing. Whatever it was, human nature revolted against it . . . Nothing in the Islamic faith permits women to participate in this art form . . . It's no part of Islamic literature to have plays dealing with Islamic history, its caliphs and devout men, acted out in public in a fashion which makes use of love and singing as its basic attractions. (quoted from Allen, *A Period of Time* (1992), p. 369)

It is worth our while to pause for a moment at this point and observe the extent to which tensions that still impact upon the drama genre in Arabic today are present at the outset. For, by the turn of the century one can already see an obvious split in the medium of theatre performance between the essentially comic fare that is expressed in the spoken language of the audience and the more serious, literary intentions of those who aspire to a higher form of art performed in the written language of the cultural heritage of Arabic, a theatrical mode that is accompanied by interludes of music and singing. Of these two it is the comic that has always proved the more popular, a fact that continues to arouse the complaints of the theatre establishment in Egypt.

It was during the early decades of this century that many of the issues connected with this confrontation of different heritages and cultural values were explored by playwrights and the troupes who performed their works. Indeed playwrights found a good deal of inspiration for their works in the cultural confrontation itself. Faraḥ Anṭūn (*d.* 1922), a Lebanese Christian journalist and writer who was a member of the community living in Egypt, criticises the aping of Western bourgeois values in *Miṣr al-jadīdah wa-Miṣr al-qadīmah* (Modern Egypt, Old Egypt, 1913). Anṭūn was one of the earliest playwrights to experiment with the issue of levels of language to be used in dramatic works. His solution, that of scripting the high-class roles in the standard written language and the low-class ones in the colloquial, was one that proved effective within the theatrical milieu of the times; it was imitated by a number of writers.

The most important figure of the period, however, is Muḥammad Taymūr (1891–1921), who set himself to identify criteria for good drama and performance of it, ruing in particular the prevalence of performances of translated works and the lack of what can only be termed local colour in the indigenous tradition, most notably in the matter of language. As if to prove his point, Taymūr appears to have completely recast his play, *Al-ʿUsfūr fī al-qafaṣ* (Bird in the Cage, 1918) – in which a miserly landlord finds himself out-manoeuvred by his Levantine maid and his own son – from a first version in the written language to an expanded four-act work in the colloquial. With another play, *ʿAbd al-Sattār Efendī* (1918) – a more farcical piece involving a usual cast of characters: hen-pecked husband, shrewish wife, marriageable daughter, and manipulative and nubile maid – Taymūr sets himself to provide a counter to the popularity of the roles being played by actors such as Najīb al-Rīḥānī.

This period saw the heyday of a number of theatre companies, many of which were offshoots from the Syrian troupes that arrived in the latter decades of the nineteenth century: those of Iskandar Faraḥ (who counted among his protégés Najīb al-Rīḥānī, ʿAzīz ʿĪd, and the famous singer, Shaykh Salāmah al-Ḥijāzī (*d.* 1917)), and of Jūrj Abyaḍ (*d.* 1959). By contrast, a host of actors and troupes – Yūsuf Wahbī, ʿAlī al-Kassār, and ʿAzīz ʿĪd, for example – concentrated on more popular fare. Another of these troupes was that of the two brothers ʿAbdallāh and Zakī ʿUkāshah, who built a theatre alongside the Ezbekiyya Gardens in 1920, and used it to offer performances that would endeavour to strike some kind of balance between the various extremes that the combination of language and cultural attitudes had engendered.

BEGINNINGS ELSEWHERE IN THE ARAB WORLD

Numerous commentators on the development of drama in the area of Ottoman Syria (thus including Lebanon) have pointed out that the dampening effects that censorship was almost bound to have on creativity (well illustrated by the case of Abū Khalīl al-Qabbānī noted above), when coupled with the departure of large numbers of Christian writers – beginning in the 1860s and continuing well into the twentieth century – had deleterious consequences for the theatre. After what one writer has termed a series of 'false starts', it was not until the period following the Second World War that a tradition of drama began to develop in the region.

In other regions of the Arab world, the initial stimulus in establishing local traditions of drama was provided by visits from touring theatre companies. An Egyptian troupe visited Tunis, for example, as early as 1908, and by 1932 there were four local companies in existence. One of them visited Morocco in 1923 and aroused sufficient interest for a local company to be created in the following year. Jūrj Abyaḍ's famous

Egyptian troupe toured widely and had a similar impact during a visit to Iraq in 1926. However, there remained much to be learned about the drama genre in all of these countries, and the complexity of the process was such that many decades were required to bring Arabic theatre in these regions to genuine fruition.

THE ACHIEVEMENTS OF TAWFĪQ AL-ḤAKĪM

Tawfīq al-Ḥakīm must be reckoned one of the most significant figures in twentieth century Arabic literature. The triumphs and failures that are represented by the reception of his enormous output of plays are emblematic of the issues that have confronted the drama genre as it has endeavoured to adapt its complex modes of communication to the societies of the Arab world. Sent to Paris in 1925 to complete a doctorate in law, al-Ḥakīm chose instead to steep himself in Western culture, imbibing the sense of the role and power of the dramatic medium in its Western form and determined to replicate it in the context of his own society. He returned to Cairo in 1928 without a law degree, but filled with ideas for literary projects, some of them already in draft form.

The cause of 'serious' drama, at least in its textual form, was in the process of being given a boost by one of the Arab world's greatest littérateurs, Aḥmad Shawqī, 'the prince of the poets', who during his latter years penned a number of verse dramas with themes culled from Egyptian and Islamic history; these included *Maṣraʿ Kliyūbatrā* (The Death of Cleopatra, 1929), *Majnūn Laylā* (the name of a famous *ghazal* poet, 1931), *Amīrat al-Andalus* (The Spanish Princess, 1932), and *ʿAlī Bey al-kabīr* (a ruler of Egypt during the eighteenth century), a play originally written in 1893 and later revised. However, between the popular traditions of farcical comedy and melodrama and the performance of translated versions of European dramatic masterpieces, there still remained a void within which an indigenous tradition of serious drama could develop. Al-Ḥakīm's desire to replicate the European tradition was thus timely in the extreme, and it is for that reason that the publication and performance of his play, *Ahl al-Kahf* (The People of the Cave, 1933) is such a significant event in Egyptian drama.

The story of 'the people of the cave' is to be found in the eighteenth *sūrah* of the Qurʾān as well as in other sources. It concerns the tale of the seven sleepers of Ephesus who, in order to escape the Roman persecution of Christians, take refuge in a cave. They sleep for three hundred years, and wake up in a completely different era – without realising it, of course. In its use of overarching themes – rebirth into a new world and a predilection for returning to the past – al-Ḥakīm's play obviously touches upon some of the broad cultural topics that were of major concern to intellectuals at the time, and, because of the play's obvious seriousness of purpose, most critics have chosen to emphasise such features.

Within a year al-Ḥakīm produced another major work, *Shahrazād* (Scheherazade, 1934). While the title character is, of course, the famous narrator of the *Thousand and One Nights* collection, the scenario for this play is set after all the tales have been told. Now cured of his vicious anger against the female sex by the story-telling virtuosity of the woman who is now his wife, King Shahrayār abandons his previous ways and embarks on a journey in quest of knowledge, only to discover himself caught in a dilemma whose focus is Shahrazād herself; through a linkage to the ancient goddess, Isis, Shahrazād emerges as the ultimate mystery, the source of life and knowledge.

When the National Theatre Troupe was formed in Egypt in 1935, the first production that it mounted was *The People of the Cave*. The performances were not a success; for one thing, audiences seemed unimpressed by a performance in which the action on stage was so limited in comparison with the more popular types of drama. It was such problems in the realm of both production and reception that seem to have led al-Hakīm to use some of his play-prefaces in order to develop the notion of his plays as '*théâtre des idées*', works for reading rather than performance. However, in spite of such critical controversies, he continued to write plays with philosophical themes culled from a variety of cultural sources: *Pygmalion* (1942), an interesting blend of the legends of Pygmalion and Narcissus; *Sulaymān al-ḥakīm* (Solomon the Wise, 1943), and *Al-Malik Ūdīb* (King Oedipus, 1949).

Some of al-Hakīm's frustrations with the performance aspect were diverted by an invitation in 1945 to write a series of short plays for publication in newspaper article form. These works were gathered together into two collections, *Masraḥ al-mujtamaʿ* (Theatre of Society, 1950) and *al-Masraḥ al-munawwaʿ* (Theatre Miscellany, 1956). The most memorable of these plays is *Ughniyyat al-mawt* (Death Song), a one-act play that with masterly economy depicts the fraught atmosphere in Upper Egypt as a family awaits the return of the eldest son, a student in Cairo, in order that he may carry out a murder in response to the expectations of a blood feud.

Al-Ḥakīm's response to the social transformations brought about by the Egyptian Revolution of 1952 was the play *Al-Aydī al-nāʿimah* (Soft Hands, 1954). The 'soft hands' of the title refer to those of a prince of the former royal family who finds himself without a meaningful role in the new society, a position in which he is joined by a young academic who has just finished writing a doctoral thesis on the uses of the Arabic preposition *ḥattā*. The play explores in an amusing, yet rather obviously didactic, fashion, the ways in which these two apparently useless individuals set about identifying roles for themselves in the new socialist context. While this play may be somewhat lacking in subtlety, it clearly illustrates in the context of al-Ḥakīm's development as a playwright the way in which he had developed his technique in order to broach topics of contemporary interest, not least through a closer linkage between the pacing of dialogue and actions on stage. In 1960 al-Ḥakīm was to provide further illustration of this development in technique with another play set in an earlier period of Egyptian history, *al-Sulṭān al-ḥāʾir* (The Sultan Perplexed). The play explores in a most effective manner the issue of the legitimation of power. A Mamlūk sultan at the height of his power is suddenly faced with the fact that he has never been manumitted and that he is thus ineligible to be ruler. By 1960 when this play was published, some of the initial euphoria and hope engendered by the Revolution itself, given expression in *al-Aydī al-nāʿimah*, had begun to fade somewhat. The Egyptian people found itself confronting some unsavoury realities: the use of the secret police to squelch the public expression of opinion, for example, and the personality cult surrounding the figure of ʿAbd al-Nāṣir (Nasser). In such a historical context al-Ḥakīm's play can be seen as a somewhat courageous statement of the need for even the mightiest to adhere to the laws of the land and specifically a plea to the ruling military regime to eschew the use of violence and instead seek legitimacy through application of the law.

While al-Ḥakīm's earlier plays were all composed in the literary language, he was to conduct a number of experiments with different levels of dramatic language. In the play, *al-Ṣafqah* (The Deal, 1956), for example – with its themes of land ownership and the exploitation of poor peasant farmers – he couched the dialogue in something he termed 'a third language', one that could be read as a text in the standard written language of literature, but that could also be performed on stage in a way which, while not exactly the idiom of the colloquial dialect, was certainly comprehensible to a larger population than the literate élite of the city. There is perhaps an irony in the fact that another of al-Ḥakīm's plays of the 1960s, *Yā ṭāliʿ al-shajarah* (1962; *The Tree Climber*, 1966), was one of his most successful works from this point of view, precisely because its use of the literary language in the dialogue was a major contributor to the non-reality of the atmosphere in this absurdist drama involving extensive passages of non-communication between husband and wife. Al-Ḥakīm continued to write plays during the 1960s, among the most popular of which were *Maṣīr ṣarṣār* (The Fate of a Cockroach, 1966) and *Bank al-qalaq* (Anxiety Bank, 1967).

Tawfīq al-Ḥakīm is one of the major pioneer figures in modern Arabic literature. In the particular realm of theatre, he fulfils an overarching role as the sole founder of an entire literary tradition, as Ṭāhā Ḥusayn had earlier made clear. His struggles on behalf of Arabic drama as a literary genre, its techniques, and its language, are coterminous with the achievement of a central role in contemporary Arab political and social life.

EGYPTIAN DRAMA AFTER THE REVOLUTION

Following the Egyptian Revolution of 1952 a complete generation of younger playwrights came to the fore who were able to build and expand upon the basis that had been laid by al-Ḥakīm himself and by other prominent pre-revolution dramatists such as Maḥmūd Taymūr (*d.* 1973) and ʿAlī Aḥmad Bākathīr (*d.* 1969). A number of theatres and companies received financial backing from the Ministry of Culture; several excellent directors returned from study and practice abroad to apply their craft in new and experimental ways; and a cadre of drama critics was provided, through the journal *al-Masraḥ*, with a means of discussing the theoretical issues involved in production and of criticising the performances themselves.

First among this new generation was Nuʿmān ʿĀshūr (*d.* 1987). His play, *An-Nās illī taḥt* (Downstairs Folk), was produced in 1956 and was an instant sensation. Here was a work of Egyptian drama that addressed itself to a serious contemporary subject, namely the modes of interaction between people from a variety of professions and classes, all of whom inhabit a single building owned by Bahīga Hānem. The play is written in a colloquial dialect that allows for a good deal of verbal repartee while retaining the authenticity of the social functions that each character represents. With the deft use of a comedy that has been liberated from the more physical stage actions associated with popular farce, ʿĀshūr managed to present his audiences with a play in which they could recognise the problems and foibles of their neighbours and themselves.

The 1960s proved to be a particularly fertile decade in Egyptian dramatic production, with distinguished contributions from such writers as Saʿd al-dīn Wahbah (*b.* 1925), Maḥmūd Diyāb (*d.* 1983), and ʿAlī Sālim (*b.* 1936). Both Wahbah and Diyāb concentrated initially on the life of the village. Most notable among Wahbah's plays of this type is *al-Sibinsā* (The Guard's Van/Caboose, 1963), a heavily symbolic play that revolves around the discovery in a provincial village of a 'bomb' and its subsequent disappearance; the true nature of this bomb and the role of the title in symbolising the processes of social transformation are made clear as the action of the play draws to its inexorable conclusion. Diyāb's *Al-Ẓawbaʿah* (The Storm, 1964) that portrays the tensions that are aroused in a village community by the news that Ḥusayn Abū Shāmah, a villager who has been framed for a crime he did not commit and has spent the last twenty years in jail, is about to be released and has vowed vengeance. ʿAlī Sālim's mode of confronting the unpleasant realities of his intellectual and political surroundings has been through comedy, seen at its most enjoyable in his pointed satire of the all-pervasive triumph of bureaucracy. His sarcasm finds its readiest target in *Bīr al-qamḥ* (The Wheat-pit, 1968), in which the archaeological discoveries of an amateur Egyptologist, ʿAmm Ḥusayn (who is a waiter in normal life), lead to a take-over of the dig by the official academic and governmental bureaucracy and to a chaos so complete that the importance of Ḥusayn's original discovery is itself buried. While Sālim's talent clearly lies in the medium of satire, he has also written a number of more serious dramas, of which *Kūmīdiyā Ūdīb aw anta illī ʾatalt al- waḥsh* (The Comedy of Oedipus, or You're the One Who Killed the Beast, 1970) is the most accomplished. In this play, Sālim takes the characters from the Greek myth of Oedipus, but places them in the environment of the ancient Egyptian city of Thebes. They are used as a vehicle for the exploration of the ways in which political authority can be manipulated and the media can be exploited to persuade and mislead the populace.

Most of the dramatists whom we have considered thus far write on the assumption that the question of language use has been resolved in favour of the colloquial. However, for those playwrights who wish to continue al-Ḥakīm's efforts by carrying Arabic drama to a broader Arab world audience, the problem of language remains. One dramatist who has addressed himself to this issue is Alfred Faraj (*b.* 1929). *Ḥallāq Baghdād* (The Barber of Baghdād, 1963), while not his first contribution to the drama, was the work that secured him a popular audience. The play actually consists of two separate tales, one from the *Thousand and One*

Nights and the other from a collection attributed to the great classical littérateur, al-Jāḥiẓ (discussed above in Chapter 4). Disguised caliphs, damsels in distress, tyrannical viziers, and incredible twists of fate are all orchestrated around the meddlesome prattle of a barber who vows to see justice done in spite of the best efforts of authority – a theme, needless to say, with echoes in modern, as well as earlier, times. Faraj's opinions on the language of Arabic drama are of considerable interest:

a new, fully dramatic language will only emerge through serious efforts in the spheres not only of written and colloquial languages but also in the middle languages between the two poles. (*Al-Majallah* July 1965: 127)

Faraj also enjoyed considerable success with *Sulaymān al-Ḥalabī* (Sulaymān from Aleppo, 1965), a complex and fast-moving drama about a young Syrian student who murders the French General Kléber in Cairo during the brief French occupation of the country at the end of the eighteenth century, and *al-Zīr Sālim* (Prince Sālim, 1967), based on the events of the famous popular narrative set in pre-Islamic times (mentioned in Chapter 5). However, Faraj's most accomplished play from all points of view takes him for his source materials back to the *Thousand and One Nights*: *ʿAlī Janāḥ al-Tabrīzī wa-tābiʿuhu Quffah* (ʿAlī Janāh from Tabrīz and Quffah, his Henchman, 1969). Once again, a theme from the classical heritage – that of a 'wealthy' merchant whose caravan laden with fabulous goods has been delayed and who needs 'temporary credit' – conveys its message very directly to a contemporary audience. Those watching the action of the play – as merchants fall over themselves to grant credit, as the king marries his daughter to ʿAlī the merchant, as the justifiably suspicious vizier is constantly subverted in his attempts to discover the truth, and as ʿAlī himself dispenses all his wealth to the poor of his host city – needed no additional cues to see this picture of an idealist dreamer surrounded by greedy opportunists and yes-men as both a wonderfully entertaining and well-structured piece of drama and as an allegory of their own contemporary political realities.

We began this chapter with a reference to some articles on Egyptian drama written by Yūsuf Idrīs. His two-act play, *al-Farāfīr* (The Farfūrs, 1964), invokes features of drama from a number of sources: the traditional genres that we have described above; the *théâtre en ronde* with actors placed within the audience itself; and the more farcical aspects of popular comedies. The persona of the 'author' who opens the performance gradually loses control of proceedings, and the audience finds itself involved – seemingly literally – in a wide-ranging discussion of the nature and justification of authority and the use of employment in a futile search for meaning in life. As the twin characters of the Master, born to give orders, and the Farfūr, a stooge doomed to everlasting submission to commands, argue about possible jobs in the face of their wives' demand that they earn money, the possibilities for humorous repartee are endless. The following extract from the first act is taken from a succession of such exchanges:

FARFŪR: How about being an intellectual?
MASTER: And what are they supposed to do?
FARFŪR: Absolutely nothing.
MASTER: How can that be?
FARFŪR: If you need to ask that question, you're clearly not going to be an intellectual!

In spite of Idrīs's success in using his plays to depict some of the socio-political problems confronting modern man, each of the works shows structural flaws, particularly an unwillingness to exert some editorial control over length. A greater mastery of dramatic economy is shown by Mīkhā'īl Rūmān (1927–73), whose images of contemporary man as a victim of 'the system', mostly notably in *al-Wāfid* (The New Arrival, 1965), are brilliant and chilling visions of the callous anonymity beloved of mindless bureaucracy.

This period of efflorescence in Egyptian drama coincided with an increase of scholarly and governmental interest in the revival of the heritage of Egyptian folklore. Among those associated with this movement were at least two dramatists, Shawqī ʿAbd al-Ḥakīm and Najīb Surūr (*d.* 1978). ʿAbd al-Ḥakīm found inspiration in the popular heritage for several plays, including *Ḥasan wa-Naʿīmah* (Ḥasan and Naʿīmah, 1960), *Shafīqah wa-Mitwallī* (Shafīqah and Mitwallī, 1961), and *Mawlid al-Malik Maʿrūf* (King Maʿrūf's Birthday, 1965). The first of these, concerning a country girl who is forced into prostitution and murdered by her brother for the sake of family honour, was a *cause célèbre* when during the 1970s it was presented in the ancient Ghūriyyah hostelry in Cairo under the direction of Laila Abou Seif. The theme of Ḥasan and Naʿīmah, also involving a murder but this time of the male lover, was also the subject of *Min ayn agīb nās?* (Where Will I Get the People From? 1976), a verse play by Najīb Surūr, who was one of the most notable and complex participants in the Egyptian theatre scene during the 1960s and 1970s.

The mention of Surūr here brings back into focus the issue of verse drama in Arabic. We noted above the early tendency of theatre directors to incorporate musical episodes into performances and the desire of early pioneers to move away from the apparent inevitability of this association in audience expectations. Aḥmad Shawqī's plays, full as they were of beautiful poetry, tended to follow this practice. During the golden age of Egyptian drama that we have been exploring here, at least two writers, ʿAbd al-raḥmān al-Sharqāwī (*d.* 1987) and Ṣalāḥ ʿAbd al-Ṣabūr (*d.* 1981), succeeded in making contributions that both avoided the linkage with music and were successfully performed on stage. Of the two ʿAbd al-Ṣabūr was certainly the more accomplished, most especially in his remarkable play, *Maʾsāt al-Ḥallāj* (The Tragedy of al-Ḥallāj, 1965), which retells the true story of the famous mystic, al-Ḥallāj, who was crucified in AD 922

RECENT TRENDS ELSEWHERE IN THE ARAB WORLD

Syria, Lebanon, and Palestine

Sharīf Khazandar, the prominent French-trained Syrian authority on the theatre, indulges in what seems like a little dramatic gesture of his own when he writes in 1967 that Syrian drama is only seven years of age. He and other critics see the real beginning as only occurring with the foundation of the National Theatre Troupe in 1958. The same sense of timing characterises discussions of the recent tradition of theatre in Lebanon, with the foundation of the National Theatre in 1960 and the emergence of a number of troupes during that decade, including those of Munīr Abū Dibs, Roger ʿAssāf, and the Raḥbānī brothers (who were much aided in performances of their operettas by the spectacularly beautiful voice of the world-famous singer, Fayrūz). In the case of Lebanon, particular mention needs to be made of two important littérateurs who composed dramas that made significant contributions to the societal acceptability of the genre. Within the *émigré* (*mahjar*) environment of the United States, Mīkhāʾīl Nuʿaymah published *Al-Ābāʾ wa-al-banūn* (Fathers and Sons, 1916), a play set within the Christian Lebanese community that explores the complexities of corruption, arranged marriages, and true love. Another contributor to the literary tradition of Lebanese drama is the renowned symbolist poet, Saʿīd ʿAql (*b.* 1912), who is clearly reflecting his well-known concern with the Phoenician aspect of Lebanese nationalism in composing a verse drama on the theme of *Qadmūs* (1944), a tale culled from Greek myth about the quest of Cadmus to rescue his sister, Europa, who has been carried off by Zeus.

In the period immediately preceding the 1948 'disaster' – as the

Palestinians term the war that followed the creation of the State of Israel – there was a large number of theatre troupes in Jerusalem. The dispersal of Palestinian intellectuals to other Arab countries served to enrich cultural life elsewhere, but their departure, when coupled with a particularly severe system of military censorship within Israel (and, after 1967, the Occupied Territories as well), rendered any notion of founding, let alone sustaining, a theatre tradition problematic in the extreme. As a result, the plays which Palestinian littérateurs composed tended to be contributions to the more literary and intellectual side of the dramatic tradition. Their works relied to a significant extent on the symbolic power of the re-enactment on stage of incidents of tyranny, cunning, and revolt culled from history: for example, *Thawrat al-zanj* (The Zanj Revolt) and *Shamsūn wa-Dalīlah* (Samson and Delilah) by Muʿīn Basīsū (*d.* 1984), and *Qarqāsh* by Samīḥ al-Qāsim (*b.* 1939). However, one troupe that has confronted the realities of this fraught political and social situation in a fashion which is as creative as it is courageous is the Palestinian Al-Ḥakawātī troupe, founded in 1977 and taking its name from the function of that most traditional of public performers, the story-teller (*ḥakawātī*). Performing in theatres whenever the censorship authorities allow or else becoming itinerant players with performances in public squares and village meeting-places, the Ḥakawātī troupe gather together stories from a variety of sources, present and past (such as that of the great hero cavalier-poet, ʿAntar), and turn them into solo or group performances that comment on the injustices of the present. This same technique of taking drama to the people and indeed of creating 'plays' in the process of collecting and re-enacting stories was also adopted by Roger ʿAssāf in Lebanon during the protracted fighting of the Lebanese civil war. The vast disruption of communal life, particularly that of the Shīʿī communities in the south, provided a rich store of material for these presentations.

In view of the relative newness of the modern drama tradition in both Lebanon and Syria, not to mention the shortage of theatres in which to mount productions, it is not surprising that such an unsettled political and social environment has not been conducive to the natural development of that aggregation of elements that are needed to promote a popular tradition of drama performance. However, one Syrian writer, Saʿdallāh Wannūs (*d.* 1997), managed to make a major contribution to the advancement of drama not only in his own country but also on a much broader scale. Playwright, director, drama critic and theorist, Wannūs succeeded in his plays in combining classical themes and modern techniques in order to create works that possess immediate contemporary relevance.

While Wannūs had written some short plays before 1967, it was *Ḥaflat samar min ajl al-khāmis min Ḥuzayrān* (Soirée for the 5th of June 1968), a searing criticism of the attitudes of Arab society that were so cruelly exposed by the June War, that really brought him into the public eye. The acting troupe presents the set of scenes that they have prepared for a play that is supposed to illustrate the official version of what happened during the June War. However, 'members of the audience' continually interrupt the action, coming up on stage to give their own personal accounts. As the reality of the defeat is underlined with increasing clarity, the 'officials' of the Ministry of the Interior who are sitting in the front row become more and more agitated. Eventually, the performance is stopped, the theatre is declared closed, and the entire audience is 'arrested' and escorted out.

This play marks the beginning of Wannūs's concern with some of the theoretical dimensions of modern drama, most especially the relationship between the actors in the play and the audience. In an introduction to *Maghāmarat ra's al-Mamlūk Jābir* (The Adventure of the Mamlūk Jābir's Head, 1970), the author informs readers that the script is to be regarded as merely a blueprint for performance; the text should be translated into the colloquial dialect of whichever region is to be the location of performance, and the appropriate local music is to be incorporated within the intervals between scenes and acts. The actors are instructed to come out on to the stage and engage the audience in dialogue before the performance starts. Orchestrating the events of the play and the interaction between the actors serving as café audience and others playing parts in the inner story is, once again, the figure of the *ḥakawātī* (story-teller). He tells his listeners a gruesome tale of opportunism and treachery set during an unsettled period of the ʿAbbāsī caliphate when rival factions were engaged in a struggle for power. A Mamlūk (slave) is sent from Baghdād to Persia with a secret message inscribed on his head, requesting that the King send forces to help one side in the struggle. Unbeknown to the Mamlūk, the message also instructs the King to get rid of the messenger. At the moment when Jābir the Mamlūk imagines his mission to be complete, he is taken away to be executed. As the play concludes, the actors advance towards the audience; such is the reward, they announce, of all people who are prepared to go on saying 'anyone who marries our mother we call uncle'.

Both these plays were clearly a major challenge to the theatre tradition in the Arab world in the expectations that they placed on the audience itself. Comments on productions make it clear that the kind of interaction for which Wannūs was searching did not occur. He now proceeded to explore this dilemma further by composing another play that examines the issue of audience in the context of the experiences of Abū Khalīl al-Qabbānī, his nineteenth-century predecessor. *Sahrah maʿa Abī Khalīl al-Qabbānī* (An Evening with Abū Khalīl al-Qabbānī, 1972) takes the form of a play within a play: the outer play depicts al-Qabbānī in Ottoman Damascus in the 1880s struggling to produce a play in the face of conservative opposition, continually changing Ottoman regulations, and unruly audiences. The inner play consists of *Hārūn al-Rashīd maʿa Qūt al-qulūb wa-Ghānim ibn Ayyūb* (Hārūn al-Rashīd with Qūt al-Qulūb and Ghānim ibn Ayyūb), one of al-Qabbānī's works culled from the *Thousand and One Nights* collection concerning the caliph and the love story between his favourite slave-girl and her lover.

Wannūs's next work, *al-Malik huwa al-malik* (The King's the King, 1977), finds its inspiration in the *Thousand and One Nights*, this time the tale of 'Abū al-Ḥasan al-mughaffal'. In Wannūs's version of the story, a king and his minister overhear a merchant (now named Abū ʿIzzah) wishing to find solutions to problems with his business and his shrewish wife. They decide to take the man back to the palace and make him king for a day. However, their plans for entertainment go sadly awry: no one, including the actual king's wife, appears to notice any difference, and Abū ʿIzzah himself takes to his new role as though 'to the palace born'.

In confronting questions of language, of theatre semiotics, of acting technique, and of production through both his plays and critical writings, Wannūs fulfilled an invaluable role in the continuing process of developing an Arabic drama that is both lively and relevant. No other dramatist in Syria and Lebanon has managed to match the comprehensive nature of his contribution to the Arabic theatre tradition, but several other playwrights have written significant dramas. In Lebanon, mention should be made of Raymond Jabbārah (*b.* 1935) and ʿIṣām Maḥfūẓ (*b.* 1939), and, in Syria, Muḥammad al-Maghūṭ (*b.* 1934), Walīd Ikhlāṣī (*b.* 1935), and Mamdūḥ ʿAdwān (*b.* 1941).

The Maghrib: Tunisia, Algeria, Morocco

Of the countries that are included within the region known as the Maghrib it was Tunisia that had made the earliest gestures in the development of a drama tradition. From initial efforts that followed visits by

Egyptian troupes in 1908 several theatre troupes were founded that performed regularly in the period before independence (1956). In 1964 an Arab Theatre Festival was established, which has served as the focus of much discussion concerning the nature and direction of the drama genre in the Arab world. One of the participants in such discussion was ʿIzz al-dīn al-Madanī (*b.* 1938), who has written a series of plays that take as their theme popular revolution: in order of publication they are *Thawrat ṣāḥib al-ḥimār* (The Donkey-owner's Revolt, 1971), *Riḥlat al-Ḥallāj* (Al-Ḥallāj's Journey, 1973), *Dīwān al-Zanj* (The Zanj Collection, 1974), and *Mawlay al-Sulṭān al-Ḥasan al-Ḥafṣī* (Our Lord, Sultan al-Ḥasan the Ḥafṣī, 1977). The staging of the third of these works, set during the period of the Zanj slave revolt in Iraq in the latter half of the ninth century, conveys some idea of the author's experiments with dramatic form. The stage is virtually subdivided into three segments: the first is used to present the action of the play; in the second the 'author' comments on the nature of revolutions; and in the third extracts are read from documents contemporary with the events themselves, most famous of which is undoubtedly the famous poetic elegy of Ibn al-Rūmī (cited in Chapter 4).

In Algeria and Morocco, the pace of development has been slower; the reasons involve a complex of issues, including those of language use and educational policy and not excluding, of course, the political dimensions of such a public cultural activity. While a number of Algerian writers have made contributions to popular drama in the colloquial dialect of the region – not least the renowned novelist, Kātib Yāsīn – the process of 'Arabising' (*taʿrīb*) the cultural and educational systems in the country is still underway. In Morocco two writers have played a central role in the fostering and expansion of a theatre tradition. Aḥmad Ṭayyib al-ʿIlj (*b.* 1928) emulated the earlier example of ʿUthmān Jalāl in Egypt by transferring to the Moroccan environment Molière's *Tartuffe* under the title *Walī Allāh*, a work that was presented with great success in the Theatre Festival in Tunisia in 1968. Al-ʿIlj's colleague, al-Ṭayyib al-Ṣiddīqī (*b.* 1938), is a man of the theatre in every sense: playwright, producer, and actor. His play, *Dīwān Sīdī ʿAbd al-raḥmān al- Majdhūb* (The Collection of Sīdī ʿAbd al-raḥmān al-Majdhūb, 1966), tells the story of an itinerant poet, a role that he has often taken himself, while in *Maqāmāt Badīʿ al-zamān al-Hamadhānī* (The Maqāmāt of 'the Wonder of the Age' al-Hamadhānī, 1971) he explores in contemporary dramatic form the long-appreciated potential of the picaresque episodes written ten centuries earlier by al-Hamadhānī (discussed in Chapter 5).

Iraq and the Gulf States

While the theatre tradition in Iraq owes a good deal to the pioneering efforts of Ḥaqqī al-Shiblī who founded a theatre troupe in 1927, joined the famous Egyptian troupe of Fāṭimah Rushdī, and later studied drama in Paris, there can be little doubt that Yūsuf al-ʿĀnī (*b.* 1927) has been the predominant figure in Iraqi theatre during the modern period. In his concern for and involvement in every aspect of the drama, he stands within the Iraqi tradition as the equivalent of Wannūs, al-Madanī, and al-Ṣiddīqī in theirs. Al-ʿĀnī invokes all the emotive power of the colloquial dialect of the region in *Anā ummak yā Shākir* (I'm Your Mother, Shākir, 1955) to provide an accurate reflection in dramatic form of the period that preceded the bloody Iraqi revolution of 1958; the principal character, Umm Shākir, sees her children suffer and die in the struggle for liberation but insists on the rightness of the nationalist cause. *Al-Miftāḥ* (The Key, 1968) is a more accomplished piece of theatre. A popular song is introduced to invoke the tale of a young married couple, symbolically named Ḥayrān and Ḥayrānah (the masculine and feminine forms of the adjective meaning 'perplexed'). They have determined not to become parents until they have discovered a fulfilling role in life; they are in quest of a key to a magical box, but at every turn they are thwarted in their efforts.

The level of official support and popular interest for theatre in the other nations of the Gulf region has, at least thus far, been considerably less than in the countries we have discussed above. With the expansion of educational and cultural opportunities the status of drama is changing, albeit slowly. An example of such a trend can be seen in Kuwait where initial gestures in the 1940s are now beginning to bear fruit in the plays of writers such as Ṣaqr al-Rashūd and ʿAbd al-ʿazīz Surayyiʿ.

CONCLUSION

In the Introduction to this chapter I discussed briefly the essence of drama, and especially the fact that it differs from the other genres being considered in this book in that its cultural standing within society is related not only to its place within the textual, literary tradition, but also – and perhaps more significantly – to its essential nature as performance. The above discussion of developments in modern Arabic drama, it needs to be said, is limited by the fact that it is itself based on materials available in textual form. While I am familiar with all the works discussed here as texts – through both the works themselves and critical writings about them – I have to admit to having seen only a very small sampling of them on stage, and then only in Egypt.

The pioneering work of Tawfīq al-Ḥakīm and his analogues in other regions of the Arab world has now ensured that drama has come to be regarded as a literary genre in its own right. The texts of plays written by writers across the length and breadth of the Arab world are generally available, and in many areas these texts will include works written in the colloquial dialect.

It is in the complex area of stage performance that many of the thorniest problems connected with modern Arabic drama continue to lie. The issues involved have changed surprisingly little from those which confronted the genre at the outset. There is first the major problem of censorship. While certain countries in the region – specifically Egypt between 1956 and 1967 – seem to have permitted a good deal of freedom of expression with the theatrical medium, the general principle has been one of the closest governmental control over drama, as both text and performance. When scripts have been rejected or continually blue-pencilled, when entire seasons or individual performances have been officially cancelled, and when new plays have been inadequately rehearsed or performed, the response of many dramatists has, not unnaturally, been disillusion and despair; the consequence has often been a resort to silence, another literary genre, or even exile.

Beyond these issues lies the much debated and continuing question of the nature of the desired theatre audience. The tradition of farce in the colloquial language that remains so popular today has been a part of the modern Arabic drama tradition from the outset and clearly traces its origins to earlier exemplars. Alongside it has developed a tradition of what is generally referred to as 'serious' drama, the popularity of which has rarely, if ever, rivalled that of the comic tradition. However, I would suggest that the most successful experiments in attracting a popular audience to such drama have been those that have endeavoured, in a variety of ways, to transcend the cultural and attitudinal boundaries set up by the two extremes of 'serious' and 'popular' drama and to fill part of the substantial space that lies in between the two: thus the plays of Alfred Faraj, for example, or of Saʿdallāh Wannūs.

Regarding the language of drama, it is now clear that a large number of highly accomplished Arab playwrights compose their contributions to drama in the colloquial dialect of their own region. If the myriad political and social factors involved in theatre production are working in their favour, they have a reasonable expectation of popular success. As we have shown in the sections above, every region of the Arab world can provide examples of dramatists who fit this category. However, the linguistic boundaries of each colloquial dialect virtually guarantee that any such success will be a local one. Any aspiration that the playwright may have to broaden the audience to the pan-Arab level will involve a willingness to compromise on the question of language. Some experiments in this area have clearly been declared failures, mostly because they did not represent linguistic reality; thus, early attempts to vary language level according to class. But, between the efforts of al-Ḥakīm and Faraj at finding a median level of language and Wannus's recommendation that his text is intended as a blueprint for a script in the local dialect, there is clearly plenty of room for continuing experiment.

If the world of Arabic drama shows signs of creative energy today, then that is a tribute to the amazing resilience of practitioners of the theatre in the face of considerable odds. Many of the more political and social problems involved have already been discussed. However, recent decades have introduced a further factor which may be the most powerful of all: what in the West are known as 'the media'. Arabic drama has a modern performance tradition that in certain countries is barely thirty years of age, and the process of creating *ab initio* a space for itself within a cultural environment that is daily bombarded by modern media in the form of soap operas and films that can be watched in the home is nothing less than daunting. It is here that the initiatives of the Ḥakawātī Troupe and of Roger ʿAssāf – taking drama to the people where they are – turn the necessity of an unsettled political situation into an experimental virtue.

The institution of the theatre itself has become a part of the literary and cultural milieu of the Arab world, bringing with it from the West the large number of theoretical issues that impact upon the performance of drama and adding to them a further collection of questions that are intrinsic to the Arabic environment. With Arabic drama we witness a genre in a continuing process of adaptation and development, one that, by its very nature, must confront the political, social, and cultural problems of the day. In the Arab world that can be a dangerous role, but within that broad and variegated space the struggle for creative change is a continuing process.

CHAPTER 7

The critical tradition

'Criticism is reason applied to the imagination'.

Francis Bacon

INTRODUCTION

In the previous three chapters I have surveyed the development of poetry, belles-lettres, and drama – the works of literature themselves. As I noted in the first chapter on principles, any anthologising process such as this and indeed the very utilisation of the concept of genre as a means of differentiation and organisation involve acts of interpretation that are based on modes of evaluation; to wit, criticism. Having already had frequent recourse to the views of individual Arab critics regarding these genres, schools, and authors, I will now devote this chapter to a brief survey of the critical tradition in its own right, concentrating on the often close linkage between the literary texts themselves and the critical tradition that assessed them. That such a closeness exists can be illustrated by a representative listing of Arab writers who have made important contributions to both fields; a short list would include Abū Tammām, ibn al-Muʿtazz, ibn ʿAbd Rabbihi, ibn Rashīq, al-Sharīf al-Raḍī, ibn Shuhayd, Ḥāzim al-Qarṭājannī, Ṣafī al-dīn al-Ḥillī, Mīkhāʾīl Nuʿaymah, ʿAbbās Maḥmūd al-ʿAqqād, Yaḥyā Ḥaqqī, Nāzik al-Malāʾikah, Ṣalāḥ ʿAbd al-Ṣabūr, and Adūnīs.

The process of criticism, *qua* the evaluation of literary works, is evident in abundance in every period of Arabic literary history and can be traced back to the very beginnings. On the various occasions when poets gather at fairs and verbal jousting contests, a decision is to be made as to which poet has created the better poetry. While experts may be called upon to give their verdict, the audience participates vigorously in the evaluative process, voicing their enthusiasms and evaluations just like any other type of joust or competition. Negative judgements will also be expressed, and a personal anecdote provides a useful illustration of the way in which even this becomes an opportunity for poetic creativity. As part of a festival held in Egypt in 1984, participants were invited to attend a poetry evening in Alexandria. At one point during the proceedings, an aged Alexandrian poet launched into a tediously lengthy and bombastic ode in traditional form in which a soccer match between Egypt and the (then) Soviet Union became a symbol for negative reflections on Egyptian–Soviet relations. It was not long before the poets around me decided to couch their evaluation of the poem in their own particular way; in hushed tones that were nevertheless clearly audible to those around them, they took turns in reacting instantaneously to the first half of each of the poet's lines by providing an irreverent and often ribald second half – all within the interval that it took for the poet on stage to recite his own version thereof.

The public performance of poetry and other genres of literature has thus been intimately linked to the often equally public modes of their evaluation. The other aspect of criticism mentioned above, the systematisation of those modes of evaluation into a tradition of critical scholarship, was to be yet another development in the gradual process of collection, synthesis, and codification that was explored in our second chapter within the broader context of the Islamic sciences as a whole.

FROM PHILOLOGY TO CRITICISM

The first works in Arabic that attempt to define and analyse poetry and its features date from the latter half of the ninth century. As is the case with all the literary genres that have been studied in previous chapters, the process of development that led up to the appearance of these works of systematisation can be traced back to the revelation of the Qur'ān to Muḥammad and the increasingly wide-scaled movement of intellectual exploration and cultural transformation that it instigated. The process of examining the meanings of words and the structuring of phrases and sentences in the newly recorded sacred text led philologists to collect and examine the largest extant archive of the language, the tradition of poetry that had been handed down from poet to bard (*rāwī*) for centuries. Certain collectors of poetry, Ḥammād al-Rāwiyah (*d.* 785) and Khalaf al-Aḥmar (*d.* 796), became proverbial for the amount of poetry they had memorised, and the results of their recording were turned into collections based on different organising principles: for example, the primary criterion for the most famous collection of poems, the *muʿallaqāt,* was that of length (they are often referred to as the 'long odes'); by contrast, the *al- Mufaḍḍaliyyāt* collection, named after its compiler, al-Mufaḍḍal al-Ḍābbī (*d.* 786), was compiled as a teaching anthology of shorter poems.

With the poetic repertoire now available for analysis, the task of sifting and anthologising – and thus the earliest glimpses of activity that might be termed critical – began. Among the most famous members of the community of philologists who, in addition to studies on *ḥadīth* and grammar, devoted themselves to this particular task were Abū ʿAmr ibn al-ʿAlāʾ (*d.* 770), Abū ʿUbaydah (*d.* 825), and al-Aṣmaʿī (*d.* 831). It was their task to familiarise themselves with the work of the transmitters and recorders (like Khalaf al-Aḥmar), to consider the different versions of poems and – analogous to the process of *ḥadīth* scholarship described in Chapter 2 – to check on the authenticity of the recording process. From such concerns with the validity of the corpus at their disposal, they moved on to the processes of analysis and classification. Abū ʿAmr ibn al-ʿAlāʾ, for example, subdivided the poetry into four major topic areas: boasting (*fakhr*), eulogy or panegyric (*madīḥ*), lampooning (*hijāʾ*), and love (*nasīb*). Abū ʿUbaydah, whose familiarity with the poetic tradition was proverbial (he was said by one contemporary to be 'a head stuffed full of learning'), wrote a work, *Majāz al-Qurʾān* (Figurative Language in the Qurʾān), which serves as an early example of what was to become a major strand in Arabic literary criticism: the relationship between the inimitable language of the Qurʾān and the varieties of literary language.

It will be recalled that one of the most typical organising matrices in use during this particular phase in the development of the Islamic sciences was the 'class' (*ṭabaqah*). Al-Aṣmaʿī, himself the compiler of a collection of poetry known as *al-Aṣmaʿiyyāt*, composed a work under the title *Fuḥūlāt al- shuʿarāʾ* (Champion Poets) in which he categorises poets, while one of his students, ibn Sallām al-Jumaḥī (*d.* 847), produced a similarly titled work, *Ṭabaqāt fuḥūl al-shuʿarāʾ* (Classes of Champion Poets).

This poetic corpus is the major focus of the earliest contributions to literary criticism. The great polymath, al-Jāḥiẓ (*d.* 869), merits inclusion in this context, as in so many others. Firstly, there is his famous collection, *Kitāb al-ḥayawān* (Book of Animals), a collection of poetry and anecdote that also included a number of observations on poets and poetry and a most perceptive section on the impossibility of translating poetry. However, it is in an anthology of both poetry and prose entitled *Kitāb al-*

bayān wa-al-tabyīn (Book on Clarity and Eloquence), as well as in a number of shorter treatises, that he expands the framework of critical discussion by making the base of his observations the question of eloquence (*balāghah*) and the unique properties of the Arabic language – an opinion that once again looks to the Qur'ān as its yardstick and justification. In *Kitāb al-bayān* al-Jāḥiẓ's discussion sets the groundwork for a number of debates that are to preoccupy his successors: the relative roles of form (*lafẓ*) and meaning (*ma'nā*), the different attributes of poetry and prose, and the question of coherence within a single composition. The balance between poetry and belles-lettres was also taken up by al-Mubarrad of al-Baṣrah (*d.* 898), the compiler of another famous literary anthology, *al- Kāmil* (The Complete).

The broad interests of ibn Qutaybah led him to delve into a large number of different intellectual spheres – the education of bureaucrats, for example, and the difficulties of language in the Qur'ān – and he is also much involved in these early efforts aimed at classifying poets and poetry and developing analytical criteria. His *Kitāb al-shi'r wa-al-shu'arā'* (Book on Poetry and Poets) is yet another large, analytical anthology, the title of which announces its intention of discussing poetry as well as its practitioners. The work is prefaced with an introduction that offers some important new principles: that poetry should not be judged by its time-period but on its own merits – in other words, more ancient poetry was not automatically to be judged superior to modern poetry; and, most famously of all, that 'some people of learning' maintained that the *qaṣīdah* had an internal structural logic of its own, one that gave the performance of such poems a function similar to a communal rite.

Viewed in retrospect, the works of writers such as ibn Sallām and ibn Qutaybah cannot be regarded as literary criticism, as the modern Egyptian critic, Muḥammad Mandūr (*d.* 1965) points out in his important study of classical criticism, *Al-Naqd al-manhajī 'inda al-'Arab* (Methodical Criticism Among the Arabs, 1948). They do, however, serve as important transitional figures. The same holds true of Tha'lab (*d.* 904), the grammarian of al-Kūfah, to whom is attributed a work entitled *Qawā'id al-shi'r* (The Rules of Poetry). The discussion focuses on four types of poetic expression – imperative, prohibition, statement, and interrogative – but Tha'lab moves beyond the purely grammatical to elaborate on the topic areas of poetry identified by Abū 'Amr and to devise some categories for the analysis of poetic tropes that appear to have been the basis of later works on the subject.

MAJOR CRITICAL DEBATES

After the transfer of the caliphal capital from Damascus to Baghdād in the mid-eighth century, Baghdād rapidly became not only the locus of an elaborate court system and the vast bureaucracy that went with it but also a glittering cultural centre that came to rival the intellectual prestige of the twin cities of al-Kūfah and al-Baṣrah. It is within this intellectual environment that the creations of Arab poets who have been designated modernist (*muḥdath*) must be placed. Bashshār, Abū Nuwās, and Muslim ibn al-Walīd (*d.* 823) are the names most frequently cited as the originators in this move to break away from the normative expectations regarding poetry, and especially its language, that had been established as part of the process of philological canonisation noted above. Al-Jāḥiẓ himself appears to have been the first to apply the term *badīʿ* (new, novel – from the verbal root that also provides the word for heresy, *bidʿah*) to describe their approach to poetic language. However, it was to be ibn al-Muʿtazz who managed to reflect the debates of the era by analysing the phenomenon in detail.

Ibn al-Muʿtazz and Qudāmah ibn Jaʿfar

The very title of ibn al-Muʿtazz's work, *Kitāb al-badīʿ* (Book on *badīʿ* – translatable perhaps as 'figurative language') announces an approach that will focus on one aspect of the use of a particular level of language in literary texts; it thus can be seen as marking a beginning of what we might term an Arabic poetics. He identifies five elements of *badīʿ*: metaphor, paranomasia (the use in the same line of a similar word or verbal root with two different meanings); antithesis (for example, black and white, or sword and pen); *radd al-aʿjāz* (internal repetition within the line); and lastly the most problematic category – *al-madhhab al-kalāmī* which, some modern scholars specialising in Arabic criticism maintain, is best rendered as 'the replication of the speculative discourse of theology' (*kalām*). To these five principal categories of trope ibn al-Muʿtazz adds twelve examples of what he terms 'discourse embellishments'. However, in spite of the significance of ibn al-Muʿtazz's work-most particularly the way in which his analysis moves from the level of grammar and theme towards a consideration of how poetic discourse functions, we need to return to the general intellectual environment in order to place the impact of his contributions into context. As we noted above, the element of *badīʿ* and some of its features had already been identified and discussed by previous writers such as al-Jāḥiẓ and Thaʿlab, and indeed the phenomenon had become associated with certain poets. However, it was Abū Tammām (*d.* 845), who was to carry the potentialities of this new concern with poetic ornamentation to a higher level of complexity, and it is his poetry that is most often cited in ibn al-Muʿtazz's *Kitāb al-badīʿ*, mostly with disapproval. We can illustrate the nature of the latter's concerns by citing a line of poetry by Abū Tammām. One of his most famous odes, a eulogy composed on the occasion of the victory against the Byzantines at the Battle of Amoreum in Anatolia, opens with the following line:

> The sword brings more accurate news than books; in its edge lies
> the dividing line between serious and frivolous.

Here we notice firstly the antitheses between 'sword' and 'book', and 'serious' and 'frivolous'; secondly, instances of two separate types of the verbal puns of paronomasia: a complete similarity between the Arabic words meaning 'edge' and 'dividing line' (*ḥadd*, *ḥadd*) and the partial similarity between those meaning 'edge' and 'seriousness' (*ḥadd*, *jidd*). It is the increased emphasis that the application of the principles of *badīʿ* was placing on the use of poetic devices and an elaboration of language that causes ibn al-Muʿtazz's clearly expressed unease. He invokes citations from the texts of the Qur'ān, *ḥadīth*, and the early poets in order to demonstrate that the phenomenon termed *badīʿ* (with the literal meaning of 'new') is in fact not new; what is different and, in ibn al-Muʿtazz's opinion, of questionable desirability is the extent to which modernist poets and one in particular – Abū Tammām – are using its repertoire of devices in their poetry. Seen in such a light, ibn al-Muʿtazz's work seems to fulfil a Janus-like function: on the one hand it can be viewed as the base from which much future critical writing would develop; on the other, it is a call for moderation that underlines the historical precedents of *badīʿ* rather than its radical extremes.

The other famous figure in criticism during this period was Qudāmah ibn Jaʿfar (*d.* 948). In *Naqd al-shiʿr* (Poetic Criticism) he sets out to describe the craft of poetry and to provide a manual for its description and evaluation; as he candidly observes, 'So far I have not discovered a single work of poetic criticism that distinguishes good from bad poetry'. He then proceeds to provide a definition of poetry: 'discourse [the word *kalām* implies 'speech'] that is metred, rhymed, and conveys meaning'. This terse definition of what constitutes poetry (and by implication what does not) is to serve as a prescriptive yardstick, to be invoked by students of Arabic poetry for many centuries. In the assessment of the poetic craft, Qudāmah provides a schema through which judgements can be made. Four categories are involved: words, meaning, metre, and rhyme. They can be combined in eight different ways to provide a basis for the evaluation of good and bad poetry; thus, a poem in which the combined categories are all good is thus a very good poem, but, as weak points emerge in one or more category, so does the poem fit into a descending scale towards 'badness'.

A cluster of dichotomies

The basic framework adopted by the majority of critics continues to revolve around questions concerning the nature of poetry, its themes, tropes, and language, and the evaluation of its practitioners and their works. There is firstly much discussion of the relative priority to be assigned to form and content; the very process of differentiating these two entities and considering their relative 'merits', coupled to the enormous antipathies expressed regarding certain poets such as Abū Tammām and al-Mutanabbī, leads to the development of an elaborate literature on plagiarism. Secondly, the community's fervent belief in the 'truth' of its canonical texts and the process of checking their authenticity is combined with the Qur'ān's expressed disapproval of the statements of poets to produce some rigorous comparisons between the 'veracity' of the poetic message and that of other categories of text. This results in the incorporation into many critical works of a discussion of the role of truth and lies in poetry. The third pair of terms contrasts the merits of the qualities of 'naturalness' and 'artifice, craft' (*tab*ʿ and *ṣanʿah*, or, in adjectival form, *maṭbū*ʿ and *maṣnū*ʿ), attributes the discussion of which intensified, needless to say, as the *badī*ʿ poets began to craft – in written form, perhaps – their complex creations.

The continuing focus on the desired characteristics of poetry is exemplified by *ʿIyār al-shiʿr* (The Yardstick of Poetry) of ibn Ṭabāṭabā (*d.* 934), a work that neatly mirrors some of the tensions mentioned above. For, while his emphasis on meaning as a separable entity and his distaste for all but the most transparent of metaphors link his views firmly to those of earlier critics, his concern with units of composition beyond the single line marks a new trend. Indeed, in his discussion of the element of cohesion within segments of the poem he makes particular use of the qualities of the (prose) epistle – its concision, awareness of beginnings and endings, and purity of language (*faṣāḥah*) – as yardsticks in poetic construction. Here we find ourselves presented with evidence of the role that the emerging tradition of *adab* and its repertoire of manuals on epistolography were beginning to play within the domain of criticism, a trend reflected in later works – to be discussed later in this chapter – that place the discussion of the qualities of 'the two arts' into a broader framework.

Poets in the balance

We will begin by examining the large number of studies that were devoted to two of Arabic's most famous poets, Abū Tammām and al-Mutanabbī. The process of developing modes of comparative analysis by which they were to be judged is, not unnaturally, the occasion for several notable advances in critical method. The first work we will discuss is *Kitāb al-muwāzanah bayn al-Ṭā'iyyayn* (The Book of Weighing the Two Ṭā'ī Poets [Abū Tammām and al-Buḥturī] in the Balance) by Abū al-qāsim al-Āmidī (*d.* 987). Al-Āmidī adopts the basic structure of the *qaṣīdah* as outlined by ibn Qutaybah and goes through the thematic segments of the poem – the deserted encampment, the departure, love sentiments, and so on – concentrating in particular on opening lines in order to illustrate the ways in which al-Buḥturī's poetry is more in line with the norms of the classical tradition (for which he uses the term *'amūd al-shi'r*) than is Abū Tammām's. For al-Āmidī, of course, the bases of that taste were firmly rooted in what he saw as the natural poetry of the ancient poets, and his critical stance thus emerges as a conservative one. Even so, the somewhat biased nature of al-Āmidī's comparative method should not obscure the extent of his achievement. By focusing his attention exclusively on specific poets and developing a system for the evaluation of actual segments of poems, he provides the critical enterprise with a greater methodological rigour.

The critical furore created by Abū Tammām's complex imagery was but a prelude to the one that developed around the career and work of his pre-eminent successor, al-Mutanabbī. The title of a second comparative work, *Kitāb al-wasāṭah bayn al-Mutanabbī wa-khuṣūmihi* (Book of Mediation Between al-Mutanabbī and His Antagonists) by 'Alī al-Jurjānī (*d.* 1002), reflects the fact that al-Mutanabbī's highly developed sense of his own importance (that we noted in the chapter on poetry) was quite sufficient to attract enemies, quite apart from the consequences of more literary debates concerning the merits of his poetic output. This al-Jurjānī was himself a judge (*qāḍī*), and he is thus usually known as al-Qāḍī al-Jurjānī in order to distinguish him from ʿAbd al-qāhir al-Jurjānī, the eminent critic whose works we will consider below. Like al-Āmidī, al-Qāḍī al-Jurjānī prefaces his 'mediating' section with examples of poetic devices, including three of ibn al-Muʿtazz's five – metaphor, paronomasia, and antithesis – thus indicating perhaps an early realisation of the problematic nature of the other two. After a section in which he examines the properties of al-Mutanabbī's poetry, he turns to a mammoth survey of plagiarism (which he dubs 'an ancient disease').

With al-Mutanabbī the topic of plagiarism had become a major growth industry, and so here is probably an appropriate place to pause for a brief consideration of the topic. The principles of plagiarism analysis were firmly grounded in the twin notions of word and meaning mentioned above: a précis of them is provided by Abū Hilāl al-ʿAskarī whose manual on poetry and prose will be discussed below:

> I've heard it said that anyone who adopts a concept word for word is a [full-scale] plagiarist; anyone who takes part of one is [designated] an inserter; and anyone who takes one and adorns it with words that are better than the original is more worthy than his predecessor.

The final category refers to the process known as *muʿāraḍah* whereby a poet would gain kudos by consciously adopting a line by a predecessor and improving on it.

Al-Āmidī and al-Qāḍī al-Jurjānī made major contributions to the field of poetic criticism, but at the same time both clearly express an anxiety about change; not so much the process itself as the pace and direction of the modernist poets. Both alluded to a set of principles, termed *ʿamūd al-shiʿr*, which served as locus for the classical ideals in which they both believed. Those ideals were elaborated by al-Marzūqī (*d.* 1030) as part of his commentary on the *al-Ḥamāsah* (Collection of Poetry on Chivalry) of Abū Tammām. He sets out to explore the elements that make poetry good and, more specifically, to identify the particular characteristics that have made the early poetic corpus into a model of 'naturalness', and then elaborates on his preference in a listing of the elements of *ʿamūd al-shiʿr*. Poetry, he says, should possess nobility and soundness of meaning; polished and appropriate wording; apposite description; and closeness of resemblance in simile (none of those far-fetched examples of Abū Tammām). These categories had already been identified by al-Qāḍī al-Jurjānī, and to them al-Marzūqī appends: tight cohesion of segments and pleasant metre; appropriateness of similarity in the two elements of a metaphor; and suitable choice of wording in accordance with the demands of rhyme. These criteria, needless to say, serve to canonise the normative function of ancient poetry as the classical model of naturalness; they form the yardstick against which the contemporary swings of modernist poets between naturalness and craft are to be evaluated.

The Qur'ān as miracle: different discourse

The challenge to record, codify, and understand the Qur'ān, as we have noted above, presented the Muslim community with a clear set of research priorities in the fields of lexicography, philology, and grammar. As part of this process, scholars such as Abū ʿUbaydah and ibn Qutaybah identified those elements of the sacred text that showed elements of difference or difficulty. However, from these concerns with interpreting the Qur'ān and its discourse features scholars moved on to another topic, one that finds its origins in the text itself when, in response to a challenge to produce a miracle, Muḥammad is inspired to retort that the Qur'ān itself is miraculous. This revelation is the origin of a school of critical writing that sets out to prove *iʿjāz al-qur'ān*, that the Qur'ān is the supreme example of Arabic discourse, different from and superior to the literary genres composed by humans.

In a short treatise entitled *al-Nukat fī iʿjāz al-Qur'ān* (Comments on the Miraculous Nature of the Qur'ān) the Muʿtazilī grammarian al-Rummānī (*d.* 994), makes *iʿjāz* the highest of three categories of eloquence. Examining ten different tropes (including simile and metaphor), he notes that only the Qur'ān has features that place it alone into the highest category. The title of al-Khaṭṭābī's (*d.* 988) work on this same topic, *Bayān iʿjāz al-Qur'ān*, neatly encapsulates the focus of al-Rummānī's argument, and to it the former adds sections on words and meanings and an important gesture whereby the two are fused into the concept of arrangement (*naẓm*), which is to be brought to its finest elaboration in the work of ʿAbd al-qāhir al-Jurjānī. However, the staunchest of these early proponents of *iʿjāz al-Qur'ān* is al-Bāqillānī (*d.* 1013) who in a work of that title launches himself undaunted into a proof of the Qur'ān's superiority through a comparison of its discourse with that of two prominent poets, one ancient – Imru' al-Qays – the other contemporary – al-Buḥturī. Imru' al-Qays's famous *muʿallaqah* is shown not only to lack cohesion but also to contain some tasteless and morally offensive passages; furthermore his use of a large number of place-names is found otiose to the purposes of the poem. The structure and contents of al-Buḥturī's ode are found to be likewise deficient.

ʿAbd al-qāhir al-Jurjānī

The critic who made a significant contribution to the analysis of *iʿjāz al-Qur'ān* is ʿAbd al-qāhir al-Jurjānī (*d.* 1079), without doubt the major figure in Arabic literary criticism and one whose contributions to the history of criticism in general deserve much wider recognition. His two great works are *Dalā'il al-iʿjāz* (Features of *Iʿjāz*) and *Asrār al-balāghah* (The Secrets of Eloquence).

Al-Jurjānī was a grammarian, and the contents of *Dalā'il al-iʿjāz* reveal that aspect of his expertise through a detailed analysis of those elements of syntax (tense, negation, and connection, for example) and stylistics (word order, use of tropes) that contribute to the qualities of proper usage of Arabic (*faṣāhah*) and eloquence. However, when he moves to the notion of *iʿjāz* itself, he takes his syntactic analysis beyond the level of the word and sentence into a discussion of the function of meaning. Language, he writes, conveys meaning through the way in which words are organised into contextualised sets of semantic relationships. As a consequence, the dichotomy, much belaboured by earlier critics, between word and meaning, is deemed to be a false one. Furthermore, since language operates in this fashion, figurative language and imagery need to be viewed as another mode of conveying meaning and to be incorporated within the same analytical process. Such a mode requires that we consider not merely the meaning but 'the meaning of the meaning' (*maʿnā al-maʿnā*); thus, when, for example, the poet speaks in context about 'stars of guidance', the listener needs to move beyond the surface meaning of the words in order to appreciate that it is religious scholars who are being described.

In his second major work, *Asrār al-balāghah*, al-Jurjānī addresses himself to the poetic image (*ṣūrah*) and its functions. He categorises images in terms of similarity (metaphor and simile) and contiguity (allusion and devices involving substitution such as synecdoche – for example, that the notion found in Arabic, as in English, of 'giving someone a hand' implies doing someone a favour). Al-Jurjānī devotes the bulk of his attention to the categories of similarity, simile (*tashbīh*) and metaphor (*istiʿārah*). He identifies two types of meaning, one that resorts to the intellect *ʿaqlī*, the other to the imagination (*takhyīlī*); each has several subcategories. The first consists of what is considered rationally justifiable and objective, linkages that appear to be verifiable; the second type involves what is not truthful; it is not intended to be deliberately false, however, but is simply unverifiable.

The integration of critical thought brought about by al-Jurjānī's principle of arrangement (*naẓm*) was to have a profound effect on the way in which his successors studied the Qur'ān. Among those who composed works on the subject in the pre-modern period are al-Zamakhsharī (*d.* 1143), ibn Abī al-Iṣbaʿ (*d.* 1256), ibn Qayyim al-Jawziyyah (*d.* 1350), al-Zarkashī (*d.* 1392), and al-Suyūṭī (*d.* 1505). The later encounter between traditional approaches to the study of the Qur'ān, especially those founded on the principles of *iʿjāz*, and critical methods that Arab scholars acquired through a European education almost inevitably led to confrontations that have engendered some of the most famous controversies in the intellectual life of the region during the twentieth century. In 1925, for example, Ṭāhā Ḥusayn wrote a study of the earliest period of Arabic literature, *Fī al-shiʿr al-jāhilī* (On Pre-Islamic Poetry) – to be examined below – in which he suggested that certain stories in the Qur'ān appear to be fables. In 1995, another Egyptian scholar, Naṣr Ḥāmid Abū Zayd, who in his *Naqd al-khiṭāb al-dīnī* (Critique of Religious Discourse, 1992) attempts to apply contemporary modes of critical analysis to religious discourse, was declared divorced from his wife since his ideas had shown him to be a heretic.

THE CONTRIBUTION OF GREEK THOUGHT

The precise nature and extent of the role of Greek thought in the development of Arabic literary criticism has been the focus of considerable discussion; indeed, the debate is not confined to more recent times. Ḍiyā' al-dīn ibn al-Athīr (*d.* 1239), whose work will be examined below, makes little effort to disguise his feelings as he endeavours to prove the minimal influence of the Greek tradition. With the cosmopolitan atmosphere of Baghdād during the heyday of the ʿAbbāsī caliphate (ninth and tenth centuries) in mind, not to mention the research activities fostered by the Baghdād library, *Bayt al- Ḥikmah* (the 'House of Wisdom'), this seems not a little extreme, and yet it also seems clear that those aspects of Greek learning that did make their way into Arabic literary discourse as a result of cultural contacts and translation were assimilated into a critical tradition, the basic parameters of which had already been firmly established within the context of the early priorities of the Muslim community and especially of the hermeneutics of the Qur'ān.

The great philosopher, al-Fārābī (*d.* 950), contemporary of the poet al-Mutanabbī at the court of Sayf al-dawlah al-Ḥamdānī at Aleppo, composed a *Risālah fī qawānīn ṣināʿat al-shuʿarāʾ* (Epistle on the Canons of the Poets' Craft) in which he attempted a synthesis of the principles gleaned from a reading of the far from satisfactory Arabic early translation of Aristotle's *Poetics* with the poetic tradition of the Arabs. What is interesting about al-Fārābī's presentation of aspects of the poet's craft in this way is that, having used Aristotle's mode of categorisation to present his system, he then shows a clear preference for the more conservative tendencies of the Arab tradition of his day by stressing the virtues of naturalness over those of craft.

Ibn Sīnā (*d.* 1037), the renowned physician-philosopher, discussed the nature and role of poetry in several of his works; his major philosophical treatise, *al-Shifāʾ* (The Healing) incorporates a commentary on Aristotle's *Poetics* entitled *Fann al-shiʿr* (The Art of Poetry). Ibn Sīnā noted that poetry, besides its more obvious features of rhyme and metre, can be defined by the way in which it invokes the imagination. Thus the analysis of poetry should not concern itself with issues of morality or a semblance of reality, but with the process of utilising imitation (*muḥākāh*) as a means of arousing a sense of delight, a sensation that produces in the listener a feeling of harmony and assent with what is being expressed.

Another Arab philosopher whose name was renowned in Christian Europe was ibn Rushd (*d.* 1198), who served as physician and judge in Spain and Morocco. One of the most famous interpreters of Aristotle's corpus, he wrote several commentaries, including one on the *Poetics* entitled *Takhlīṣ kitāb Arisṭūṭalīs fī al-shiʿr* (A Summary of Aristotle's Poetics). He makes clear at the outset that the purpose of his summary is not to discuss Aristotle's views as a whole, but only those that can be extrapolated into general principles and thus applied to the tradition of Arabic poetry. Like ibn Sīnā, ibn Rushd views poetry as being the invoker of the imagination, its principal topics being praise and invective (reflecting man's proclivity for either virtue or vice).

Ḥāzim of Cartagena (al-Qarṭājannī) was a well-known poet. However, his famous and mostly successful attempt at making a synthesis of the Aristotelian and Arabic traditions of poetics, *Minhaj al-bulaghāʾ wa-sirāj al-udabāʾ* (Course for the Eloquent and Beacon for the Literate), focuses on literary discourse, combining thereby rhetoric – with its task of persuasion (*iqnāʿ*) – and poetry – aimed at invoking the imaginary (*takhyīl*). The work is subdivided into four major sections, beginning with an analysis of two categories very familiar to Arabic literary criticism, words and meanings, and then proceeding to two other sections that discuss combinations of the first two: the joining of words (*naẓm*) and of meanings (*uslūb*). Poetry's purpose of *takhyīl* is achieved, he writes, through a combination of factors; one of the most important is mimesis (*muḥākāh*), which at its best arouses in the listener a sense of wonderment at its extraordinary qualities and therefrom of pleasure.

In spite of the existence of this impressive attempt to present a systematic study of the creative and receptive processes of poetry and the structure(s) of the Arabic *qaṣīdah*, the primary focus of critical attention remained the increasingly elaborate and exhaustive analyses of the devices of *badīʿ* and of the elements that contributed to eloquent usage (with the Qurʾān's *iʿjāz* as its supreme model).

COMPILATIONS OF CRITICAL OPINION

Alongside the more particular trends in criticism that we have investigated above there are also a number of works that endeavour to keep score, as it were, on the critical tradition. The organising principles of these works vary, but the primary goal is summative. The case of poetic tropes provides a ready example. The *Kitāb al-badīʿ* of ibn al-Muʿtazz had, it will be recalled, identified five tropes and fifteen so-called 'embellishments'. A section of *Kitāb al-ṣināʿatayn: al-kitābah wa-al-shiʿr* (The Book on the Two Arts: [prose] writing and poetry) by Abū Hilāl al-ʿAskarī (*d. c.* 1009), analysed more than thirty, and by the time of al-Suyūṭī (*d.* 1505) the figure had topped two hundred.

In the case of al-ʿAskarī we are definitely dealing with a summary of the works of others, a kind of handbook on the craft of writing. Al-ʿAskarī's goal is to describe and codify the elements of *balāghah* (correct usage, good style), and thus another direct link is established to the goals and methods of exegesis (*tafsīr*), jurisprudence (*fiqh*), and grammar (*naḥw*). His examination of good writing involves detailed catalogues of literary genres and concepts, of types of expression, and of plagiarism. There is an interesting discussion of parallelism and rhyming prose (*sajʿ*) in the context of Qurʾānic discourse which leads into the lengthy section of *badīʿ* and its – now – thirty-five subcategories (including such figures as hyperbole). This how-to-do-it manual ends with a section on appropriate beginnings and endings.

Another critical compilation is ibn Rashīq's (*d. c.* 1065) *al-ʿUmdah fī maḥāsin al-shiʿr wa-adabihi wa-naqdihi* (The Pillar Regarding Poetry's Embellishments, Proper Usage, and Criticism); in a short aside, it is interesting to note the way in which the word *adab* is used here in the context of poetry to describe the normative values of the tradition. Like the works of his predecessors, ibn Rashīq's survey of the elements of poetry brings together within a single, undifferentiated format information of a wide variety: the principles of metre and rhyme, structural elements (beginnings and endings), characteristics of eloquence, poetic tropes (continuing the numerical expansion yet further), and genres (eulogy, elegy, lampoon). The extent to which *al-ʿUmdah* becomes a frequently quoted source regarding the Arabic poetic tradition is a tribute not only to the thoroughness with which he sets out to reflect the work of his predecessors (yet again, not always traceable to their actual source) but also to his attempts to find a more critically sophisticated middle-ground between the series of dichotomies that we discussed above.

If al-ʿAskarī and ibn Rashīq express a predilection for poetry in their discussion of 'the two arts', then with *Al-Mathal al-sāʾir fī adab al-kātib wa-al-shāʿir* (The Current Ideal For the Literary Discipline of the Secretary and Poet) by Ḍiyāʾ al-dīn ibn al-Athīr (*d.* 1239) we appear to encounter a tilt in the other direction. Ibn al-Athīr's aim, he tells his readers, is to explore the nature of clear expression (*bayān*) in both poetry and prose; in describing his overall purpose he expresses his admiration for two previous writers in particular, al-Āmidī and ibn Sinān al-Khafājī (*d.* 1073), the author of an earlier work entitled *Sirr al-faṣāḥah* (The Secret of Proper Discourse). The practical goals of this manual are immediately apparent. The syntax of the sentence is explored from the simple to the more complex; the advantages of memorising the texts of the Qurʾān and *ḥadīth* are pointed out; the basic features of poetry – metre and rhyme – are discussed as well as the (still increasing) number of tropes; and different skills associated with the scribal profession – types of beginning and ending, suitable rebuttal techniques, and methods of précis – are discussed and illustrated. While in most of these fields ibn al-Athīr is gathering into a huge compilation the views and attitudes of his predecessors, there is one in which he does appear to offer something unusual, namely an attempt to formulate the basic framework for a poetics of rhyming prose (*sajʿ*).

While ibn al-Athīr's discourse manual seems to have been widely known, the great historian, ibn Khaldūn (*d.* 1406), expresses a clear preference for ibn Rashīq's *al-ʿUmdah* in the section of his *Muqaddimah* that deals with poetry. Ibn Khaldūn includes within his frame of reference examples of literary genres that had remained outside the purview of previous critics: not only segments of popular narrative but also the

Andalusian strophic poetry that had been the subject of an earlier study, *Dār al-ṭirāz* (The House of Embroidery), by the Egyptian critic, ibn Sanāʾ al-Mulk (*d.* 1210). With such apparent innovations in mind, it is something of a surprise to note quite how conversative ibn Khaldūn's opinions about poetry actually are: form is emphasised over meaning and the line of poetry is regarded as the major unit of analysis.

If ibn al-Athīr begins his analyses in *al-Mathal al-sāʾir* with the basic sentence, then Jalāl al-dīn al-Suyūṭī (*d.* 1505) goes one better in *al-Muzhir fī ʿulūm al-lughah wa-anwāʿihā* (The Luminous Work Concerning the Language Sciences and Their Categories) by beginning at the level of the phoneme, working outwards through the entire morphology of the language, and including sections on those who communicate through it, the non-native speakers who have learned it and even the colloquial usages to be encountered in its different social registers.

These manuals and compendia, which conveniently brought together a wealth of information from a number of sources and venues, provided the most available source for Arab scholars in the nineteenth century who, in the light of cultural developments that were affecting the Middle East region, set themselves to re-examine the Arabic literary heritage. One such figure was the Egyptian, Ḥusayn al-Marṣafī (*d.* 1890), who converted his lectures at the *Dār al-ʿulūm* (House of Sciences) into a book entitled *al-Wasīlah al-adabiyyah ilā al-ʿulūm al-ʿArabiyyah* (The Literary Way to the Arabic Sciences, 1872–75). Taking large segments from al-ʿAskarī's *Kitāb al-ṣināʿatayn*, he follows his predecessors in beginning with a definition of the concept of *bayān* and then proceeding to the analysis of words, morphology, and syntax. A second volume investigates the figurative level of language (*majāz*), the syntactic features of the sentence, then includes a large section on the categories of *badīʿ* before finishing with sections on poetic metres and rhyme (the last incorporating a discussion of the rhyme schemes of both *muwashshaḥ* and *zajal*). Al-Marṣafī's work is thus a genuine piece of neo-classicism, but we need to recall that, in spite of the work's essentially retrospective qualities, it was al-Marṣafī for whom Ṭāhā Ḥusayn (*d.* 1973), one of the greatest figures in twentieth-century Arabic criticism, expressed enormous respect. Ṭāhā Ḥusayn is in many ways one of the symbols of the profound changes that were to have a major impact on the direction and nature of Arabic literary criticism. The pedagogical manual of his revered teacher can thus be seen as a fitting symbol of the turbulent era of cultural change during which it was composed.

CONTACTS WITH THE WEST AND THE TENSIONS OF CHANGE

The aesthetic principles espoused by the system of criticism that has just been described – with selections of the theories and opinions of its famous individual contributors gathered together in widely used compilations – were to serve as a strong conservative bastion against the incursion of new ideas of Western provenance that reached the Arab world during the nineteenth and early twentieth centuries.

In 1898, Aḥmad Shawqī (*d.* 1932), the Egyptian court poet, published his collected poems (*Dīwān*) and prefaced them with a statement of his views about poetry. Looking at the classical tradition of Arabic poetry, he says, all he found were bombastic *qaṣīdas* by the ancients and others imitating them. It was only when he turned to Europe and encountered Lamartine and La Fontaine that his ideas on poetry were truly formed. Such a statement could not and did not go unchallenged; it was taken up in a famous series of articles by Muḥammad al-Muwayliḥī (*d.* 1930), the author of *Ḥadīth ʿĪsā ibn Hishām* discussed in Chapter 5. Shawqī is criticised for his poor choice of poets as exemplars of the classical tradition, but above all for his failure to realise that the composition of poetry consists of that time-honoured pair, words and meanings, and must thus inevitably involve a resort to the Arabic language and its poetic tradition. Among contemporaries of Shawqī who are mentioned in his Introduction is Khalīl Muṭrān (*d.* 1949), who emigrated to Egypt from Lebanon. He also prefaced his collected poems (published in 1908) with an introduction in which he also declares his frustration with the classical tradition, both the poetry itself and criticism of it.

Arabic romantic poetry was to find its more radical early voice among the distant emigrant communities of the United States (*al-mahjar*, 'the *émigrés*'), but the formulation of the critical principles of romanticism was most prominently elaborated in the Arab world itself by three Egyptian writers: Ibrāhīm ʿAbd al-qādir al-Māzinī (*d.* 1949), ʿAbbās Maḥmūd al-ʿAqqād (*d.* 1964), and ʿAbd al-raḥmān Shukrī (*d.* 1958). All three writers penned a number of articles in which they called for an end to the traditional artifice and rhetoric of poetry and sought instead a greater emphasis on poetic unity and the role of the individual poet (and thus an end to patronised verse forms), and on the centrality of emotion and the subjective in creating poetry. In citing these principles to advocate a new approach to poetry, these critics were, needless to say, mounting a direct assault on the bastion of neo-classical poetry as personified in Egypt by the work of such illustrious poets as Aḥmad Shawqī and Ḥāfiẓ Ibrāhīm. Their attacks reached an acme in a two-volume publication that appeared in 1921 under the title *al-Dīwān*. While al-Māzinī used the occasion to savage the sentimental and somewhat pompous prose musings of Muṣṭafā Luṭfī al-Manfalūṭī (*d.* 1924), al-ʿAqqād took on a relatively easy target – one of Shawqī's sonorous occasional odes (an elegy of the nationalist hero, Muṣṭafā Kāmil). Rearranging the lines with minimal effect, he showed in pedantic detail that the poem is 'a disjointed collection of verses with only rhyme and metre as a unifying factor' (*al-Dīwān* II (1921), p. 45).

The work of al-ʿAqqād and his colleagues served a crucial role in the development of modern Arabic poetry by weakening the ties that bound it to the classical tradition and thereby opening up the field to new ideas and directions. It is indeed a sign of al-ʿAqqād's important position as a critic that he was asked by Mīkhāʾīl Nuʿaymah (*d.* 1988), the most prominent critic of the *mahjar* school, to write the introduction to his own significant contribution to the early development of modern Arabic literary criticism, *al-Ghirbāl* (The Sieve), which appeared in 1923. The spirit of romanticism is clearly reflected in Nuʿaymah's complaint that in the Arab world the poet tends to speak with the tongue and not the heart; the poet, he suggests, needs to be someone who 'feels' (the literal meaning of *shāʿir*, 'poet'), and it should be the role of poetry to convey an emotion from the soul of the poet to that of the listener.

Turning now to a consideration of what might be dubbed the 'French' school, we can begin with that young Egyptian student, Muḥammad Ḥusayn Haykal (*d.* 1956), who, as was noted in Chapter 5, returned from his period of study in France with the text of a novel, *Zaynab*. Under the initial tutelage of Aḥmad Luṭfī al-Sayyid (*d.* 1963) – an Egyptian journalist and intellectual who, through his positions as editor of the newspaper, *al-Jarīdah*, and university educator, was to serve as mentor to a whole generation of young Egyptian writers – Haykal caught the nationalist mood of the times by supporting the notion of an Egyptian literature (and other national literatures) that would reflect the spirit of each nation. The Egyptian example would permit its writers to exploit the continuity of its cultural history from Pharaonic times to the present, the former being much in the public eye following the discovery of Tutankhamun's tomb in 1922. Haykal also acknowledges a direct debt to Hippolyte Taine (*d.* 1893) in advocating the need for an objective, scientific critical method, based on the study of works of art as a product of their social and temporal environment.

Blind from the age of two, Ṭāhā Ḥusayn initially received a thoroughly traditional Islamic education, attending al-Azhar mosque-university in Cairo where he came under the influence of Ḥusayn al-Marṣafī (whose *al-Wasīlah al- adabiyyah* was noted above), then studying at the new secular university (now the University of Cairo) where in 1914 he had completed a doctoral degree with a thesis on the blind poet, Abū al-ʿAlāʾ al-Maʿarrī. Sent to France for further study, he returned to Egypt in 1919 with a second doctorate (on ibn Khaldūn), eager to apply to the Arabic literary heritage some of the objective principles he had studied in France. The topic he chose to illustrate these ideas could hardly have been more controversial: his renowned work, *Fī al-shiʿr al-jāhilī* (On Pre-Islamic Poetry, 1926), examines the texts of the Qurʾān itself and pre-Islamic poetry and concludes not only that the Qurʾān contains narratives that are fables but also that portions of the corpus of pre-Islamic poetry appear to date from the Islamic period and thus to be fake. This attack by a Western-educated Muslim son of Egypt on the sanctity of the Qurʾān itself and the poetic tradition that preceded it aroused a firestorm of controversy, as a result of which the book had to be withdrawn; it was reissued in revised form as *Fī al- adab al-jāhilī* (On Pre-Islamic Literature, 1927), with the offending section on the Qurʾān removed, but the other parts expanded.

This incident and its consequences made Ṭāhā Ḥusayn the *bête-noire* of the establishment and hero of the younger generation. He now proceeded to use his prominent position in the cultural life of his country as a platform through which to educate an entire generation about the treasures of the Arabic literary heritage. Following his studies of al-Maʿarrī and ibn Khaldūn, he addressed himself to a number of classical figures in both poetry and prose; his weekly talks on radio devoted to prominent figures and genres in Arabic literary history were gathered together into volumes under the title *Ḥadīth al-arbaʿāʾ* (Wednesday Talk, 1926 *et seq.*). From the classical period, topics include the *muʿallaqah* poets, the love poem (*ghazal*), a series of chapters on the clash between the 'ancients' and 'modernists' that we have discussed above, and perceptive analyses of the work of individual poets such as Bashshār ibn Burd. In the third collection, he considers some contributions to modern literature, and here his critical comments assume a tone more redolent of a schoolmaster's function. In 1938 this didactic aspect took the form of a broad-scaled assessment of Egypt's cultural status, *Mustaqbal al-thaqāfah fī Miṣr* (The Future of Culture in Egypt), in which he suggested that, in order to become part of the modern world, Egypt should stress its more

Mediterranean aspect and use the virtues of European culture – cultural, societal, and political – as models for emulation.

During the course of his long career as a teacher Ṭāhā Ḥusayn trained many illustrious students. One of them was Muḥammad Mandūr (*d.* 1965), whose doctoral thesis, later published as *al-Naqd al-manhajī ʿinda al-ʿArab* (Systematic Criticism Among the Arabs, 1948), traces the predominant trends in classical criticism; he decries the influence of Qudāmah ibn Jaʿfar, while assigning al-Āmidī and his *al-Muwāzanah* a key role in the development of 'systematic criticism'. Returning from a period of study in Paris that was interrupted by the Second World War, Mandūr wrote articles for the cultural magazine, *al-Thaqāfah*, some of which were collected in a very influential book, *Fī al-mīzān al-jadīd* (In the New Balance, 1944). The collection contains significant sections on the work of the playwright Tawfīq al-Ḥakīm, a renewed look at the critics of the earlier period and especially ʿAbd al-qāhir al-Jurjānī, and a segment on metrics; but the one that attracted the most critical attention discusses what he terms 'whispered poetry' (*al-shiʿr al-mahmūs*). Here Mandūr examines the various schools of romantic poetry; he extols its more muted qualities as opposed to the loud, rhetorical tones of traditional poetry as revived by the neo-classical poets.

The bulk of critical attention among these central figures in the development of modern Arabic criticism was devoted to poetry, the genre that had predominated during the pre-modern period. Among the pioneers in the analysis of prose genres from the earlier period was yet another Egyptian returnee from study in Paris, Zakī Mubārak, who is remembered for his pioneering study, *La prose arabe au IVe siècle de l'Hégire (Xe siècle)* (Paris, 1931). In the study of modern prose the situation was also changing: the new genres of fiction were steadily gaining in popularity and, at some undefined point in the post-independence period, were to become the most popular form of literary expression.

THE AFTERMATH OF INDEPENDENCE: COMMITMENT AND BEYOND

As we noted in Chapter 2, the decade of the 1950s was one during which many Arab states achieved the independence for which they had long struggled. While certain members of the older cultural élite tended to become politically marginalised (for example, at the time of the Egyptian Revolution, Ṭāhā Ḥusayn himself was serving as Minister of

Education), a new generation set itself to develop a significant role for literature and its evaluation within the context of the new political and social realities. The rallying-cry of the era was 'literature with a purpose' (*al-adab al-hādif*), gathered around the concept of commitment (*iltizām*). While much inspiration was drawn at the time from Sartre's *Qu'est-ce que c'est que la littérature?* (1947) and its notion of *engagement*, the inspiration for the movement can be traced back to an earlier period. The ideas of socialism, introduced into the Arab world by such pioneers as Shiblī Shumayyil (*d.* 1917) and Faraḥ Anṭūn (*d.* 1922), had been developed in the writings of Salāmah Mūsā (*d.* 1947), a Coptic intellectual who aroused the ire of conservative scholars by suggesting that much of the heritage of Arabic literature consisted of writings for the élite that were of little relevance to the needs of the Arab world in his generation. In periodicals and books, a number of intellectuals introduced Marxist notions regarding the function of literature and the littérateur in society: in Lebanon Ra'īf al-Khūrī and Ḥusayn Muruwwah (*d.* 1987), and in Syria ʿUmar al-Fakhuri, who, besides editing a journal, *al-Ṭalīʿah* (The Vanguard), published a work under the title *al-Adīb fī al-sūq* (The Littérateur in the Market, 1944).

A major turning-point in this process of transformation occurs in January 1953, with the appearance of the first issue of *al-Ādāb*, the Beirut monthly edited by Suhayl Idrīs, which announced the principles of commitment as its guiding criteria and has served in the intervening period as a major advocate and reflector of change in Arabic literature. A new generation of creative writers took to the task of advocating and reflecting such change with relish, and a number of 'realistic' works in a variety of genres, many of them establishing new levels of technical excellence, began to appear. Such enthusiastic advocacy of *engagé* literature by the critics noted above and others led, not surprisingly, to some notable debates that pitted the younger generation against the guardians of the traditional heritage. In 1955, two Egyptian critics, ʿAbd al-ʿaẓīm Anīs and Maḥmūd Amīn al-ʿĀlim, published *Fī al-thaqāfah al-Miṣriyyah* (On Egyptian Culture) in which they encapsulated many of the arguments that had been debated in a newspaper-article joust with, among others, Ṭāhā Ḥusayn and al-ʿAqqād. Literature, they suggested, could no longer adopt an 'ivory-tower' attitude and indulge in the detached effusions of romantic (and especially symbolist) poets or the lengthy philosophical contemplations of al-Ḥakīm's plays. For Anīs and al-ʿĀlim, and indeed for other critics like Khūrī and Ḥusayn Muruwwah, the littérateur was under an obligation to write for a general public.

The nature and pace of the changes represented by these debates inevitably had a significant effect on the relationship between creative writing and criticism. To cite just one illustration, two Iraqi poets, Badr Shākir al-Sayyāb (*d.* 1964) and Nāzik al-Malā'ikah (*b.* 1923), simultaneously but separately composed poems in 1947 that challenged the longstanding criteria of Qudāmah ibn Jaʿfar regarding the metre and rhyme of Arabic poetry. While indeed these poems did represent a radical shift away from the prescriptive dictates of the classical tradition of criticism, giving the Arabic poem a completely new look on the page and inevitably arousing the opposition of conservative critics, poets who had now seen the floodgates of innovation and change opened by this and other gestures were not content with the prospect of replacing one set of rules with another. When Adūnīs, Arabic's most radical contemporary poet, announces that the purpose of poetry is to change the meanings of words and that the content of each individual poem will determine afresh what its structure will be, he is, among other things, confirming the end to any notion of prescriptive criticism.

CONCLUSION

As is the case with the literary genres examined in previous chapters, developments in modern Arabic literary criticism constitute a process of blending whereby an awareness of Western ideas (and particularly those associated with disciplines such as linguistics, folklore, and psychology) has interacted with a re-examination of the heritage of the past. In addition to works that have appeared in book form, the principal avenue through which these new ideas have been fostered has been the pages of a number of distinguished literary journals; a short list, in addition to the already mentioned *al-Ādāb*, would include *Alif*, *al-Aqlām*, *Fuṣūl*, *al-Fikr*, *Mawāqif*, and *al-Mawqif al-adabī*.

The principles of linguistics provide a basis for the work of many contemporary Arabic critics, an apt reflection of the situation in the West; among several possible examplars we would list Salāḥ Faḍl, Kamāl Abū Dīb, and Maurice Abū Nāḍir. For other interpreters of modern Arabic literature, the theoretical underpinnings are less specific: ʿIzz al-din Ismāʿīl, Muḥammad Bannīs, and Jābir ʿUṣfūr with poetry; Laḥmadāni Ḥamīd, Ṣabrī Ḥāfiẓ, and ʿAbd al-fattāh Kilīṭo with prose. As critic, Adūnīs has endeavoured to take in the entire literary tradition in a sweeping survey, most notably in *al- Thābit wa-al-mutaḥawwil* (The Static and Dynamic) but also in other, more recent, works. From the perspective of a contemporary Arab writer who is a student of cultural traditions and the way they change, he insists that the past cannot be treated as a fixed entity forever frozen in time, but must be reinterpreted in accordance with the ideologies and methods, and therefrom with the insights, of the present. It is in the very act of (re-)discovering the essence of that past, he suggests, that the Arab writer will become aware of the nature of the 'modern'.

Guide to further reading

2 THE CONTEXTS OF THE LITERARY TRADITION

In writing this background chapter, I have made use of a very large number of sources. Even a bibliography restricted to works in English would be enormous. The works cited below are intended as a representative sample, selected for their comprehensive approach:

al-Azmeh, Aziz, *Arabic Thought and Islamic Societies*, London: Croom Helm, 1986.

Badran, Margot, and Miriam Cooke (eds.), *Opening the Gates: A Century of Arab Feminist Writing*, London: Virago Press, 1990.

Barakat, Halim, *The Arab World: Society, Culture, and State*, Berkeley: University of California Press, 1993.

Beeston, A. F. L. *et al.* (eds.) *Arabic Literature to the End of the Umayyad Period.* Cambridge History of Arabic Literature 1, Cambridge University Press, 1983.

Bosworth, C. E., *The Islamic Dynasties*, Islamic Surveys 5, Edinburgh University Press, 1967, 1980.

Boullata, Issa J., *Trends and Issues in Contemporary Arabic Thought*, Albany, New York: State University of New York Press, 1990.

Caton, Steven C., *Peaks of Yemen I Summon*, Berkeley: University of California Press, 1990.

Endress, Gerhard, *An Introduction to Islam*, trans. Carole Hillenbrand, New York: Columbia University Press, 1988.

Eph'al, Israel, *The Ancient Arabs: Nomads on the Borders of the Fertile Crescent 9th–5th Centuries BC*, Leiden: E. J. Brill, 1982.

Hourani, Albert, *History of the Arab Peoples*, New York: Warner Books, 1991.

Lapidus, Ira, *A History of Islamic Societies*, Cambridge University Press, 1988.

Laroui, Abdallah, *The Crisis of the Arab Intellectual*, trans. Diarmid Cammell, Berkeley: University of California Press, 1976.

Makdisi, George, *The Rise of Colleges*, Edinburgh University Press, 1988.

The Rise of Humanism, Edinburgh University Press, 1990.

Meisami, Julie Scott and Paul Starkey (eds.), *Encyclopedia of Arabic Literature*, 2 vols., London: Routledge, 1998.

Rosenthal, Franz, *Knowledge Triumphant*, Leiden: E. J. Brill, 1970.

A History of Muslim Historiography, Leiden: E. J. Brill, 1968.
Schacht, Joseph, and C. Edmund Bosworth (eds.), *The Legacy of Islam*, Oxford: Clarendon Press, 1974.
Watt, Montgomery, *Islamic Philosophy and Theology*, Islamic Surveys 1, Edinburgh University Press, 1962, 1964.

3 THE QUR'ĀN: SACRED TEXT AND CULTURAL YARDSTICK

Even if listings are restricted mostly to works in English, the number of publications devoted to the Qur'ān that might be included here is enormous. The works that are listed are those that are pertinent to a literary approach to the text of the Qur'ān.

ENGLISH VERSIONS OF THE QUR'ĀN (A SELECTION)

Arberry, A. J., *The Koran Interpreted*, London: George Allen & Unwin Ltd., 1955; New York: Macmillan Publishing Co., 1986.
The Koran, trans. N. J. Dawood, London: Penguin Classics, 1956.

STUDIES ON THE QUR'ĀN

Bellamy, James, 'The Mysterious Letters of the Koran: Old Abbreviations of the *Basmalah*', *Journal of the American Oriental Society* Vol. 93 (1973): 267–85.
Burton, J., *The Collection of the Qur'ān*, Cambridge: Cambridge University Press, 1977.
Gätje, Helmut (ed.), *Grundriss der Arabischen Philologie: II Literaturwissenschaft*, Wiesbaden: Reichert Verlag, 1987, pp. 96–135.
Graham, William A., *Beyond the Written Word: Oral Aspects of Scripture in the History of Religion*, Cambridge: Cambridge University Press, 1987.
Hawting, G. R., and Abdul-Kader A. Shareef (eds.), *Approaches to the Qur'ān*, London: Routledge, 1993.
Heinrichs, Wolfhart (ed.), *Neues Handbuch der Literaturwissenschaft: Orientalisches Mittelalter*, Wiesbaden: AULA-Verlag, 1990, pp. 166–85.
Jeffrey, Arthur, *The Foreign Vocabulary of the Qur'ān*, Baroda: Oriental Institute, 1938.
Martin, Richard (ed.), *Approaches to Islam in Religious Studies*, Tucson, Arizona: University of Arizona Press, 1985.
Mir, Mustansir, 'Humor in the Qur'ān,' *Muslim World* 81/3–4 (July–Oct. 1991): 179–93.
'The Qur'ān as Literature,' *Religion and Literature* 20/1 (Spring 1988): 49–64.
'The Qur'ānic Story of Joseph: Plot, Themes, and Characters,' *Muslim World* 76 (Jan. 1986): 1–15.
Nelson, Kristina, *The Art of Reciting the Qur'ān*, Austin, Texas: University of Texas Press, 1985.

Neuwirth, Angelica, *Studien zur Komposition der mekkanischen Suren*, Berlin: Walter de Gruyter, 1981.

Rippon, Andrew (ed.), *Approaches to the History of the Interpretation of the Qur'ān*, Oxford: Clarendon Press, 1988.

Sells, Michael, 'Sound, Spirit, and Gender in *Sūrat al-Qadr*,' *Journal of the American Oriental Society*, 111/2 (April–June 1991): 239–59.

'Sound and Meaning in *Sūrat al-Qāriʿa*,' *Arabica* 40 (1993): 403–30.

Stewart, Devin, '*Sajʿ* in the Qur'ān: Prosody and Structure,' *Journal of Arabic Literature*, 21/2 (Sept. 1990): 101–39.

Wansbrough, J., *Qur'ānic Studies: Sources and Methods of Scriptural Interpretation*, Oxford University Press, 1977.

Watt, W. Montgomery, *Bell's Introduction to the Qur'ān*, Islamic Surveys 8, Edinburgh University Press, 1970.

4 POETRY

ANTHOLOGIES IN TRANSLATION AND EDITIONS

Beeston, A. F. L. (ed.), *Selections from the Poetry of Bashshar*, Cambridge University Press, 1977.

Clouston, W. A., *Arabian Poetry for English Readers*, London: Darf Publishers, 1986.

Desert Tracings, trans. Michael A. Sells, Middletown: Wesleyan University Press, 1989.

Jones, Alan (ed.), *Early Arabic Poetry*, vol. 1: *Marāthī and Ṣuʿlūk Poems*, Reading: Ithaca Press, 1992; vol. 2: *Select Poems*, ed. Reading: Ithaca Press, 1996.

Jayyusi, Salma Khadra (ed.), *Modern Arabic Poetry: An Anthology*, New York: Columbia University Press, 1987.

Monroe, James T. (ed.), *Hispano-Arabic Poetry: A Student Anthology*, Berkeley: University of California Press, 1974.

Nicholson, Reynold A., *Translations of Eastern Poetry and Prose*, Cambridge University Press, 1922.

STUDIES

Abū-Lughod, Lila, *Veiled Sentiments: Honor and Poetry in A Bedouin Society*, Berkeley: University of California Press, 1986.

Adonis, *An Introduction to Arab Poetics*, trans. Catherine Cobham, London: Saqi Books, 1990.

Ashtiany, Julie, et al. (eds.), *Abbasid Belles-Lettres*, Cambridge History of Arabic Literature 2, Cambridge University Press, 1990, esp. chs. 9–19.

Badawi, M. M., *A Critical Introduction to Modern Arabic Poetry*, Cambridge University Press, 1975.

Badawi, M. M. (ed.), *Modern Arabic Literature*, The Cambridge History of Arabic Literature 4, Cambridge University Press, 1992, esp. chs. 1, 2, 3, 4, and 14.

Bailey, Clinton, *Bedouin Poetry from Sinai and the Negev*, Oxford: Clarendon Press, 1991.

Bannīs, Muḥammad, *Al-Shiʿr al-ʿArabī al-ḥadīth: bunyatuhu wa-ibdālātihā*, 4 vols., Casablanca: Dār Tubqāl, 1989–91.

Beeston, A. F. L. et al. (eds.), *Arabic Literature to the End of the Umayyad Period*, Cambridge History of Arabic Literature 1, Cambridge University Press, 1983, esp. chs. 2, 18, 20, and 21.

Bencheikh, Jamaleddine, *Poétique arabe*, Paris: Editions Anthropos, 1975.

Caton, Steven C., *Peaks of Yemen I Summon: Poetry as Cultural Practice in a North Yemeni Tribe*, Berkeley: University of California Press, 1990.

Gätje, Helmut (ed.), *Grundriss der Arabischen Philologie: II Literaturwissenschaft*, Wiesbaden: Reichert Verlag, 1987, pp. 7–95.

Hamori, Andras, *On the Art of Medieval Arabic Literature*, Princeton University Press, 1974.

Heinrichs, Wolfhart (ed.), *Neues Handbuch der Literaturwissenschaft: Orientalisches Mittelalter*, Wiesbaden: AULA-Verlag, 1990, pp. 142–65, 216–41, 284–300, 409–22, 440–64, 482–523.

Homerin, Th. Emil, *From Arab Poet to Muslim Saint: Ibn al-Farid, his Verse, and his Shrine*, Columbia: University of South Carolina Press, 1994.

Jacobi, Renata, *Studien zur Poetik der altarabischen Qaside*, Wiesbaden: Franz Steiner, 1971.

Jayyusi, Salma Khadra, *Trends and Movements in Modern Arabic Poetry*, 2 vols., Leiden: E. J. Brill, 1977.

Kennedy, Philip, *The Wine Song in Classical Arabic Poetry*, Oxford: Clarendon Press, 1997.

Kheir Beik, Kamal, *Le mouvement moderniste de la poésie arabe contemporaine*, Paris: Publications Orientalistes de France, 1978.

Kurpershoek, P. M., *Oral Poetry and Narratives from Central Arabia*, 3 vols., Leiden: E. J. Brill, 1994–99.

Meisami, Julie S., *Medieval Persian Court Poetry*, Princeton University Press, 1987.

Moreh, S., *Modern Arabic Poetry 1800–1970*, Leiden: E. J. Brill, 1976.

Sperl, Stefan, and Christopher Shackle (eds.), *Qasidah Poetry in Islamic Asia & Africa*, vol. 1: *Classical Traditions & Modern Meanings*; vol. 2: *Eulogy's Bounty, Meaning's Abundance: An Anthology*, Leiden: E. J. Brill, 1996.

Stetkevych, Suzanne P. (ed.), *Reorientations/Arabic and Persian Poetry*, Bloomington: Indiana University Press, 1994.

Reynolds, Dwight, *Heroic Poets, Poetic Heroes*, Ithaca: Cornell Press, 1995.

Schimmel, Annemarie, *As Through a Veil: Mystical Poetry in Islam*, New York: Columbia University Press, 1982.

Sowayan, Saad A., *Nabati Poetry*, Berkeley: University of California Press, 1985.

Stetkevych, Jaroslav, *The Zephyrs of Najd: The Poetics of Nostalgia in the Classical Arabic nasib*, University of Chicago Press, 1993.

Stetkevych, Suzanne P., *Abū Tammam and the Poetics of the ʿAbbāsid Age*, Leiden: E. J. Brill, 1991.

The Mute Immortals Speak: Pre-Islamic Poetry and the Poetics of Ritual, Ithaca: Cornell University Press, 1993.

Zwettler, Michael, *The Oral Tradition of Classical Arabic Poetry*, Columbus: The Ohio State University Press, 1978.

5 BELLETRISTIC PROSE AND NARRATIVE

TRANSLATIONS

The Arabian Nights, trans. Husain Haddawy, New York: W. W. Norton & Co., 1990.

Arabic Short Stories, trans. Denys Johnson-Davies, Berkeley: University of California Press, 1994.

Badran, Margot, and Miriam Cooke (eds.), *Opening the Gates: A Century of Arab Feminist Writing*, London: Virago Press, 1990.

The Book of the Thousand Nights and a Night, trans. R. F. Burton, 10 vols., Benares, 1885.

Dunn, Ross E., *The Adventures of Ibn Battuta, a Muslim Traveler of the 14th century*, Berkeley: University of California Press, 1989.

al-Hamadhani, Badiʿ al-zaman, *The Maqamat of Badiʿ al-zaman al-Hamadhani*, trans. W. J. Prenderghast, London: Curzon Press, 1973.

al-Hariri, al-Qasim, *Makamat or Rhetorical Anecdotes of al Hariri of Basra*, trans. Theodore Preston, London: W. H Allen & Co., 1850 (reprint: Gregg International Publishers Ltd., 1971).

Ibn Shuhayd, *Treatise of Familiar Spirits and Demons*, trans. James T. Monroe, Berkeley: University of California Press, 1971.

Kassem, Ceza, and Malak Hashem (eds.), *Flights of Fantasy: Arabic Short Stories*, Cairo: Elias Modern Publishing House, 1985.

The Laṭāʾif al-maʿārif of Thaʿālibī, trans. C. E. Bosworth, Edinburgh University Press, 1968.

Lewis, Bernard (ed.), *Islam from the Prophet Muhammad to the Capture of Constantinople*, 2 vols. New York: Harper and Row, 1974.

The Life of Muhammad: A Translation of Ishaq's Sirat Rasul Allah, trans. A. Guillaume, London: Oxford University Press, 1955.

Lichtenstadter, Ilse, *Introduction to Classical Arabic Literature*, New York: Twayne Publishers Inc., 1974.

Les Mille et Une Nuit [*sic*], trans. Antoine Galland, Paris, 1726.

Manzalaoui, Mahmoud (ed.), *Arabic Writing Today: The Short Story*, Cairo: American Research Center in Egypt, 1968.

Modern Arabic Short Stories, trans. Denys Johnson-Davies, Oxford University Press, 1967.

Al-Qushayri, *Principles of Sufism* trans. B. R. von Schlegell, Berkeley: Mizan Press, 1990.

Al-Tabari, *The History of al-Ṭabarī*, 38 vols., New York: SUNY Press.

The Thousand and One Nights, trans. E. W. Lane, 3 vols., London, 1877.

STUDIES

Allen, Roger, *The Arabic Novel: An Historical and Critical Introduction*, 2nd edn, Syracuse University Press, 1995.

Modern Arabic Literature, Library of Literary Criticism Series, New York: Ungar, 1987.

Ashtiany, Julia, *et al.* (eds.), *'Abbasid Belles-Lettres*, Cambridge History of Arabic Literature 2, Cambridge University Press, 1990, esp. chs. 1–8.

Beeston, A. F. L. *et al.* (eds.), *Arabic Literature to the End of the Umayyad Period*, Cambridge History of Arabic Literature 1, Cambridge University Press, 1983, esp. chs. 3, 4, 5, 10, 11, 13, 15, 16, 17 and 19.

Badawi, M. M. (ed.), *Modern Arabic Literature*, The Cambridge History of Arabic Literature 4 Cambridge University Press, 1992, esp. chs. 1, 5, 6, 7, 8, and 11.

Bencheikh, Jamal Eddine, *Les Mille et Une Nuits ou la parole prisonnière*, Paris: Gallimard, 1988.

Blachère, Régis, *Histoire de la littérature arabe des origines à la fin du XVe siècle de J-C*, vol. 3, Paris: Adrien-Maisonneuve, 1966, esp. troisième partie, chs. v and vi.

Bosworth, C. Edmund, *The Mediaeval Islamic Underworld*, Leiden: E. J. Brill, 1976.

Burgel, J. C., 'Repetitive Structures in Early Arabic Prose,' *Critical Pilgrimages: Studies in the Arabic Literary tradition* [= *Literature East and West*] ed. Fedwa Malti-Douglas, Austin, Texas: Department of Oriental and African Languages and Literatures, 1989, pp. 49–64.

Gätje, Helmut (ed.), *Grundriss der arabischen Philologie II: Literaturwissenschaft*, Wiesbaden: Reichert Verlag, 1987, pp. 208–63.

Gerhardt, Mia, *The Art of Storytelling*, Leiden: E. J. Brill, 1963.

Ghazoul, Ferial, *The Arabian Nights: A Structural Analysis*, Cairo: Associated Institution for the Study and Presentation of Arab Cultural Values, 1980.

Hafez, Sabry, *The Genesis of Arabic Narrative Discourse: A Study in the Sociology of Modern Arabic Literature*, London: Saqi Books, 1993.

Heinrichs, Wolfhart (ed.), *Neues Handbuch der Literatur-Wissenschaft 5: Orientalisches Mittelalter*, Wiesbaden: AULA-Verlag, 1990, esp. pp. 326–45.

'Ḥikāya', in *Encyclopedia of Islam*, 2nd edn, Leiden: E. J. Brill, 1954.

Irwin, Robert, *The Arabian Nights: A Companion*, London: Penguin Books, 1995.

Kilito, Abdelfattah, *L'auteur et ses doubles: essai sur la culture arabe classique*, Paris: Edition du Seuil, 1985.

L'oeil et l'aiguille, Paris: Editions La Decouverte, 1992.

Kraemer, Joel L., *Humanism in the Renaissance of Islam*, Leiden: E.J. Brill, 1986.

Leder, Stefan, and Hilary Kilpatrick, 'Classical Arabic Prose Literature: A Researcher's Sketch Map,' *Journal of Arabic Literature* 23/1 (March 1992): 2–26.

Lyons, M. C., *The Arabic Epic: Heroic and Oral Story-telling*, 3 vols., Cambridge University Press, 1995.

Makdisi, George, *The Rise of Humanism in Classical Islam and the Christian West*, Edinburgh University Press, 1990.

Malti-Douglas, Fedwa, *Structures of Avarice: The Bukhalaʾ in Medieval Arabic Literature*, Leiden: E. J. Brill, 1985.
al-Maqdisī, Anīs, *Taṭawwur al-asālīb al-nathriyyah fī al-adab al-ʿArabī* [The Development of Prose Styles in Arabic Literature], Beirut: Dār al-ʿilm li-al-malāyīn, 1968.
Monroe, James T., *The Art of Badīʿ al-Zamān al-Hamadhānī as Picaresque Narrative*, Beirut: American University of Beirut, 1983.
Mubarak, Zaki, *La prose arabe au IVe siècle de l'Hégire (Xe siècle)*, Paris: Maisonneuve, 1931.
Pellat, Charles (ed.), *The Life and Works of Jāḥiẓ*, trans. D. M. Hawke, Berkeley: University of California Press, 1969.
Pinault, David, *Story-telling Techniques in the 'Arabian Nights'*, Leiden: E. J. Brill, 1992.
Rosenthal, Franz, *A History of Muslim Historiography*, Leiden: E. J. Brill, 1968.
Slyomovics, Susan, *The Merchant of Art: An Egyptian Hilali Oral Epic Poet in performance*, Berkeley: University of California Press, 1987.
Young, M. J. L. *et al.* (eds.) *Religion, Learning and Science in the ʿAbbasid Period*, Cambridge History of Arabic Literature 3, Cambridge University Press, 1990, esp. chs. 5, 6, 11, 12, 13, and 17.

6 DRAMA

TRANSLATIONS

Anthologies

Arabic Writing Today: The Drama, ed. Mahmoud Manzalaoui, Cairo: The American Research Center in Egypt, 1977
Mahmoud Taymour, 'The Court Rules'; Tewfiq al-Hakim, 'Song of Death' and 'The Sultan's Dilemma'; Mahmoud Diyab, 'The Storm'; Shawky Abdel-Hakim, 'Hassan and Naima'; Youssef Idris, Flipflap and His Master [= *al-Farāfīr*]; Farouk Khorshid, 'The Wines of Babylon'; Mikhail Roman, 'The Newcomer'; Mohammed Maghout, 'The Hunchback Sparrow.'
Egyptian One-act Plays, trans. Denys Johnson-Davies, London: Heinemann, and Washington: Three Continents Press, 1981.
Farid Kamil, 'The Interrogation'; Alfred Farag, 'The Trap'; Abdel-Moneim Selim, 'Marital Bliss'; ʿAli Salem, 'The Wheat Well'; Tawfiq al-Hakim, 'The Donkey Market.'
Modern Egyptian Drama, ed. Farouk Abdel Wahab, Minneapolis & Chicago, 1974.
Tawfiq al-Hakim, 'The Sultan's Dilemma'; Mikhail Roman, 'The New Arrival'; Rashad Rushdy, 'A Journey Outside the Wall'; Yusuf Idris, 'The Farfoors.'
Modern Arabic Drama, ed. Salma al-Jayyusi and Roger Allen, Indiana University Press, 1995
ʿIsam Mahfouz, 'The China Tree'; Mamdouh Udwan, 'That's Life';

Saʿdallah Wannus, 'The King is the King'; Walid al-Ikhlasi, 'The Path'; 'Izz al-din al-Madani, 'The Zanj Revolution'; the Balalin Troupe, 'Darkness'; 'Abd al-ʿAziz al-Surayyiʿ, 'The Bird Has Flown'; Yusuf al-ʿAni, 'The Key'; Salah ʿAbd al-Sabūr, 'Night Traveller'; Alfred Farag, 'Ali Janah al-Tabrizi and His Servant Quffa'; ʿAlī Salim, 'The Comedy of Oedipus, or You're the One who Killed the Beast'; Mahmoud Diyab, 'Strangers Don't Drink Coffee'.

Pagine di teatro siriano, trans. Rosella Dorigo (Supplemento 1, *Quaderni di studi arabi*) Venice: Universita degli studi, 1983.

Individual writers

Ṣalāḥ ʿAbd al-Ṣabūr, *Murder in Baghdad* [Maʾsāt al-Ḥallāj], trans. Khalil I. Semaan, Leiden: E. J. Brill, 1972.

Night Traveller, trans. M. M. Enani, Cairo: General Egyptian Book Organization, 1980.

Now the King is Dead . . ., trans. Nehad Selaiha, Cairo: General Egyptian Book Organization, 1986.

Tawfīq al-Ḥakīm, 'The Donkey Market', trans. Denys Johnson-Davies, in *Egyptian One-Act Plays*, Arab Authors Series 18. London: Heinemann, 1981, pp. 101–18.

'The Donkey Market', trans. Roger Allen, in *Arab World* (October–February 1971–72): 20–28. reprinted in *Small Planet*, New York: Harcourt Brace Jovanovich, 1975, 70–81.

Fate of a Cockroach and Other Plays, trans. Denys Johnson-Davies, Arab Authors Series 1, London: Heinemann, 1973. 'Fate of a Cockroach,' 'The Song of Death,' 'The Sultan's Dilemma,' 'Not a Thing out of Place.'

Plays, Prefaces and Postscripts of Tawfiq al-Ḥakīm, trans. W. M. Hutchins, Washington: Three Continents Press, 1981. 'The Wisdom of Solomon,' 'King Oedipus,' 'Shahrazad,' 'Princess Sunshine,' 'Angel's Prayer'.

The Tree Climber, trans. Denys Johnson-Davies, Arab Authors Series 17. London: Heinemann, 1980.

SOURCES

Roger Allen, 'Egyptian Drama after the Revolution,' *Edebiyat* 4/1 (1979): 97–134.

'Drama and Audience: The Case of Arabic Theater,' *Theater Three* 6 (Spring 1989): 7–20.

M. M. Badawi, *Early Arabic Drama*, Cambridge University Press, 1988.

Modern Arabic Drama in Egypt, Cambridge University Press, 1988.

Badawi, M. M. (ed.), *Modern Arabic Literature*, Cambridge History of Arabic Literature 4 Cambridge University Press, 1992.

Jean Fontaine, *Aspects de la littérature tunisienne (1975–83)*, Tunis: RASM, 1985.

Gätje, Helmut (ed.), *Grundriss der arabischen Philologie II: Literaturwissenschaft*, Wiesbaden: Reichert Verlag, 1987, pp. 244–48.

Al-Khozai, Mohamed A. *The Development of Early Arabic Drama 1847–1900*, London: Longmans, 1984.

Landau, Jacob M., *Studies in the Arab Theater and Cinema*, Philadelphia: University of Pennsyvlania Press, 1958.

Moosa, Matti, *The Origins of Modern Arabic Fiction*, Washington: Three Continents Pres, 1983.

Moreh, Shmuel, *Live Theatre and Dramatic Literature in the Medieval Arabic World*, Edinburgh University Press, 1992.

al-Rāʿī, ʿAlī, *Al-Masraḥ fī al-waṭan al-ʿarabī*, Kuwait: ʿĀlam al-maʿrifah, 1980.

Slyomovics, Susan, 'To Put One's Finger in the Bleeding Wound': Palestinian Theatre under Israeli Censorship,' *The Drama Review* 35/2 (Summer 1991): 18–38.

Tomiche Nadia (ed.), *Le théâtre arabe*, Louvain: UNESCO, 1969.

SPECIFIC AUTHORS

Roger Allen, 'Arabic Drama in Theory and Practice: The Writings of Saʿdallāh Wannūs,' *Journal of Arabic Literature* 15 (1984): 94–113.

de Moor, C. M. (ed.) *Un oiseau en cage*, Amsterdam: Rodopi, 1991.

Fontaine, Jean, *Mort-resurrection: une lecture de Tawfiq al-Hakim*, Tunis: Editions Bouslama, 1978.

Long, Richard, *Tawfiq al-Ḥakīm Playwright of Egypt*, London: Ithaca Press, 1979.

Reid, Donald M., *The Odyssey of Faraḥ Anṭūn*, Minneapolis and Chicago: Bibliotheca Islamica, 1975.

Starkey, Paul, *From the Ivory Tower: A Critical Study of Tawfiq al-Ḥakīm*, London: Ithaca Press, 1987.

7 THE CRITICAL TRADITION

ʿAbbās, Iḥsān, *Tārīkh al-naqd al-adabī ʿinda al-ʿArab* [History of Literary Criticism Among the Arabs], Beirut: Dār al-thaqāfah, 1971.

Abū Deeb, Kamal, *Al-Jurjānī's Theory of Poetic Imagery*, Warminster, Wilts.: Aris & Philllips, 1979.

Adonis, *An Introduction to Arab Poetics*, trans. Catherine Cobham, London: Saqi Books, 1985.

Ajami, Mansour, *The Alchemy of Glory*, Washington: Three Continents Press, 1988.

The Neckveins of Winter, Leiden: E. J. Brill, 1984.

Allen, Roger, *Modern Arabic Literature*, A Library of Literary Criticism Series, New York: Ungar Publishing Company, 1987.

Ashtiany, Julia, *et al.* (eds.), *ʿAbbasid Belles-Lettres* Cambridge History of Arabic Literature 2, Cambridge University Press, 1990, chs. 20 and 21.

Badawi, M. M. (eds.), *Modern Arabic Literature*, The Cambridge History of Arabic Literature 4, Cambridge University Press, 1992, ch. 12.

Bonebakker, Seeger A., 'Aspects of the History of Literary Rhetoric and Poetics in Arabic Literature,' *Viator* 1 (1970): 75–95.

'Poets and Critics in the Third Century A.H.,' in *Logic in Classical Arabic Culture.*

Brugman, J., *An Introduction to the History of Modern Arabic Literature in Egypt*, Leiden: E. J. Brill, 1984.

Cantarino, Vicente, *Arabic Poetics in the Golden Age*, Leiden: E. J. Brill, 1975.

Gätje, Helmut (ed.), *Grundriss der arabischen Philologie II: Literaturwissenschaft*, Wiesbaden: Reichert Verlag, 1987, pp. 177–207.

Gelder, G. J. H. van, *Beyond the Line: Classical Arabic Literary Critics on the Coherence and Unity of the Poem*, Leiden: E. J. Brill, 1982.

Heinrichs, Wolfhart, and Roger Allen, 'Arabic Poetics,' in *The New Princeton Encyclopedia of Poetry and Poetics*, Princeton University Press, 1993.

Semah, David, *Four Egyptian Literary Critics*, Leiden: E. J. Brill, 1974.

Stetkevych, Suzanne, *Abū Tammām and the Poetics of the ʿAbbasid Age*, Leiden: E. J. Brill, 1991.

Young, M. J. L. *et al.* (eds.), *Religion, Learning and Science in the ʿAbbasid Period*, Cambridge History of Arabic Literature 3, Cambridge University Press, 1990, esp. chs. 4, 8, 22, and 23.

Index

NOTE: The majority of technical terms in this index are listed under their English names, with cross-references to their Arabic equivalents (as far as they exist).